THE MAKING OF THE ENGLISH LANDSCAPE
Edited by W. G. Hoskins and Roy Millward

THE MAKING OF THE WELSH LANDSCAPE
Edited by W. G. Hoskins and Roy Millward

THE MAKING OF THE ENGLISH LANDSCAPE

The Hertfordshire Landscape

by

LIONEL M. MUNBY

HODDER AND STOUGHTON
LONDON SYDNEY AUCKLAND TORONTO

To

W. Branch Johnson

Preface

ANY BOOK ON such a wide ranging subject as the landscape and its history must draw largely on the work of others. The many printed sources on which I have relied are revealed in the text and in footnotes, but almost more important has been what I have gained from personal contact and discussion. First and foremost this work owes much to W. Branch Johnson, who should have been its author and to whom it is dedicated. I can only hope that it is in a small measure an effective expression of gratitude for his generosity and for what he has done for Hertfordshire history. My debt to the many people who have been in my extramural classes on local history during the last twenty-seven years is immeasurable. Almost every page of this book contains for me the memory of some apt comment or idea contributed in discussion, for any worthwhile adult education is always a partnership in learning. The few whose particular assistance I will mention must stand for many others. Mrs Crawley drew my attention to Norton in Letchworth, the Hon. Baron Dimsdale gave me much information about Meesden, while Mr Tomkins shared his landscape researches with me.

Other local historians have helped me. Miss Eileen Lynch was kind enough to read and correct my manuscript, freely giving me the benefit of her wide knowledge of Hertfordshire. In the two aspects of landscape history about which I am most ignorant, archaeology and architecture, I have relied heavily on the advice of others, though I must take full responsibility for what I have written. Mr John Moss-Eccardt and Mr Tom Jeffrey have given me archaeological information and corrected my grosser errors. Mr Peter Richards has been kind enough to let me see the early conclusions which he has reached in his research into the field archaeology of Braughing Hundred. Mr Graham Bailey has made available to me, as to others, the work of many years study of domestic architecture; his generosity has not always been sufficiently appreciated. The section of chapter seven which deals with timber-framed houses is largely based on his work, though whether he will recognise what I have made of his researches I am not sure!

The non-expert is always liable to misunderstand and mis-interpret what he hears. I have found myself skating on the thinnest of ice in trying to give distinct names or descrip-tions and even approximate dates to the early settlers in Hertfordshire: where can the line be drawn between the 'Bronze Age' and the 'Iron Age'? and how can one relate Celtic and Germanic language speakers to particular mate-rial cultures or human physiques? The dating of vernacular buildings and the making of subtle distinctions between different modes of construction or different plans seem full of traps.

During the last few years, and largely in 1974 to 1975, I have visited, looked at, driven round or walked over very nearly all the places mentioned in this book. The judgments which I express are my own, but the help of my wife, Diana, has been incalculable. She has been my fellow driver, map reader, and note-taker, typist and proof reader, but above all has helped by commenting on confusions in the text. I have tried to say what I have to say simply and without too much academic pretension, for any worthwhile look at the landscape must be for all readers and not for specialists. I have tried to include as many particular examples, from as many parts of the county, as possible without losing sight of the general themes which they have been chosen to illustrate. Two themes, however, have been lightly treated, churches and country houses, because access to information about them is so easily available, and it seemed better to use a limited space for comment on subjects which are not normally treated in guidebooks or other widely accessible sources. That is why much of this book deals with the pattern of fields and the shape of villages and towns, and with the impact of industrialisation and urbanisation on the county's appearance.

Without sabbatical leave during the winter of 1974-5, I doubt whether this book would ever have been finished. I am, therefore, especially grateful to my employers, the University of Cambridge's Board of Extramural Studies, and, in particular, to John Andrew, Director and Secretary. No one can work on Hertfordshire history without appreciating the service provided by the County Archivist Peter Walne, and his staff. One only wishes that appreciation for this service would lead the electors of Hertfordshire to find money for modern accommodation to allow the County Record Office to make its unrivalled collections of documents and maps even more widely available than they already are. I shall always be grateful to Prof. W. G. Hoskins for encouraging me to write this book, and I am only too well aware of how much Mr Roy Millward's editorial advice has improved it; the edited version is a substantial improvement on the first draft.

In reading this book anyone who does not know the Hertfordshire countryside very well would be wise to make use of the new 1:50,000 Ordnance Survey maps, sheets 153, 154, 165, 166 and 167. Map references for the places mentioned are given in the index.

Contents

List of Plates

Acknowledgments

The author wishes to thank the following for permission to use their photographs:

The Committee for Aerial Photography, Cambridge: Plates 1, 2, 3, 4, 5, 6, 11, 12, 17, 18, 24 (photographs by Prof. J. K. St Joseph, Cambridge University Collection: copyright reserved).
The National Monuments Record: Plate 32.
Hertfordshire County Council: Plates 13, 14 (photographs by F. Day); Plate 19 (photograph by Bob Norris: copyright reserved).
Mr Graham Bailey: Plates 26, 27, 28, 29, 31 (copyright reserved).
Mr Brian Long: Plates 38, 39.
Mr Percy Birtchnell: Plate 37 (copyright reserved).
Miss J. A. Clarke: Plates 20, 22, 25, 34, 35, 36, 41 (copyright reserved).
Mr Peter Clarke: Plates 8, 9, 21, 23, 30, 33, 40, 42, 43, 44 (copyright reserved).
Plates 7, 15, 16 are old prints.
Plate 10 is from Dury and Andrews *A Topographical Map of Hertfordshire*.

List of maps and plans

Most of the traces on which these diagrams are based were produced by Sandra Bicknell.

Editor's Introduction

THIS SERIES OF books on The Making of the English Landscape originated in 1955 with my own pioneer book under that title. A few county volumes were published under the same format (Cornwall, Leicestershire, Gloucestershire, and Lancashire), but a new and better format was worked out from 1970 onwards, beginning with Arthur Raistrick's *West Riding of Yorkshire* and Christopher Taylor's *Dorset*. Since then there has been a steady flow of such county studies, aiming at covering the whole country eventually. Already there have been volumes as far apart as Northumberland and Sussex; and books are in preparation ranging from Kent in the east to a revised edition of Cornwall in the far west.

Purists might object that the geographical county has no particular unity except for administrative purposes, that the 'region' would be more appropriate. Apart from the fact that few would agree about what constituted a 'region', the primary fact is that the geographical county is a unity so far as the documentary material is concerned; but, more than that, it evokes local patriotism, and again each English county (one ought to say 'British' in view of the fact that Wales has been brought within the orbit of the series) contains a wide variety of landscapes each interesting and appealing in its own right. Every county presents a multitude of problems of Landscape History and their very contrast is illuminating. Even little Rutland has such contrasts, though naturally on a more limited scale; and a large county like Devon has almost every kind of landscape. One other point: when the reorganisation of local government took place a few years ago, and some entirely new names appeared on the administrative map of England, such as Avon and Cleveland, I had to consider whether we should stick to the old counties as we have always known them or adopt the new set-up. As the series was by then so far advanced under the old and well-loved names, we decided to retain them and go on as before. There were other good reasons, besides the sentimental one, for sticking to the original plan.

It is a well-worn truism that England is a very small country with an almost infinite variety of rocks, soils, topography, and watercourses by the tens of thousands: all these things create what one might call micro-landscapes at the risk of importing a little professional jargon into something which is meant to be enjoyed and explained in plain English. One look at the coloured map of the geology of England and Wales and above all the way in which the colours change every few miles, is enough to excite the visual imagination. This is especially true when one crosses the grain of a piece of country, instead of travelling along it. There is for example the major grain, so to speak, which runs from the southwest coast in Dorset north-eastwards to the Yorkshire coast round Whitby. If you cut *across* this geological grain, going from south-east to north-west the landscapes change every few miles. On a smaller scale but nearly as complicated, the south-eastern corner of England, running from, say, Newhaven northwards to the Thames estuary, presents rapid and very contrasted changes of landscape—in soils, building stones (and hence buildings themselves), in vernacular building—the architectural equivalent of the once-rich variety of local dialects in this country—in land-forms, in farming, in almost everything that is visible.

Most of us enjoy some widespread view from a hilltop or on some grand coast: we enjoy it as 'scenery' but this is really a superficial enjoyment. What I prefer to call 'landscape' as distinct from 'scenery' is that a landscape to me asks questions: why is something like this at all, why does it differ from another view a few miles away? It is the difference perhaps between what an amateur portrait painter sees and puts on paper and what a skilled surgeon sees when he contemplates and reflects over a human body. He sees things, even on a superficial examination, because of his training and his long experience, that the layman never sees. So it is with *landscape*. To see it thus, seeing beneath the surface and the obvious, is to increase one's enjoyment of the English countryside enormously. The great English painter John Constable makes this point in one simple sentence in one of his *Discourses on Landscape*, a sentence I shall never tire of quoting: "*We see nothing till we truly understand it.*" Constable's *Discourses* were an attempt to justify landscape-painting as an end in itself. If we take his great dictum as our text, Landscape History becomes an end in itself, transmuting the textbook facts of rocks and soils, landforms, economic history, industrial archaeology—words calculated to deter all but the most determined reader—into a different way of looking at perhaps commonplace things, into a different language. The art is to use these academic disciplines in a concealed way, never to let them obtrude or, if so, to some essential purpose so that the visual is always paramount.

When I wrote my own book now more than twenty years ago I did not answer all the possible questions by a long way, though it still stands as a good introduction to a new field of history. Landscape History is now, I think, a well-accepted and respectable discipline, taught in some universities and in schools, and the subject of theses. I did not answer all the questions for the simple reason that I did not then know what they all were. And even now, after so many books and articles and theses have been written, there is so much that remains unknown, and no doubt questions that I, and others, have still not perceived. This, to me, is one of the great values of these landscape books, treated county by county. Local studies in depth, to use a fashionable phrase, but for once a useful one, will not only enlarge our generalisations about the major changes in the landscape, but also because of their detail bring new lights into the picture. Ideally, as editor of this series , I would like each writer on a particular county to pick out an even smaller area for special examination under the microscope, having in mind such revealing studies as Professor Harry Thorpe's masterly essay on Wormleighton in Warwickshire (*The Lord and the Landscape*, published in 1965) and Dr Jack Ravensdale's *Liable to Floods* (1974) which deals with three Fen-Edge villages in Cambridgeshire. Not only are the topographical settings of these two studies so completely different, but one is concerned with 'peasant villages' and the landscapes they created. So social structure also enters into the many hidden creators of a particular bit of England and the vision it presents.

Some major problems remain virtually unsolved. I myself in my first book fell into the trap, or rather accepted the current doctrine, that until the Old English Conquest most of this country was uncleared woodland or undrained marsh or in many parts primeval moorland. To a large extent I was deceived by the overwhelming evidence of the number of Old English place-names on the map, or, if not these, then the powerful Scandinavian element in the eastern parts of England. I am no longer deceived, or perhaps I should say that I have become much more sceptical about the ultimate value of this treacherous evidence. Thanks to archaeological advances in the past twenty years (and partly thanks to the opportunities offered by the odious onwards march of the motorways—their only value in my eyes) we know very much more about the density of settlement and of population in prehistoric times right back to the Mesolithic of seven or eight thousand years ago. There is evidence for forest clearance and to some extent for settled farming as early as this, and to an even greater extent by Neolithic times when one thinks of the axe-factories two thousand or more feet up on the wildest mountains of Lakeland. Forest clearance was going on at this height, and axes were being exported as far south as the coast of Hampshire. We now need a completely fresh study of the distribution of woodland by, say, Romano-British times. Not only woodland clearance, but the river gravels which have been exploited by modern man for his new roads have changed our whole concept of prehistoric settlement. The gravels of the Welland valley, almost in the heart of the Midlands, have been particularly intensively studied and have changed our entire thinking in these parts.

That is one aspect of the English landscape which I greatly under-estimated when I first wrote and I welcome every fresh piece of evidence that proves me misguided. Yet all the same the outlines of the main picture remain unchanged, and I stand by that first book subject to such changes of emphasis as I have mentioned.

There are other problems waiting to be worked out, some special to particular bits of England, others of a more general nature. Of the special problems I think of the number of isolated parish churches in the beautiful county of Norfolk: why are they there, stuck out all alone in the fields? Somebody could write a wonderful book on Churches in the Landscape. And there are other special aspects of the landscape wherever one walks in this most beloved of all countries: so much to do, so little done. These closer studies of England county by county will add enormously to our knowledge. Already the study of Landscape History has attracted a growing literature of its own, a great deal of it scattered in local journals and periodicals. Soon, perhaps in ten years' time, we shall need a Bibliography of the subject. This makes it sound dull and academic, but in the end I look upon it as an enlargement of consciousness, a new way of looking at familiar scenes which adds to the enjoyment of life. For those who have eyes to see, the face of Britain will never look the same again.

Exeter, 1976   W. G. HOSKINS

1. Hertfordshire

'England meditative'. The shape of the county. The London communication network and Hertfordshire's regions.

'England meditative'

HERTFORDSHIRE IS SMALL; only six of the forty ancient English counties were smaller. It seems very ordinary; no stranger would think of holidaying here. The traveller passes rapidly through the county along a motorway or in an Inter-City train and, if he looks out of the window, will see new houses, new factories, New Towns. He will not stop. There is no mountain scenery, no moorland, no downs, no fenland; there are no stone villages, no soaring spires. But the more observant eye will notice the undulating fields and hedgerows between the new buildings. Anyone who does stop and turn off the main roads or get out of the train, as E. M. Forster's Schlegels did at Stevenage, will be surprised. Forster described Hertfordshire as "England at its quietest, with little emphasis of river and hill; it is England meditative", a theme which runs through the writings of all those who have known the county.[1] There are no obvious edges in the landscape, no sudden contrasts, but there are immense differences. One landscape shades delicately into another.

From the northern end of the village of Barley a sweeping, open panorama covers north-east Hertfordshire, north-west Essex and south Cambridgeshire. In these large arable fields barley has long been a major crop; the village name, however, commemorates not corn but an ancient burial place. At one time saffron was cultivated in rotation with

---

[1] *Howard's End*, Penguin, 1960, p. 185.

barley over an area stretching from Sawbridgeworth in south-east Hertfordshire to Saffron Walden in Essex and on to the southern outskirts of Cambridge. If one turns round and looks south and west from Barley, there are woods, small hedged fields and much grass. This is close, almost secretive country. Six kilometres to the west of Barley and slightly north, on Therfield Heath, is one of the eastern-most long barrows in Britain. Standing here, or higher on the ridge to the south near Therfield village, and looking westwards there seem to be miles of open grassland (Plate 1). Corn has replaced the grass, especially towards Baldock, but early in the spring the appearance remains. This light, chalky soil is natural grassland, grazing for sheep; it became some of the best barley land in the country. Still further westwards along the Icknield Way, beyond Hitchin, is more downlike country, with deep dry valleys and an impressive view over Bedfordshire. Bunyan knew this country well and surely thought of it when he described the Delectable Mountains.

> Now there was on the tops of these Mountains, shepherds feeding their flocks . . . The pilgrims therefore went to them . . . they asked, "Whose Delectable Mountains are these? And whose be the sheep that feed upon them?" *Shepherds*: "These Mountains are Immanuel's Land and they are within sight of his City."[2]

Only sixteen kilometres south-west from Lilley and Hexton, from the downs, is Ashridge and the Gaddesdens, with beechwoods and lanes that twist and run up and down on the edge of the Chilterns. Redbourn, twelve kilometres south-east of Ashridge, has a beautiful village green which has only just lost the long line of elms stretching across it from the church to Watling Street. Cricket has been played here for a century and a half. Verulamium lies to the south and

[2] John Bunyan, *Pilgrim's Progress*, ed. Roger Sharrock, 1965, pp. 157–8.

from the grass which covers its ruins one can look up at St Albans Abbey. Nine kilometres to the east is Hatfield house in a park and wooded landscape (Plate 2). Still further to the east, from the Hadhams to Sawbridgeworth, are sunken, winding lanes with high hedgebanks and wandering streams with the remains of watercress beds.

Following the minor roads which accompany a stream like the Beane, from its source near Rushden to where it joins the River Lea at Hertford, brings an intimate acquaintance with the interior of the county. To reach the source from the Icknield Way the chalk escarpment has to be passed to the southern end of Wallington. The Cat Ditch flows north, into the Ouse; the Beane's waters which rise scarcely a kilometre south of the Cat Ditch reach the Thames. The road is at first shut in. It rises and falls as it takes short cuts over the tongues of higher land, around which the Beane flows. Remnants of the ridge and furrow of the open fields can still be seen at Cumberlow Green, on the top of one of these spurs; there are few such survivals in Hertfordshire.

Further south the road follows the river more closely. At Walkern it becomes the village street, while near the beautiful village of Benington it follows the side of the valley between the village and the river. From this road the Beane valley can be clearly seen: it slopes steeply down from the road and uphill across the other side of the river to Aston. At Watton-at-Stone the valley widens and its sides are wooded and emparked in places. At Hertford the Beane and the Lea run side by side for nearly a kilometre and this is the area around which the county town grew.

This journey from north to south covers twenty kilometres and there is a great variety of scenery; the uses man has made of the landscape have been as diverse. A journey of the same distance from east to west, from Standon to Graveley near Stevenage passing over the Beane at Walkern, is like moving on a switchback, as one crosses the plateaux between the Rib, the Old Bourne, the Beane, and their tributary streams. The roads zigzag crazily but give constant glimpses of enchanting scenery. Another journey of half the length, from Radlett to Hatfield, in the south-west of the county reveals a subtly different landscape. This is the valley of the upper Colne, before it is joined by the Ver. The feel of the countryside is different; it is a low lying, more open landscape although there are still woods and parks. There is much more evidence of suburbia, and trunk roads criss-cross the ground. What appears to be a long medieval abbey roof rises abruptly from the flatlands between the road and the river near Broad Colney. There is an interesting piece of local history to be uncovered in such a building for it is not in fact medieval. Extraordinary pieces of fairly modern Gothic revival building like this are not uncommon in south-west Hertfordshire. There is an equally fantastic, but very different piece of nineteenth-century Gothic on what was once Caldecote Lane but is now a built up area between Bushey and Elstree. It is the Rosary Priory High School.

Exploring Hertfordshire can bring surprises and delights once the eye is attuned to the undramatic variety. Almost from parish to parish the scenery changes and much of it is still lovely. The physical landscape makes possible the variety, but the loveliness is the work of man. Almost four hundred years ago Camden described Hertfordshire as a county with 'more footsteps of antiquity' than most others.[3] Since Camden wrote, Hertfordshire has been changed fundamentally; its remaining open fields have disappeared; its farming has been transformed; and from the nineteenth century people have poured into the county, into Garden Cities and New Towns, housing estates and garden villages. There were just under 102,000 people in Hertfordshire in 1801, perhaps twice the population of Camden's youth. By 1901 there were 250,350 but the population increase had been

---

[3] W. Camden, *Britannia*, 1586. There are various versions of this passage in the many English editions which followed, but the sense is the same. This is taken from the 1695 edition by Edmund Gibson, p. 292.

very much in line with that of the country as a whole. Between 1901 and 1951 the county's population more than doubled, a rate of growth over four times that of England and Wales. There were 561,445 people in Hertfordshire in 1951, and the growth has continued: by 1971 the county population was 924,632. London's expansion was directed northwards and Hertfordshire has received London factories and Londoners in great numbers. Very much of the landscape of Hertfordshire is new. No study of the county can neglect this.

New Stevenage is as important as the 'gracious Old Market Town with roots in the fifteenth century', which the Residents' Protection Association in 1947 feared would be 'crucified on the cross of progress'.[4] Both are the handiwork of man and both are part of the landscape. The landscape is a palimpsest: Welwyn Garden City stands on Iron Age farmsteads; two farms in King's Langley were carved out of a royal park in the seventeenth century, a park which replaced arable open fields before 1290; in Hatfield a triangle of built-up land north of a road called The Common is crossed by paths, called the Rights of Way, one of which still follows the curves of the open field strips. Every change has divided opinion. How effectively the scars made by motorways and New Towns will heal and the new growth come in time to merge with the traces left by man's earlier surgery no one can for certain prophesy. But it would be an illusion to believe that surgery is new; we can still see the scars of man's earlier operations. The attractive main streets of Buntingford or Redbourn were once brash new buildings, with decaying and abandoned settlements in the countryside behind them. Church ruins like those of Chesfield or Layston are a reminder. Sometimes, as at Broadfield near Cottered and at Wakeley, even the ruins of the church have gone.

[4] Harold Orlans, *Stevenage: a sociological study of a New Town*, 1952, p. 70.

The shape of the county

Hertfordshire is roughly the shape of a rhomboid on a north-east, south-west axis; the longest sides are those on this axis. The county boundaries are, for the most part, artificial, though a great deal of the eastern boundary is formed by the River Lea and its northern tributary, the Stort. The northern boundary of the county lies on and to the north of the water-shed between the Wash rivers and the Thames. While almost all the rivers that rise in Hertfordshire flow into the Thames through the Colne or the Lea, the little Hiz at Hitchin and the Ivel at Baldock flow into the Ouse, and the Rhee or Cam has its source in Ashwell. In fact the northern county boundary, in many places, extends over the crest of the chalk ridge which marks this watershed. Ashwell and its neighbouring villages lie on the edge of the Cam valley, and Hexton lies on the edge of the Bedfordshire plain. The western side of Hertfordshire reaches the Chilterns. The southern boundary extends well into the London clay, heavily wooded country that formed an almost impenetrable belt separating what was to become Middlesex from what was to become Hertfordshire.

There are three upland areas in the county (Fig. 1). The London clay forms one such small area between Bushey and Oxhey, the Barnets, south Hatfield and Haileybury. To the north the valleys of the Colne, Lea and Stort form a broad lowland belt, from Rickmansworth to Ware, which separates this plateau from the other two. A second plateau, boulder-covered, lies in the north-east of the county. This is divided from the third plateau in the west by a narrow belt of lower ground which stretches from Hitchin through Watton and Stevenage to Ware. The largest upland area of Hertfordshire stretches eastwards from the Chilterns to this Hitchin gap.

When the glaciers of the last Ice Age over-rode the northern chalk ridge which links the East Anglian heights with the Chilterns, they left behind the raw materials from which the soils of Hertfordshire have evolved. These were spreads of boulder-clay, mixtures of gravel, flints and other stones. Lumps of glacial conglomerate, Hertfordshire pudding stone, were deposited to become the focus of many myths,

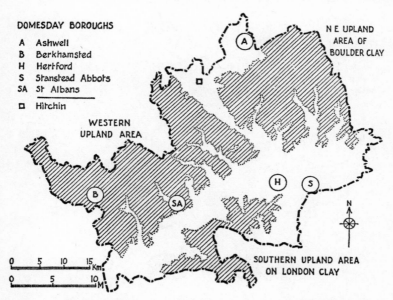

Fig. 1. Hertfordshire: relief. From 'Hertfordshire' in *The Domesday Geography of S. E. England* edited by H. C. Darby and E. M. J. Campbell.

ancient and modern. The soil which covers Hertfordshire today is of two kinds (Fig. 2): alkaline or neutral, chalky soils predominate in the north and east of the county; more or less acid, leached soils cover some three-quarters of the centre and west of the county. The natural vegetation of the eastern area was "moist oakwood, usually with hazel, ash, or hornbeam coppice. The field layers include brambles." The northern chalk ridge was, probably, covered with beechwoods and typical chalk grassland or scrub. The west

31

of Hertfordshire has a well-drained, brown earth cover with natural beech and oak woodland on the Chilterns. The centre of the county has less well-drained gley soils which "carry considerable areas of semi-natural woodland, mainly of oak, with hazel or hornbeam coppice . . . the ground vegetation

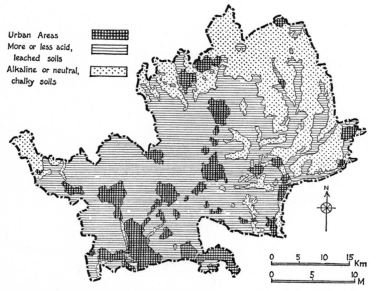

Fig. 2. Soil map. From *The Soils of Hertfordshire* by A. J. Thomasson and B. W. Avery.

includes brambles, bracken, honeysuckle, bluebells and creeping soft-grass as common species, with rushes or sedges on the wettest sites".[5] In sum almost all the county except its northern ridge was densely covered before man cleared the woodland. The commons of West Hertfordshire, at places like Berkhamsted and King's Langley, have begun since the Second World War to revert towards this older landscape. A patch of Broadbalk Field on the Rothamsted Experimental Station farm at Harpenden has been left

[5] A. J. Thomasson and B. W. Avery, *The Soils of Hertfordshire*, 1970, pp. 3–7.

untouched since 1882. What is emerging is the kind of dense woodland which must have covered a great deal of the clay plateaux and valley slopes of Hertfordshire two thousand five hundred years ago. This must have been very unattractive to early settlers who were few in number and had plenty of space to choose from.

Along the northern chalk escarpment trees and undergrowth may have been thinner. The gravel, sand and alluvium deposits along the little river valleys were easier to clear of vegetation than the clay plateaux. So there were two ways into or through this uninviting forest area. One was along the chalk ridge which joins the Wash with the Thames valley near Dorchester and continues on to the Salisbury Plain area. The other was up the rivers which flow into the Thames from the north to their sources. Both these routes were used by early men, though the chalk ridge was far more popular; for a long time the area of Hertfordshire was a place to get through or by, rather than somewhere in which to settle. Old Stone Age hunters used the river valleys; flints and deer antlers used as tools are found in the gravels and alluvium. This does not compare with the amount of use made of the chalk ridge. By the Bronze Age the chalk country of Hertfordshire and this alone was heavily settled.

Prehistoric peoples moved through and settled in the area using the natural routes. All later movement has been dominated by and to some extent distorted by the creation of trunk routes radiating from London northwards.

The London communication network and Hertfordshire's regions

The landscape of Hertfordshire is so much the work of man that it cannot be understood simply in geological and geographical terms. While local physical conditions may explain the minutiae of the landscape, they cannot explain the broad sweeps. Human decisions, and often decisions taken outside the county, have created the bone structure, the skeleton of

Hertfordshire's landscape. The sweep of motorways, the Gade valley route followed by Hertfordshire's only canal and first railway line, were no more pre-determined by geography than was the line of Roman roads. The site of St Albans was as much the result of a conscious human choice as is the location of Garden Cities and New Towns. The fundamental determinant of Hertfordshire's landscape in historical times has been the growth of London at the lowest crossing of the River Thames.

The spread of Iron-Age settlement led to the development of the only effective, man-made, east-west communication route the county has ever enjoyed. This was the track which linked pre-Roman Verulamium, with Wheathampstead, Welwyn, Braughing and Colchester, thus connecting three of the main Belgic settlements in the south-east of England. Once Roman roads were built, radiating from Londinium, this trackway faded out of existence; parts of it are not even country roads today. New Town and County planners talked of a North Orbital road and at one time after the Second World War an east–west railway link through north Hertfordshire was mooted. What has actually been constructed is M1 and A1(M) and the electrification of railway routes north from London; they follow what had become the traditional orientation of communications across the county.

While the modern physical environment has been so often determined by external forces, the people who live in the county do not always follow the pattern of life which the dreamers have planned for them. There is a great deal of movement to work between Hemel Hempstead, Luton just outside the county to the north, and Stevenage, as well as in and out of the surrounding villages. But this has not been catered for by road improvements; only in the mid-1970s is the old road between Luton and Hitchin, and its continuation between Baldock and Royston, being double-tracked and improved. This road is parallel to the line of the Icknield Way, the oldest trackway in the county and one which

follows a natural communication route. Its improvement
has been neglected because it has no function as a London
link, although men and women have persisted in wanting to
travel in this direction.

One particular man-made influence on the local landscape,
that of the London communication network, has been em-
phasised at the beginning of this book, though it will be
qualified in detail later. It is the factor which seems to explain
the dominant cultural pattern in Hertfordshire history, the
continuation of a strong contrast between the north-east and
south-west, long after the geographical and geological influence which first created it had ceased to matter. While it
is possible to distinguish between many different regions
when the county's history is looked at from different angles
and at different times, this one division was predominant
until recently. Already in the high Middle Ages London
influenced Hertfordshire in the obvious way. Between 1270
and 1320 land values were determined by distance from the
capital: "the zone of high prices extends from Sawbridgeworth to Langley."

The general trend of value seems to be higher in the
southern part of the county. This was the region where
commutation was earliest, and it is tempting to regard
this as more than a coincidence; even to seek as the
efficient cause a connection with London and its markets.

By the end of the thirteenth century commutation of the
week work had taken place in the southern part of the
county; . . . Beyond the southern area commutation of
week work is found distributed rather fantastically.[6]

Since the Industrial Revolution those parts of the county
nearest to London have once more become economically
and socially differentiated from the remoter north. But this

[6] *Victoria County History*, Vol. IV, pp. 186–7 and 191.

simple north–south division, which cuts across the physical east–west division, has not been predominant.

Over long periods of time what influenced local development was not so much nearness to London as accessibility. So it was nearness to roads, waterways and railways communicating with London which had an effect on where

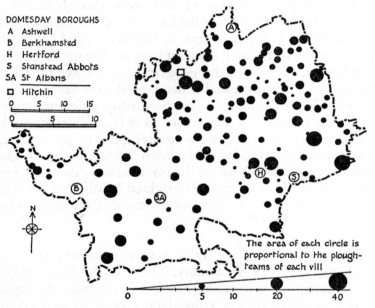

DOMESDAY BOROUGHS
A Ashwell
B Berkhamsted
H Hertford
S Stanstead Abbots
SA St Albans
□ Hitchin

The area of each circle is proportional to the ploughteams of each vill

Fig. 3. Domesday Book: distribution of ploughteams. From *The Domesday Geography of S. E. England* edited by H. C. Darby and E. M. J. Campbell.

people lived and on where they sited their businesses. In the late sixteenth and in the seventeenth centuries, when estates were changing hands fast in Hertfordshire, accessibility rather than distance from London made estates desirable. So it was that the county continued to divide into eastern and western halves rather than north–south. The dividing line was sometimes the River Lea but as often the Great North Road.

The maps with which Eila Campbell's essay on the geography of Domesday Hertfordshire is illustrated make the east–west division extremely clear (Figs. 3 and 4). There is a dividing line from Stanstead Abbots to Hertford to Hitchin. East of this line, east of the Hitchin gap, there were in 1086

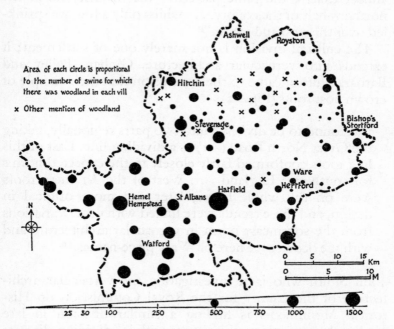

Fig. 4. Domesday Book: distribution of woodland. From *The Domesday Geography of S. E. England* edited by H. C. Darby and E. M. J. Campbell.

more settlements and more people per acre than to the west; not only was more land ploughed but the contemporary estimate of further available land for ploughing was greater than to the west. But west of the line there was far more surviving woodland.[7] The map of Hertfordshire moats which

[7] 'Hertfordshire' by Eila M. J. Campbell in *The Domesday Geography of South-East England*, ed. H. C. Darby and Eila M. J. Campbell, 1962, pp. 48–96.

Derek Renn printed (Fig. 17) shows the same concentration of moats in the east and their relative absence in the west: "the density of moats increases toward the north and east of the county, exactly as the earthwork castles do."[8] The distribution of deserted medieval villages (Fig. 18) follows almost exactly the same pattern: "the majority lie in the northern half of the county, . . . whilst only a few are sprinkled over the west and south."[9]

The cultural division is not merely one of settlement; it extends into vernacular architecture. Graham Bailey and Barbara Hutton came to the conclusion that their sample of crown post roofs (Fig. 22)

> was found to be divisible into two parts regionally, taking the Great North Road (A1) as a dividing line. East of this line roofs conformed fairly closely to the expected norms for south-east England . . . West of the A1 these roofs were on the whole fewer, later and more original in design, and these trends were linked with other variations from the south-east norm in vernacular architecture and with the occurrence here of 'Wal-' place-names.[10]

John Smith who is re-investigating the vernacular architecture of the county for the Royal Commission on Historical Monuments is finding a similar division in late medieval domestic architecture with a dividing line at Offley. To the east T-type houses are common; to the west they are rare and cruck construction is found. Of course, the cultural watershed was not always in exactly the same place but it did relate to the same points of the compass and it was reflected by the governmental divisions.

[8] Derek Renn, *Medieval Castles in Hertfordshire*, 1971, pp. 6–7.
[9] K. Rutherford Davis, *The Deserted Medieval Villages of Hertfordshire*, 1973, pp. 5 and 10–11.
[10] Graham Bailey and Barbara Hutton, *Crown Post Roofs in Hertfordshire*, 1966, p. 17.

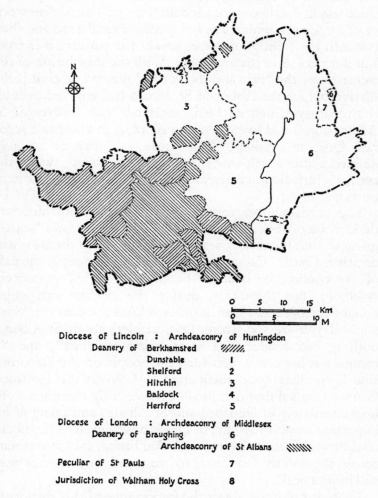

Fig. 5. Hertfordshire medieval ecclesiastical boundaries.

Diocese of Lincoln : Archdeaconry of Huntingdon
Deanery of Berkhamsted //////.
Dunstable 1
Shelford 2
Hitchin 3
Baldock 4
Hertford 5

Diocese of London : Archdeaconry of Middlesex
Deanery of Braughing 6
Archdeaconry of St Albans \\\\\\

Peculiar of St Pauls 7

Jurisdiction of Waltham Holy Cross 8

.From Saxon times until 1845 east Hertfordshire was in the diocese of London, while central and west Hertfordshire was in the diocese of Lincoln (Fig. 5). The Archdeaconry of St Albans, which was independent until 1550 and then put into the London diocese, breaks the pattern, it is true, but does not alter the argument. With the dissolution of the monasteries the 'vast and dangerous' powers of civil jurisdiction, which the Abbot of St Albans had enjoyed over all the territory which he held, vanished. The Liberty of St Albans continued in existence until 1874, in effect as a separate Quarter Sessions. "The area . . . may be roughly defined as the south-westerly part of the county, while the county's jurisdiction extended over the eastern and northern portions."[11]

The parliamentary representation of Hertfordshire was divided east–west. When the head of the Jacobite 'underground' won the county seat in 1727 support in the west was decisive. Charles Caesar's own political base was in the east of the county; he lived at Benington. So his supporters wrote to him constantly, during the election campaign, about developments 'on the other side' of the county: "Sure I am, if you are soe strong (as you hint) about St Albans, nothing can hinder you from being returned"; and "I cannot but hope well provided the people on the Dacorum side keep their good inclinations".[12] When the Hertford County Council first met in 1889 its monthly meetings were held alternately in Hertford and St Albans, and many of its important committees met in London. While all its members could travel from north to south and back, rapid movement across the county from east to west and west to east was still impractical.

There is no doubt about the importance of this east–west

[11] *Hertfordshire County Records: Sessions Records of the Liberty of St Albans Division*, Vol. IV, compiled by William Le Hardy, 1923, pp. ii–iii.

[12] Manuscript letterbooks in the possession of T. Cottrell Dormer of Rousham House, Steeple Aston, Oxon.

division but it would be an error not to realise that it was often overcome, that there was no sharp dividing line between east and west or north-east and south-west, and that there were more subtle variations in the county's landscape. These are the theme of this book.

SELECT BIBLIOGRAPHY

Lydekker, R. *Hertfordshire* (1909).
Clayton, K. M. and Brown, Joyce R. 'The glacial deposits around Hertford' in *Proceedings of the Geologists' Association*, Vol. 69 Part 2 (1958).
Thomasson, A. J. and Avery, B. W. *The Soils of Hertfordshire* (1970).
Gardner, H. W. *A survey of the agriculture of Hertfordshire* (1967).
Beach Thomas, Sir William *Hertfordshire* (1950).

2. The early settlers

Prehistory. The Catuvellauni. Roman Hertfordshire. The Anglo-Saxons.

Prehistory

THERE IS A serious difficulty in being too definite about the effect prehistoric peoples did or did not have on the local landscape. Our best information comes from excavation. Where excavation has or has not occurred is to some extent due to accident. It may be that an area of intensive settlement is only known to be such because it is an area which has been intensively explored by archaeologists. The contrasting area in which settlement is apparently scanty or non-existent may only seem so because it has not received the attention of archaeologists. An example of the latter is the area of south-east Hertfordshire within the bend of the Stort, which is only now being properly surveyed. The contrast is made clear in a report on the Hampermill site on the River Colne, near its junction with the Gade, which points out that

> the valley within a mile of Hampermill contains evidence of human settlement from many periods—Palaeolithic, Mesolithic and later prehistoric and Roman settlement, as well as the Manor of the More to the west and seventeenth-century Oxhey Lodge to the east. The Moor Park area presents evidence of an important Mesolithic-Neolithic settlement at Bathend Clump and a Roman building. These discoveries within a small area partly reflect its suitability for settlement at the south-eastern edge of the Chiltern heights; but they also signify the intensity of

archaeological work concentrated here. Merchant Taylors' School is in the centre of the area and members of its Archaeological Society have been investigating sites for more than fifteen years.[1]

During the last quarter century air photography has revealed many important archaeological sites and innumerable minor ones which were previously unknown. The countryside between Royston, Ashwell and Hitchin has been peopled by the aeroplane. Even with this knowledge, the impact of recent motorway archaeology has been shattering. The careful survey and rescue excavation of motorway routes in other parts of the country has produced a quite unexpected and almost incredible number of previously unknown archaeological sites. We would know much more about Hertfordshire archaeology if the routes of the Barnet and St Albans bypasses or of M1 had been surveyed by 'Rescue' teams with modern aids. As it is, without this kind of support, John Moss-Eccardt of Letchworth Museum and A. G. Rook of Welwyn made important discoveries in advance of the construction of A1 (M).

Historians have scarcely begun to come to terms with the implications of recent archaeological work. It would, however, not be too incautious to suggest that future discoveries are unlikely to show that either Palaeolithic or Mesolithic peoples made any considerable, permanent alteration in the natural Hertfordshire landscape. Lasting changes in vegetation were produced by climatic change rather than by human activity. Before the New Stone Age the few people who inhabited Britain were nomadic hunters. Their 'settlements' were temporary ones on the gravel or alluvium of river valleys or dry valleys. So in the area of Harpenden and Wheathampstead the evidence for the presence of primitive man consists of antlers used as tools found by the River Lea

[1] R. M. Derricourt and R. M. Jacobi, 'Mesolithic Finds from Hampermill, Watford' in *Hertfordshire Archaeology*, Vol. 2, 1970, pp. 1 and 5.

at Batford, Palaeolithic flints found in places in the Lea valley and in the gravel of a dry valley at Nomansland Common between Sandridge and Wheathampstead. Such finds have been made on many valley sites in the country. Palaeolithic implements, of different cultures, have been found, for example, at Great Gaddesden and Hitchin in the north of the county; at Knebworth in the middle; south of St Albans; and at Rickmansworth in the south-west.

The descriptions of two areas of Mesolithic settlement, from different sides of the county, give a good impression of what this kind of settlement was like. At Hampermill near Watford "the Mesolithic material would appear to represent a river valley base camp for exploiting the resources of a wider wooded area". At Bishop's Stortford two different types of Mesolithic sites have been found. A 'British Micro-lithic' site, "usually associated with light soils and hunting", was "on the edge of the plateau above the Stort valley and commanding a good view over the minor valley below, to the river beyond. There is a spring at the site". A Maglemosian site was by the riverside, appropriately for a way of life "based on fowling and fishing".[2]

The people who may have begun to change permanently the appearance of, at least a part of, Hertfordshire were the Neolithic or New Stone Age farmers who entered the north of the county somewhere about 3500 B.C. The Neolithic long barrow on Therfield Heath, Royston is one of the most easterly known. There are three in Norfolk, but apart from these the nearest group is in Bedfordshire clustered on the western escarpment of the Chilterns around the headwaters of the River Lea. The peoples who built these impressive burial mounds, probably for their leading families, were the first farmers. As such they were more likely to make lasting inroads into the natural vegetation than were hunters

[2] Derricourt and Jacobi, p. 1 and A. V. B. Gibson, 'Some evidence of two Mesolithic sites at Bishop's Stortford' in *Hertfordshire Archaeology*, Vol. 1, 1968, pp. 99 and 101–2.

and fishermen. The distribution of long barrows in southern England makes it probable that the Chiltern and Royston barrows represent an eastward movement of peoples from the great concentration on Salisbury Plain, by way of the chalk ridge.[3] A 'henge' monument near Barton Hill Farm, to the west of Hexton and just in Bedfordshire, provides further corroboration. It was not a temple of standing stones or of timber posts but another type of cemetery. The Neolithic farmers kept cattle and swine; both are naturally woodland animals and no doubt they cleared the chalk escarpment of its covering, which could have been a "mixed oak forest, with some lime and beech . . . above a lush undergrowth of hazel".[4] As the trees were cleared the grass flourished, to give nourishment to sheep. Certainly by Bronze Age times a track, the Icknield Way as it was to be called much later, was in use along the chalk ridge.

There is some evidence, in the stone axes found at Shephall and Redbourn, that Neolithic settlement spread southwards from the Icknield Way. The Redbourn axe, along with other pieces of worked flint, was discovered north-west of the church on a wide bank

of gravelly clay bordering a low-lying area of valley gravel . . . this strip formed the shoreline of a large sheet of water and marshland until comparatively recent times, doubtless providing communities which might have occupied the nearby chalk ridges with a reliable source of small game, wildfowl, and fish.[5]

Somewhere between 2000 and 650 B.C., during what has been conventionally called the Bronze Age, the northern area of Hertfordshire, between Royston and Luton, began

[3] Paul Ashbee, *The Earthen Long Barrow in Britain*, 1970, p. 10.
[4] Gordon Copley, *An Archaeology of South-East England*, 1958, pp. 54, 232 and 58.
[5] F. D. Stageman, 'A Neolithic Axe from Redbourn' in *Hertfordshire Archaeology*, Vol. 1, 1968, p. 119.

to be well occupied. There are still some of the characteristic round barrow burial mounds to be seen on both sides of the A505, the modern road on the line of the Icknield Way. More barrow sites are marked on Ordnance Survey maps and the air photography of Professor J. K. St Joseph has revealed that there were once many more. It is probable that the peoples who buried their dead in this way came into Britain via the Wash and reached north Hertfordshire in the opposite direction from their Neolithic predecessors. The Icknield Way, which may have developed as a west-east route, now became an east-west one and an invasion route, a function that it was to serve on several occasions before the arrival of the Danes in the ninth century. There is a barrow at Metley Hill in Wallington which may have become an early medieval meeting place for the local moot, but the largest group of barrows is in Therfield parish. Other cemeteries have been found at Letchworth and in Willian. A food vessel from Hinxworth suggests expansion to the north of the Icknield Way and a buried bronze hoard in Rushden which contained an axe implies movement to the south. In the area of Hitchin, pottery, a battle axe and a hoard have been found which link their owners with different parts of Europe.

While the graves of prehistoric peoples are relatively well-known and the durable objects which they used have been found in many situations, much less has been discovered about their homes. One Bronze Age home *may* have been in St Stephen's parish south of St Albans. Underneath the Roman villa found at Park Street a shallow pit with post holes for timber uprights was found. It contained a piece of pottery, belonging to a different group of people from those who occupied north Hertfordshire. Beakers have been found at Tewin and Ware, and bronze hoards at Furneux Pelham, Welwyn and Rickmansworth. A bronze sword has been found at Waltham Cross and a site excavated at Thorley Hill "on the southern slope of the valley of the small

46

stream which flows" into the River Stort, south of Bishop's Stortford.[6] The barrow, excavated at Codicote in 1956, had been built on top of a hut. The barrow stood "on the brink of the 'hanger'", on Codicote Heath, commanding "a majestic view to the south and south-west". The hut over which it was built "was circular in plan (with) a diameter of about twenty feet".[7] Other round barrows have been found near the headwaters of the Rivers Ash, Rib, Beane and Mimram. It is probable, therefore, that there was a second, independent movement of Bronze Age settlers, in addition to those who came along the Icknield Way. This second group moved up the rivers which branched off the Thames to the north. They occupied, perhaps more permanently, the kinds of sites used by the Palaeolithic and Mesolithic hunters.

It is, however, from about 650 B.C. that the human occupation of Hertfordshire really begins to make an impressive, lasting mark on the landscape. Social changes which have been associated with the gradual spread of iron led to the building of hill forts. There are three along the county's northern ridge. The fort at Wilbury on the edge of Letchworth has been largely destroyed but its southern bank can be made out in the fields south of the Wilbury Hotel and the modern cemetery. This fort was occupied early, before iron was in use; indeed there may have been a "a smaller fortified area before the construction of the larger works". The pottery finds link the fort's occupiers with wide areas of England: "the position of Wilbury astride the Icknield Way laid it open to a certain number of influences from the South-West and the Midlands, and in particular to that brought via the Chilterns".[8] Arbury Banks in Ashwell parish is a much

[6] T. W. Ellcock, 'A late Bronze Age and Romano-British site at Thorley Hill' in *Hertfordshire Archaeology*, Vol. 1, p. 103.

[7] Ernest Greenfield, 'The Bronze Age Round Barrow on Codicote Heath' in *St Albans and Hertfordshire Architectural and Archaeological Society Transactions*, 1961, pp. 5–20.

[8] John Moss-Eccardt, 'Excavations at Wilbury Hill . . .' in *Bedfordshire Archaeological Journal*, Vol. 2, 1964, pp. 44 and 46.

better preserved, oval example of these early plateau forts. Air photography has revealed hut circles within its banks (Plate 3). The site of the most impressive hill fort in Hertfordshire, Ravensburgh Castle in Hexton (Plate 4), seems to have been occupied even longer. It does not seem likely that it was the *oppidum* of Cassivellaunus, stormed by Julius Caesar in 54 B.C. as has been claimed. There is no evidence of a holocaust nor of Roman occupation and the location is far less like that which Caesar described than is the accepted site in Wheathampstead.

The intensity of human settlement along the route of the Icknield Way must have been quite remarkable. The surviving forts are only the tip of the iceberg; the numbers of early sites revealed in air photographs are astonishing. It is not yet possible to identify all of them as belonging to particular archaeological cultures or historical periods, for the little excavation that has been possible to date has, for example, revealed examples of supposedly typical 'Bronze Age' ring ditches connected with 'Iron Age' cultures. What is abundantly obvious, however, is that this whole area of the chalk was continuously occupied and heavily settled from Neolithic into Saxon times. Archaeological evidence of early Iron Age occupation has been found, for example, at Barley, Royston, Norton and Willian, at Holwell, and in a cemetery at Pirton, all along the Hertfordshire stretch of the Icknield Way, in fact. One of the most interesting sites was surveyed and excavated in 1959–61 by Miss M. D. Cra'ster at Aldwick in Barley. This has produced a good deal of evidence about farming. There are so many known sites, so near to each other, that continuity of occupation of particular places seems probable. It is, however, difficult to prove since, in a region where there is such continuous density of occupation by different peoples, the statistical probability of two different groups of people settling in much the same place at different moments in time is high.

The expansion of settlement was not confined to the

Plate 1 Royston, Therfield Heath

Plate 2 Hatfield House

Plate 3 Ashwell, Arbury Banks

Plate 4 Hexton, Ravensburgh Castle

Plate 5 Roman Road, near Cottered

Plate 6 Markyate, a Street Village

Plate 7 Braughing, 'half-hidden in a hollow'

Plate 8 Standon's Main Street, 'so much more spacious'

Plate 9 Aldbury

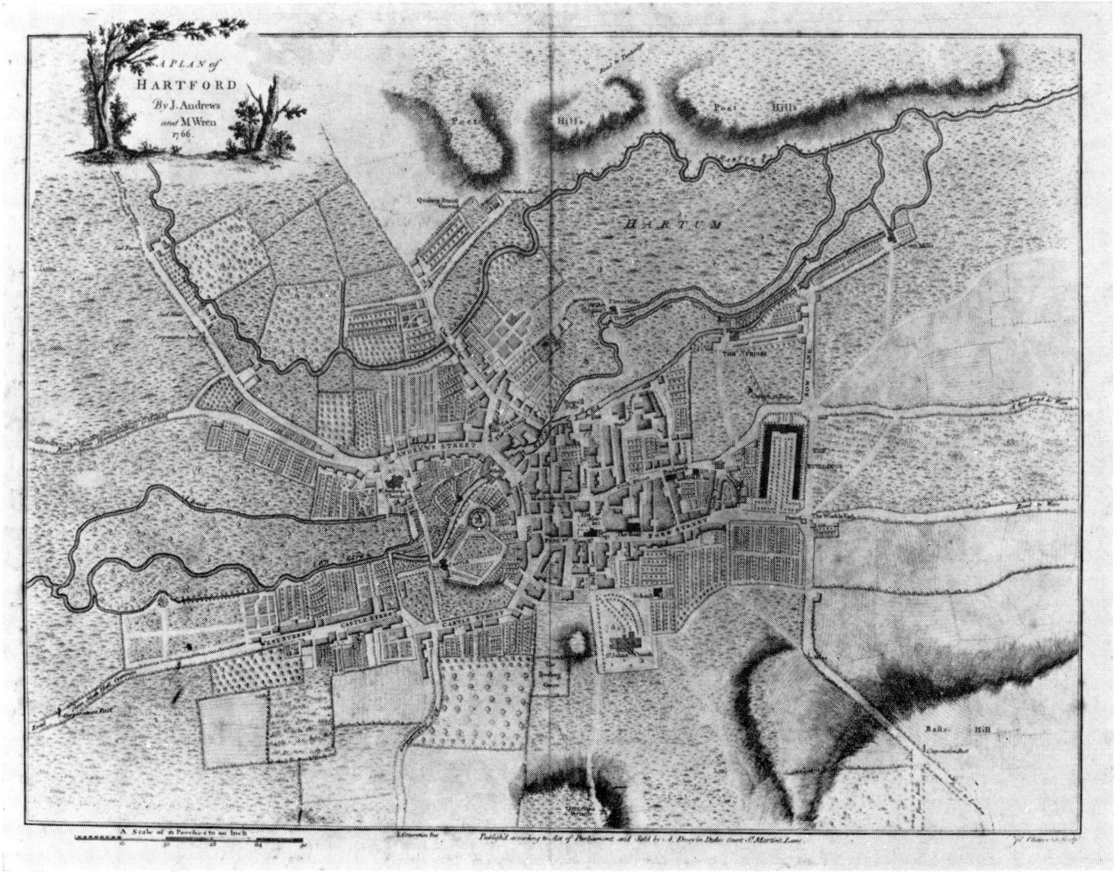

Plate 10 Hertford in 1766

northern chalk escarpment area, though this was far and away the most densely settled region of Hertfordshire. Two forts, in river valleys, are known: the Aubreys, at Redbourn, is near the Ver and Wallbury, in Little Hallingbury, is on the Essex side of the Stort opposite Spellbrook. There is other evidence for settlement along the Gade and lower down the Ver valley south to Watford. The Hampermill Mesolithic site was occupied into Roman times. Similarly the Stort and Lea valleys down to Cheshunt have produced evidence for early settlement. Olives Farm on the parish boundary between Hunsdon and Stanstead Abbots is very like an Icknield Way site with evidence of occupation in the Bronze and early 'Iron' Ages and of substantial settlement in the late Iron Age and Roman times.

What is in doubt is the extent to which early iron using peoples, or their predecessors, penetrated the woodland which covered so much of the clay plateaux of Hertfordshire. The available evidence suggests that the only sites occupied in considerable numbers were in the valleys and along the edge of the chalk ridge in the north. But the view that prehistoric settlement was limited to these kinds of areas has been challenged in other parts of England where evidence for early settlement on the clay lands is beginning to appear. So far the wooded clay belt of south Hertfordshire and the clay plateaux have not produced such evidence. This may be due to deficiencies in archaeological techniques; air photography, for example, may not be so effective in revealing earlier disturbances of clay soils. It does, nevertheless, seem probable that, even if these areas were not quite as neglected by man before the late Iron Age as has been generally assumed, any penetration made only temporary inroads in the woodland. There seems little doubt that the Celtic invaders of the late Iron Age found most of Hertfordshire still heavily wooded, as Julius Caesar found the southern clay belt in 54 B.C.

The Catuvellauni

The first historically recorded invasion of Britain began sometime after 150 B.C. Powerful and wealthy tribes from the area of the Marne valley, in the Paris basin, crossed the Channel and invaded south-east Britain. One important group of invaders moved up the Thames and the Lea and settled in central Hertfordshire. The tribe of the Belgae, known to the Romans as the Catuvellauni, steadily extended its rule from the early centres of settlement in the St Albans neighbourhood. Their first capital, the 'oppidum' which Julius Caesar successfully stormed in 54 B.C., was almost certainly in the great oval between the Devil's Dyke and the Slad at Wheathampstead. Sir Mortimer Wheeler described the Devil's Dyke as "the work of men with wealth, power, arrogance; but it is the work also of men who were still, for one reason or another, uneasy in their adopted land".[9] The Catuvellauni, ruled by Cassivellaunus, resisted Caesar in 54 B.C. but were defeated and accepted a nominal suzerainty.

For a century after Caesar's invasion Britain was left unoccupied. The Hertfordshire Celts extended their rule and settled their territories, developing trade and communication with the Roman empire. Their 'capital' had moved to Prae Wood near Verulamium by 15 B.C. when Tasciovanus, who issued coins, was the ruler of the Catuvellauni. Cunobelinus, Tasciovanus' son, succeeded to the eastern part of the Catuvellaunian territory about A.D. 10. He made his capital at Colchester, conquering the Trinovantes of Essex, and extended his rule west of Oxfordshire. It was disputes following the death of Cunobelinus which provided an opportunity for the emperor Claudius to send Aulus Plautius to conquer Britain in A.D. 43.

[9] R. M. Wheeler, 'Belgic cities of Britain' in *Antiquity*, Vol. 7, 1933, pp. 21–35; *Wheathampstead and Harpenden: I The Settlement*, ed. Lionel M. Munby, 1973, pp. 12–14.

The arc along which the successive Catuvellaunian capitals are sited is of great significance. A track from Verulamium to Colchester linked fords over the Ver, Lea, Mimram and Rib, by each of which a late Iron Age camp has been found. Wheeler described the Catuvellauni as "more than riverside villagers. They exploited the rivers, appropriated the fords, used and controlled the river system as part of a scheme of valley and cross-valley highways. This was substantially a new phenomenon in prehistoric Britain."[9] Between the Lea and the Ver and beyond the Ver towards Prae Wood the track was defended by two linear earthworks whose function was "extensive defence of a wide tract of country . . . against penetration by chariots". These earthworks may have been built when the Catuvellauni first met in conflict the established Iron Age chieftains who ruled north Hertfordshire. The Trinovantes who "occupied parts of Cambridgeshire and north Essex" had sought Julius Caesar's protection from Cassivellaunus' aggression, and there is evidence of the hasty reconstruction of the defences of Wilbury Hill just before a successful attack.[10] For a time Hertfordshire saw frontier war.

There is some archaeological evidence for the cultural contacts of the Celtic chieftains who controlled north Hertfordshire. An iron cauldron-rim discovered in 1961 in the ditch of an early Iron Age enclosure by Blackhorse Road in Letchworth is 'probably a middle La Tène type'; it was found with pottery of the mid-second century B.C. Bearers of this tradition "moved about the trade routes of southern Britain freely and . . . by the mid-second century B.C. they were of some consequence in the Chilterns, either as overlords or raiding bands".[11] Not very far away, in the middle of Baldock, the burial place of a chieftain of the first century

[10] John Holmes, 'Archaeology in the territory of the Catuvellauni' in *East Herts Archaeological Society Transactions*, Vol. XIV Part II, 1958–61, pp. 82–3 and 88.

[11] John Moss-Eccardt, 'An iron cauldron-rim from Letchworth' in *The Antiquaries Journal*, Vol. XLV, 1965, pp. 173–7.

B.C. was discovered in 1968. The burial, which has proved to be connected with a substantial Iron Age settlement, contained a bronze cauldron, a pair of iron firedogs, two bronze dishes, two wooden buckets with bronze fittings and an amphora. The burial was of the La Tène III type; extraordinarily the place where it was found is known as The Tene![12] This is extraordinary because La Tène is a place in Switzerland, whose name modern archaeologists have given to objects similar to those excavated at La Tène and to the society led by Celtic chieftains associated with these objects. This burial makes an interesting comparison with the better known chieftain's grave found on Hertford Heath in 1956 which has been dated about A.D. 40. This 'Belgic' burial contained an "amphora, glass bowl, bronze object decorated with scrolls and enamel discs, and . . . mysterious ironwork" which "are all evidence of unusual wealth". Significantly this grave was dug into an early Iron Age settlement and was enveloped by a later Romano-British cemetery. These late Iron Age chieftain burials are best known, archaeologically, from graves found in Welwyn and Welwyn Garden City most of whose contents are in the British Museum. The impression which the archaeological evidence makes is of a society in which warlike chieftains fought one another until the Catuvellaunian royal family unified the whole area of north and south Hertfordshire, finally seizing 'the existing farms in the chalk country' and occupying the hill forts.[13]

With the victory of the Catuvellauni the real settlement of Hertfordshire began, that is the expansion of existing settlement sites into the deep woods of the clay lands. As long ago as 1932 C. F. C. Hawkes pointed out that "the tendency . . . for the Belgae sometimes to prefer lowland or woodland settlement-sites, implies a beginning of the cultivation of

[12] I. M. Stead, 'A La Tène III Burial at the Tene, Baldock, Herts.' in *The Antiquaries Journal*, 1968, XLVIII, p. 306.

[13] J. Holmes and W. H. C. Frend, 'A Belgic chieftain's grave on Hertford Heath' in *East Herts Archaeological Society Transactions*, Vol. XIV, Part 1, 1955–7, p. 13; Holmes, *Catuvellauni*, p. 83.

heavier lowland soils"; lowland was in contrast to chalk uplands. John Holmes, surveying local archaeological work in the early 1960s, pointed out that "the Belgae, having a heavier plough, were the first to exploit the rich corn-growing land of our region".[14] Though the kind of plough which was used in southern Britain in the pre-Roman Iron Age is in dispute, there is no doubt that the upland areas began to be farmed. Around Welwyn there was a very heavy concentration of settlement, as the draft distribution maps based on the County Archaeological Sites and Monuments Record show. As a result, "by the beginning of the Roman occupation, most of the plateau between the Lea and the Mimram, where Welwyn Garden City now stands, had been cleared of forest". Mrs Barbara Hutton commented that

> the Belgae chose for their settlements land which has always been considered the best agricultural land in the parish (of Hatfield), and among the best, so modern farmers say, in the county. This is a wide band of rolling country, averaging about 250 feet above sea level, stretching across the northern part of the parish from Panshanger in the east to De Havillands in the west: it is divided into two parts by the valley of the Lea.

One of these farms was on the site of Welwyn Garden City Grammar School; it was surrounded by a palisade within a ditch. Archaeological evidence of other farms has been found under Roman villas, at Park Street south of St Albans and at Lockleys in Welwyn, for example.[15]

[14] T. D. Kendrick and C. F. C. Hawkes, *Archaeology in England and Wales 1914-31*, 1932, p. 203; S. W. Woolridge and D. L. Linton, 'The Loam-terrains of South-East England and their Relation to its Early History' in *Antiquity* Vol. VII, 1933, pp. 297-310; Holmes, *Catuvellauni*, p. 90.

[15] Mr David Overton, the County Planning Officer, has given me access to the draft maps, drawn by Mr T. M. Jeffrey; A. G. Rook, *Welwyn Beginning*, 1968, p. 12; Barbara Hutton, *A Thousand Years of History* (*Hatfield and its People* Part 1), 1959, pp. 26-7.

Altogether there were five major areas of settlement: apart from Welwyn, these were at Wheathampstead, in Prae Wood by Verulamium, at Baldock, and in Braughing parish. There has been considerable excavation in the Braughing area in recent years, which suggests that before the Roman conquest "occupation had already reached an urban standard" (Fig. 6). The earliest known Iron Age occupation sites were

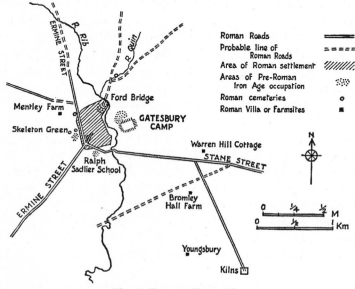

Fig. 6. Roman Braughing.

at Skeleton Green and in the area of the new sports field of the Ralph Sadlier school in Standon parish. But "numerous chance finds of British coins and pottery have been made on both sides of the river (Rib), and it seems evident that this part of Hertfordshire was intensively occupied" by the early years of the first century A.D. There was occupation to the north and west of Gatesbury Wood on the slopes facing the Rib. The earthwork in the wood and the ditched enclosures to the north-east revealed in air photographs have not yet been dated by excavation. There was occupation across the

Rib in the curve of the river south of Ford Bridge, and further west just to the east of A10 north of Puckeridge. Much of the area that was to become a Roman town (in Wickham Field) may have been occupied in the pre-Roman Iron Age.[16]

Roman Hertfordshire

Iron Age settlements and woodland clearing provided a basis on which the Romans built, in two respects. The chief sites along the Verulamium-Colchester track became the Roman centres; a Roman road was made along an Iron Age

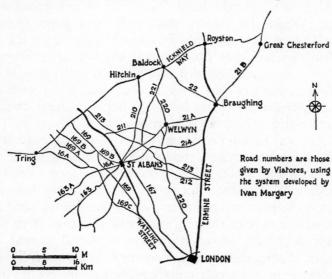

Fig. 7. Roman roads.

route. While there were many new Roman villa or farm sites, some of the most important villas grew out of earlier Catuvellaunian farms. A considerable expansion of settlement and economic growth must have taken place. The pattern of Roman roads in the county (Fig. 7, Plate 5) shows

[16] C. R. Partridge, 'Braughing' in *Small Towns of Roman Britain*, ed. Warwick Rodwell and Trevor Rowley, 1975, pp. 149–50.

the changes. The two, old east-west routes were romanised. What was significant, however, was the development of important north-south roads, Akeman Street, Ermine Street, Watling Street and, in part, what was to become the Great North Road. London had cast its shadow over Hertfordshire history, but the immediate local significance of the Roman road network lies more in the development of nuclei at road junctions. The importance of Verulamium is self-evident. Braughing was the next most important road junction. Baldock, and Welwyn were other nuclei. The continuing investigation of minor Roman roads and tracks is revealing other purely local focuses at which roads converged. While the county may well have been sparsely inhabited as compared with the high Middle Ages, the impression remains that fundamental change had occurred. Under the Romans Hertfordshire was settled by people living in communities that were in communication with one another. We are no longer looking simply at the growth of isolated settlements in the wilderness.

While some of the pre-Roman Iron Age sites were abandoned, three farms near Letchworth for example, there was far more new settlement. The general impression which the archaeological evidence conveyed until recently was that Roman settlement was much more thorough in the west and centre of the county than in the north and east. This is in contrast with the situation in the medieval period but resembles that of the twentieth century. There may, indeed, be a connection for modern archaeological interest has been focused on the south-west for much longer than on the north-east. The Viatores' study of *Roman Roads in the South-East Midlands* does not cover the area east of the Great North Road. Dr Keith Branigan published in 1973 an excellent book on 'the archaeology of Verulamium and the Roman Chilterns', *Town and Country*, which summarised much earlier work. In contrast a study of the archaeology of the Stort valley and of Braughing Hundred has only just commenced, while C. R. Partridge published the first comprehensive study of Braughing and I. M. Stead of Baldock in 1975. It may be that there was more clearing of woodland for farming in the west of the county than in the east. This would not be surprising in view of the importance of Verulamium. But recent discoveries in the Baldock and Braughing areas are beginning to suggest that there was a more even distribution of Roman settlement all over Hertfordshire.

The main features of Roman settlement are made clear by Dr Branigan. In Verulamium Hertfordshire acquired its first town and, it must be added, a town far in advance materially and culturally of anything else the area was to possess for at least a millenium and a half. Verulamium was built and rebuilt with imperial encouragement; it was not a natural, native evolution, but it long survived the departure of the legions. While the south-eastern quarter of the town, excavated by Sir Mortimer Wheeler in the 1930s, decayed in the third quarter of the fourth century A.D., Professor S. S. Frere's excavations, after the Second World War, have revealed that other parts of the town were rebuilt. One house near the forum, built between 370 and 390 with a heated room and mosaics, was used well into the fifth century. In the mid-fifth century a large buttressed building, perhaps a food store for siege conditions, was built and aligned with the roads. Roads were repaired and when the buttressed building was itself pulled down a municipal water main was laid across the site. As Keith Branigan puts it, "the continued activity and existence of a municipal authority in Verulamium in the mid-fifth century is thus well established" by archaeological evidence, as well as by St Germanus' visit in A.D. 429.[17] Indeed the English may have been kept out of the Chilterns and their south-eastern fringes until the late sixth century.

The most important influence of Roman towns on the

[17] Keith Branigan, *Town and Country*, 1973, pp. 133–4, 142 and 144.

Hertfordshire countryside, however, was indirect, through their effect on the Celtic aristocracy. Though the Belgae were not naturally town dwellers, they quickly adapted their country estates to Roman ways. Between A.D. 70 and 90 villas were built at Park Street, Lockleys in Welwyn, and Boxmoor among others. The new villa at Park Street was a replacement for the farm huts burnt down by Boudicca in A.D. 60. All these early villas were on Belgic tracks or early Roman roads which connected them with Verulamium. The town was their social centre and their local market "where the surplus from the farms could be turned into hard cash", some of which would be spent "at the blacksmiths and bronzesmiths on Watling Street". The villa owners also came to the town to take part in the local government of the region. "Verulamium and its villas were inseparably linked socially, commercially, and politically".[18]

It would not be in the least surprising if future excavation at Braughing produced a picture of survival well into the fifth century, though it is unlikely that Braughing remained for so long as Verulamium a bastion against English invaders. The first Roman site seems to have begun in ribbon development along Ermine Street, north of Puckeridge, near an area already occupied (Fig. 6). From the middle of the third century A.D. until about A.D. 400 a substantial Roman town existed at Wickham Field. It is not unlikely that future excavation will alter these dates. The Roman settlement of Baldock (Fig. 8) lasted from the first century A.D. to the fourth century at least.

An area of at least 50 acres (20 hectares) was occupied . . . the results (of excavations to date) bear little resemblance to the conventional idea of a Roman town for there are no fine houses, mosaics, temples or public buildings. Instead the site has all the features of an Iron Age farmstead, but exaggerated to an enormous scale . . . Baldock is

[18] Branigan, pp. 48–9.

significant as an Iron Age oppidum, established certainly by the first century B.C., which continued in occupation throughout the Roman period.[19]

The settlement extended on both sides of a Roman road, Pesthouse Lane or Clothall Road, and reached as far as the High Street on the south-west.

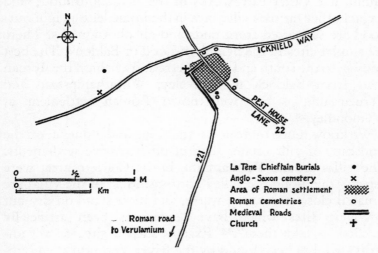

Fig. 8. Roman Baldock.

Probably Braughing and Baldock were, like Verulamium, the centres for a similar though less considerable network of country estates which had the same kind of relationship to these smaller towns. An interesting site was excavated in the mid 1960s near Bromley Hall Farm, on the parish boundary between Standon and Much Hadham. It was a group of pottery and tile kilns south of Stane Street, the Roman road from Braughing to Colchester. This industrial centre developed substantially in the third century, when the ribbon development along Ermine Street was taken over by an in-

[19] I. M. Stead, 'Baldock' in *Small Towns*, pp. 125 and 128.

dustrial community and the town in Wickham Field was prospering. A new villa appeared at Mentley Farm on the plateau above the Roman town to the west. By the fourth century the Bromley Hall potteries were servicing a wide area: a stretch of road was built from the pottery to link it with Stane Street. There was a villa, similar to that at Mentley Farm, in the south of Standon, near Youngsbury, with tumuli and other earthworks in the neighbourhood; and several other farm or villa sites in the immediate neighbourhood are suspected from finds and air photographs. There are similar sites in the neighbourhood of Baldock. The best known, to the south and a kilometre and a half off the Roman road from Baldock to Graveley, Wheathampstead and Verulamium, is the well-known Roman settlement at Wymondley.[20]

We know much more about the siting and influence on the landscape of villa estates than of other, native settlements. The villas around Verulamium, in the Chiltern area, were "strung out along the valley bottoms. Most of the villas are situated close to running water, and most stand on dry but low-lying sites which have sometimes been artificially levelled to take them".[21] Exactly such a site, as yet unexcavated, has been found by the River Ver, near the boundary of Harpenden and Redbourn by Dr Eric Humphries.[22] Similar sites were occupied on the eastern boundary of the county on "the gravel terraces of the Stort, one between Roydon and Sawbridgeworth, the other between Birchanger and Quendon". To which town, if any, these settlements in the Stort valley looked is not clear but there was a temple at Harlow. The Roman occupation of the Welwyn area provides an admirable example of the setting of such settlements. Lockleys

---

[20] Partridge, 'Braughing' and *Journal of Roman Studies*, 55, 1965, p. 211; 58, 1968, p. 194; 59, 1969, pp. 221–2.

[21] Branigan, p. 80.

[22] *Wheathampstead and Harpenden*, p. 20.

was sited on a mixture of clay and gravel over chalk, described as the 'finest barley-land in Hertfordshire' . . . Here then we see the establishment of a romanised farm on a virgin site selected both for its good barley soil and its position near a ford—a river valley site hemmed in by woods such as seldom tempted the men of the pre-Belgic Iron Age.[23]

A complete contrast is provided by another Roman site with 'overlapping rectangular enclosures' which Prof. St Joseph observed from the air, south of Guilden Morden in Cambridgeshire. It lies scarcely 800 metres north-east of the village of Ashwell and "the site is only $1\frac{1}{4}$ miles from the well-known Iron Age settlement at Arbury Banks". This place seems to offer "a chance of studying", through excavation, "the developing pattern of land use from the Iron Age to the Roman period".[24]

Keith Branigan's calculations are that since a villa in the Chiltern area was found about every two miles, their average estates consisted of some 450 acres of meadow, field and pasture together with a considerable amount of woodland. Interestingly the demesne lands of medieval estates in the Chilterns were of much the same size. Professor Applebaum credited the Great Wymondley villa with 680 acres.

It seems certain that from such villa sites romanised farmers continued to expand the area of cultivation up the valley sides on to the heavier soils of the boulder-clay covered plateaux. Sites like that of the tomb on the Rothamsted estate in Harpenden and the temple in Barkway, where silver plaques were found in 1743, suggest the occupation of the clays on the chalk dip-slope. Professor Applebaum commented on the "four or five sites along the Hertford-

[23] S. Applebaum, 'Roman Britain' in *The Agrarian History of England and Wales*, Vol. 1, II, ed. H. P. R. Finberg, 1972, pp. 65 and 11–12.

[24] J. K. St Joseph, 'Air Reconnaissance in Britain 1969–72' in *Journal of Roman Studies*, 63, 1973, p. 214.

shire border (near Meesden and Berden)" which support the idea of occupation "of the east Hertfordshire heavy clay area".[25] They may represent an advance up the Stort valley from earlier settlements or up a Roman road from Braughing.

As yet it is impossible to make any precise and comprehensive calculation of the full extent of Roman settlement in Hertfordshire, but it would be unwise to underestimate it. One cannot take it for granted that the description of the county as 'thickly wooded when the Anglo-Saxon settlement began' provides an accurate impression of its condition at the beginning of the fifth century A.D.[26] On the contrary work in recent years points to quite extensive clearances for settlement in the Romano-British Iron Age.

The Anglo-Saxons

The Roman military occupation of Britain ended in the first decade of the fifth century with the final departure of the legions. It is not possible to put a date to the English 'conquest' for there was no such thing. Infiltrating Anglo-Saxons from Northern Europe penetrated Britain over many centuries. They intermingled with the declining British population; sometimes the two peoples fought, sometimes they lived side by side. Roman culture, in its widest sense, slowly decayed and a new English society was born absorbing something from the past. How this process may have affected the local landscape is the theme of the next chapter. A brief summary of how the English took over locally will end this chapter.

Early arrivals came along the chalk ridge from the east. Archaeological discoveries in the Baldock area are suggestive of what may have happened. Around Blackhorse Road

[25] Applebaum, op. cit., p. 65.
[26] J. Gover, Allen Mawer and F. M. Stenton, *The Place-Names of Hertfordshire*, 1938, p. XIV.

in the parish of Norton in Letchworth evidence has turned up of occupation from Neolithic to Saxon times. The area is a kilometre and a half west of the centre of Baldock and just north of the Icknield Way; there is a local ditch and dike system. It seems possible that the Roman development of the Baldock area began in a movement from the Blackhorse Road site, and that a return was made to this site in the disturbed fifth century. Burials discovered between 1958 and 1966 are evidence for an early Saxon community which continued in existence from pagan into Christian times. One skeleton had an iron spearhead lodged in the chest.[27] An early Saxon hut was excavated in 1960–1 in the garden of 444 Broadwater Crescent, Stevenage to the south of Baldock. These may be fragmentary remains of the earliest Anglo-Saxon settlers. One of the smaller groups in an early Mercian tax list, the Tribal Hidage, was the Hicce from whom Hitchin got its name. Mercia was to become the dominant influence in Hertfordshire; Hertfordshire dialect is midland English and most of the west and centre of the county, except for the estates of St Albans Abbey, was in the Mercian diocese which after many changes settled its diocesan centre at Lincoln.

Most of Hertfordshire was at first in the kingdom of Essex. As late as A.D. 704 the king of Essex granted land as far to the west as Haemele (Hemel Hempstead) to the Bishop of London. London was in the Essex diocese and a significant area of east Hertfordshire remained in this diocese until 1845. Early settlers from Essex had penetrated the Stort valley and reached the Rib. Thundridge, like Baldock, may well have been a point of contact between Anglo-Saxons and Romano-Britons. The name, Thunor ridge, suggests early pagan settlement and Harlow field in Thundridge parish may commemorate a pagan Saxon burial place;

[27] John Moss-Eccardt, *Antiquaries Journal* and 'An Anglo-Saxon Cemetery at Blackhorse Road' in *Bedfordshire Archaeological Journal*, 1970, Vol. 5, pp. 27–32.

while the Roman buildings near Youngsbury are only half a kilometre north of the Rib and Thundridge Bury. Other early contacts between the two peoples may be commemorated in some of the local Wickham names. Margaret Gelling first suggested that those Wickham names which come from the Old English *wīchām* might indicate early Saxon settlement in the neighbourhood of a Romano-British settlement. She accepted that Wickham Hall in Bishop's Stortford, on the county boundary, was such a name. With proper academic caution she would not accept Wickham Hill, the site of Roman Braughing, although it was 'a very tempting specimen', because there were no 'early spellings available on which a sound etymology could be based'.[28] At the time she was writing Roman kilns at Bromley Hall Farm, four kilometres to the south-west of Wickham Hill, were being excavated at Wickham Spring.

The early Anglo-Saxon settlers in these two areas of Hertfordshire were held back from further expansion to the west and south-west by the survival of Romano-British Verulamium. The Anglo-Saxon Chronicle records a significant English victory over the British in A.D. 571 at Bedcanford and the capture of Limbury, Aylesbury, Benson and Eynsham. This English expansion into the Chilterns, from the south-west, probably ended the independence of a small Romano-British kingdom which may have already been weakened by the plague of A.D. 547.

So in two parts of Hertfordshire there were early contacts between the Romano-Britons and Anglo-Saxons which may have led to long-term peaceful coexistence, while in the west of the county this was absent. When the Anglo-Saxon conquest was complete, Essex accepted Mercian overlordship and in 793 Offa of Mercia founded St Albans Abbey on the hill across the Ver valley from Roman Verulamium, granting the abbey much land in West Hertfordshire. It is probable

[28] Margaret Gelling, 'English place-names derived from the compound wīchām' in *Medieval Archaeology*, Vol. XI, 1967, pp. 88–90.

that most of this was woodland, either never settled or covering abandoned Romano-British settlement sites.

The early diocesan boundaries and any local government units which existed were wiped out by the Danish invasions. When Alfred stabilised the division of England between himself and the Danes, the Lea was the frontier. The Danes did not keep the peace:

> It is probable that the Danish frontier was advanced . . . for the most westerly of the hundreds into which Hertfordshire was divided in 1086—a district of which nearly the whole lay to the south and west of the River Lea,— was then known as the 'Danish' hundred, presumably in contrast to adjacent English hundreds in Beds. and Bucks.

Hertfordshire was the first frontier district reconquered from the Danes by Alfred's son, Edward the Elder. Its artificial boundaries and internal organisation must date from this time. A hundred years later in 1011 the county was first mentioned by name.[29]

SELECT BIBLIOGRAPHY

Hertfordshire Archaeology (1968, 1970, 1973).

The Viatores *Roman Roads in the South-east Midlands* (1964).

Branigan, Keith *Town and Country: the archaeology of Verulamium and the Roman Chilterns* (1973).

Rodwell, Warwick and Rowley, Trevor (Ed.) *Small Towns of Roman Britain* (1975).

The Transactions both of the East Herts. and the St Albans and Hertfordshire Architectural and Archaeological Societies.

Bedfordshire Archaeological Journal.

[29] *Place-Names*, p. XVIII; *The Anglo-Saxon Chronicle*, trans. G. N. Garmonsway, 1953, p. 141.

3. English Hertfordshire

Odsey and Hitchin Hundreds: the Vale of Wringtale. East Hertfordshire: Edwinstree and Braughing Hundreds. Central and West Hertfordshire. Hertford and St Albans.

HERTFORDSHIRE WAS 'England meditative' to E. M. Forster. Sir William Beach Thomas wrote of 'its wholly English character' and to Canon Charles Raven it was 'typically the highest common factor of England'.[1] But how much of the county's appearance was due to the pioneering of its English settlers? There can be no simple answer. English settlers reached most of central, southern and western Hertfordshire at a late date. But along the northern chalk ridge and on the eastern fringe of the county they arrived much earlier. There is substantial evidence for Romano-British survival in the west and centre of the county area, centred on the capital of the Catuvellauni at Verulamium. It is not too great a flight of the imagination to see a frontier zone running through the middle of the county from south of Hitchin to north of Hertford.

The evidence for this is in the place-names. Between Walsworth, the farm of the Britons, in Hitchin and St Paul's Walden and King's Walden, the valley of the Britons, a little to the south-west, is Wain wood, on the boundary of Preston and Ippollitts' parishes. Wain wood is thought to mean the valley of the heathen worshippers, in other words, of pagan English before the conversion. Perhaps it is more than historic irony that Preston means the Priests' farm and that Ippollitts commemorates the name of a saint. Many centuries later "a thousand people have met in that dale at

---

[1] Sir William Beach Thomas, *Hertfordshire*, 1950, pp. 2 and 11.

66

midnight to hear Mr Bunyan preach".[2] To the south-east Tewin, four kilometres west of the River Beane, and Thundridge, almost the same distance to the east of the Beane, suggest early English settlement. They commemorate the pagan gods Tiw and Thunor. But the River Beane between them is given the Celtic name, *Bene ficcan*, in the Anglo-Saxon chronicle; *ficcan* is an adjective probably meaning little. Placing the adjective after the noun was a grammatical development which only took place in the Celtic tongue in the late sixth century. This suggests that a Celtic language was evidently spoken here long after the English had settled in neighbouring areas and that these were no isolated pockets of a continuing British population. It "points to a considerable period of peaceful intercourse between the English settlers of Hertfordshire and the Britons".[3]

The difficulty which the historian meets is in deciding the significance of this rather speculative evidence in relation to the problem of continuity of settlement. Is the pattern of the countryside something which the English settlers created by clearing woodland or is it closely related to earlier Iron Age and Roman settlements? If the latter, did these earlier settlements only influence the English as obvious deserted sites or was there parallel occupation? The answers can only be tentative and will be different in different parts of the county.

Odsey and Hitchin Hundreds: the Vale of Wringtale

The early Saxon settlement in Cambridgeshire, which Christopher Taylor described in *The Cambridgeshire Landscape*, spilled over into Hertfordshire along the Icknield Way route. It came early into an area already intensively settled. It is not surprising that it was in this area that Frederic Seebohm long ago pointed out the "local evidence of con-

2 W. Branch Johnson, *Companion into Hertfordshire*, 1952, p. 213.
3 *Place-Names*, pp. XV–XVI.

tinuity between Roman and English villages". Seebohm suggested that there was evidence for earlier Roman occupation of significant English settlement sites in Hitchin, Ashwell, and many of the neighbouring villages in south Bedfordshire and north Hertfordshire. But his most remarkable topographical study was of Great Wymondley. The plan which he printed is worth reproducing with the addition of more recent archaeological discoveries (Fig. 9). It is still possible to walk over the unploughed fields inside the area which Seebohm identified as a Roman holding. The hedges and earthworks convey the distinct impression of an ancient enclosed farm.

There were arable open fields in Great Wymondley which were mapped in 1803 and these fields, according to Seebohm,

> were originally divided off from the village by a stretch of Lammas land. Between this Lammas land and the church in the village lie the remains of the little Roman holding. It consists now of several fields, forming a rough square . . . and contains, filling in the corners of the square, about twenty-five Roman *iugera* . . . the extent of land often allotted . . . to a retired veteran . . . The proof that it was a Roman holding is as follows:— In the corner next to the church are two square fields still distinctly surrounded by a moat, nearly parallel to which, on the east side, was found a line of black earth full of broken Roman pottery and tiles. Near the church, at the southwest corner of the property, is a double tumulus, which . . . may have been . . . a terminal mound. In the extreme opposite corner of the holding was found a Roman cemetery . . . Over the hedge, at this corner, begins the Lammas land. How many other holdings were included in the Roman village we do not know, but that the village was in the same position in relation to the open fields that it was in 1803 is obvious.[4]

[4] Frederic Seebohm, *The English Village Community*, 1883, p. 432.

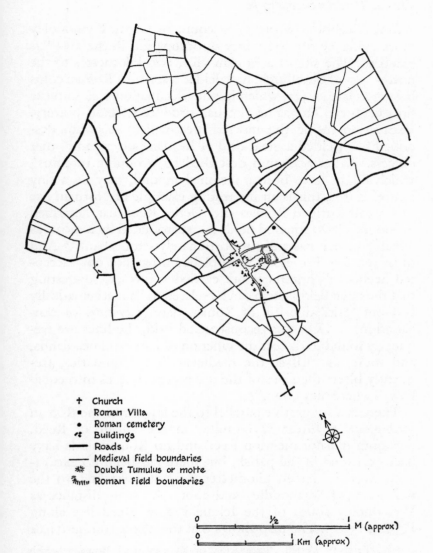

Church
Roman Villa
Roman cemetery
Buildings
Roads
Medieval field boundaries
Double Tumulus or motte
Roman field boundaries

0   ½   1 M (approx)
0   1 Km (approx)

Fig. 9. Great Wymondley.

69

Since Seebohm wrote his account of Great Wymondley more evidence for continuity of occupation in the area has emerged. The site of a Roman villa, two kilometres to the north-west of the church, has yielded a series of Roman coins lasting as late as 423, which implies occupation well into the fifth century. The same site has produced Saxon pottery. Excavation inside the moated area which Seebohm described has yielded a great deal of Roman pottery and other objects.[5] What Seebohm described as 'a double tumulus', which might have been a terminal mound, may be a tiny motte. If it is, this is an interesting example of Norman use of a small fortified Roman site. Derek Renn has described Seebohm's 'two squared fields . . . surrounded by a moat' as a bailey 'which has a disproportionately strong bank'.[6] And most recently Professor S. Applebaum has not only accepted Seebohm's argument but carried it further, suggesting that the open field system can be related to "a mathematically laid out 'grid' division of Roman date (*Limitatio* or centuriation) . . . On this reconstructed grid, the lines are frequently found to dissect the junction of lanes and headlands, and these, as well as the medieval field boundaries, frequently bisect the sides of the ten-iugera squares into equal halves where they cross."[7]

There is a suggestive parallel to the lay-out of the Roman settlement of Great Wymondley in the village of Reed. Seebohm did not mention Reed and no Roman finds have been recorded in the parish, but there has been no excavation. Reed is sixteen kilometres, in a straight line, to the north-east of Wymondley and about the same distance as Wymondley south of the Icknield Way. Reed lies along Ermine Street. The map shows that the whole southern half

[5] W. Percival Westell, 'Excavation of an uncharted Romano-British occupation-site at Great Wymondley' in *East Herts. Archaeological Society Transactions*, Vol. X, Part 1, 1937, pp. 11–15.

[6] Renn, p. 27.

[7] S. Applebaum, in Finberg, *Agrarian History*, pp. 90–8. See also V.C.H., IV, pp. 169–71.

of the parish is gridded by roads, lanes and field boundaries, and there is an astonishing number of moats and ponds (Fig. 10). Most of the rectangles into which this area is divided are of a size comparable to that of Seebohm's holding in Wymondley; they could be fitted into Professor

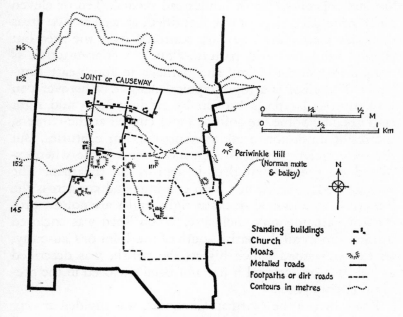

Fig. 10. Reed.

Applebaum's grid. The late R. H. Reid, who pointed out the extraordinary nature of this landscape, consciously flew in the face of what was then specialist opinion in asking whether Reed might not "have originated as an area, a very small one it is true, of Roman centuriation". He was cautious enought to add that "final proof . . . must be obtained in the hard way, by excavation".[8]

If Reed was a Roman settlement, or a British estate in-

[8] R. H. Reid, 'Reed: a topographical problem' in *Hertfordshire Past and Present*, No. 3, 1962–3, pp. 24 and 19.

fluenced by Roman 'estate management' techniques, and it is difficult to see any other explanation of its peculiar topography—then it could become a classic area for the study of continuity. The 'grid-like formation' covers a square measuring a kilometre and a half in both directions; within it is a 'unique concentration of homestead moats'. Ten or eleven different moated sites can be identified, as well as two areas of house platforms. They are scattered over the area but aligned with the grid pattern. "Such a concentration is unique in Hertfordshire" and perhaps in south-east England.[8] The place is a topographical delight. Wherever you walk the landscape is broken by straight lines and right angle bends. Some are softened and curved at the corners, the result no doubt of taking short cuts for centuries. But the rectangular pattern is even more remarkable when explored on the ground than it appears on the map. The straight hedgelines which both continue and cut across the lines of lanes and field tracks at right angles are not the product of parliamentary enclosure. When Reed was enclosed in 1808 almost all the parish south of the Joint or Causeway, an east-west road which bisects the parish, was described as 'Old Inclosures' and it had not been enclosed in the previous twenty years.

Reed, before the Norman Conquest, was divided among several Anglo-Saxon owners and, small as it is, had several manors afterwards. The chief manor, Challers, was the head of the Scales' holding in the country and there was a small castle, 'a moated mound with two small baileys' on Periwinkle Hill.[9] This castle, the outline of which can still be traced in a ploughed field, is sited, significantly, outside the gridded area of Reed and so just outside the parish boundary, in Barkway. Half a kilometre to the north-east of Periwinkle Hill seven silver votive plates and a bronze statuette of Mars were found in 1743 in a chalkpit in Barkway parish; this is the only archaeological evidence for Roman occupation of

[9] V.C.H. IV, p. 27.

the neighbourhood. Reed church has Saxon long and short
work in all four angles of the nave and in the north doorway,
and there is a block of rough masonry at the foot of the north
pier of the chancel arch which suggests an even earlier
building. Reed had a parish priest in Domesday Book.

The modern village of Reed has no nucleus and the ground
drops away to the north with magnificent views over the
Cam basin; this area was all open field until 1808 and is still
almost empty of houses. Therfield, the neighbouring parish
to the west, has many scattered settlement sites but it does
have a nucleus, around an open green. A small, unfinished
motte, sited near the church, is related to the banks and
ditches of a fortified village. The centre of Therfield is compact, very different from the open network which is Reed.
Therfield had a large area of open field which was not enclosed until 1849. Wymondley too had late surviving open
fields. Sir Henry Chauncy writing at the end of the seventeenth century described Odsey Hundred, which contains
an upside down triangle of parishes in north Hertfordshire
with Ardeley at its apex and Royston and Ashwell at each
end of its base, as 'for the greatest part Champion'.[10] The
open fields lasted longest here and to the west in Hitchin
Hundred. Most of the villages are nucleated. While north-
east Hertfordshire in general was much more heavily populated at the time of Domesday Book than the rest of the
county, in "the scarp-foot zone of the East Anglian Heights
. . . the Vale of Baldock . . . the densities of plough-teams
and of population were higher than the average for Eastern
Hertfordshire as a whole".[11] The landscape pattern is typical of the Anglo-Saxon settlements in the Midlands. So was
the whole area derelict when settled by the English? Place
name evidence could be interpreted in this way. Reed comes
from the Old English for rough ground; Therfield 'may

[10] Sir Henry Chauncy, *The Historical Antiquities of Hertfordshire*, 2nd edition, 1826, Vol. I, p. 59.
[11] Campbell, p. 95.

refer to an open stretch of dry, treeless country';[12] and Wymondley got its name from the clearing or wood of Wilmund.

But there is another possibility. The English names need not date from the earliest English settlements, *if* these were made among a considerable British population. The nucleated village with its open-field landscape might be the result of centuries of slow change from an earlier, more scattered Romano-British settlement pattern, pieces of which survive in Reed and Therfield and Wymondley. If so the present names of these villages may be late ones. There is good evidence from this very area of Hertfordshire that an apparent nucleated open-field parish developed out of quite a different settlement, though not a Roman one.

When Lilian Redstone described Bygrave in 1912, for the Victoria County History, it was 'still uninclosed' and formed

> one of the most interesting examples in this country of a concentric medieval village of the Teutonic type of settlement . . . The village is in the middle of the parish on high land. Like other early Teutonic settlements in this country it lies off the main road, about a mile and a half from the Roman road to the west and half a mile from the Icknield Way on the south.[13]

The village has changed since 1912: the broad street, once a market place, has lost its cottages and is now lined with enormous, modern barns full of machinery; a large modern house is in the centre of a moat; the strips and furlongs have gone, and a farm vanished. But it is still possible to walk the field paths and study the patterned landscape.

The centre of the village is a complex of moats. Why this has been described as a 'Palace' on Ordnance Survey maps since the nineteenth century is a mystery. The site (Fig. 11)

[12] *Place-Names*, p. 166.
[13] V.C.H. III, pp. 211–12. See also Finberg, *Agrarian History*, pp. 483–6.

consists of an inner deep moat surrounding a trapezoidal piece of ground; all this is thoroughly overgrown with woodland and undergrowth. Another moated enclosure adjoins this on the north. This enclosure contains the new house and seems to have ended south of the church; so the

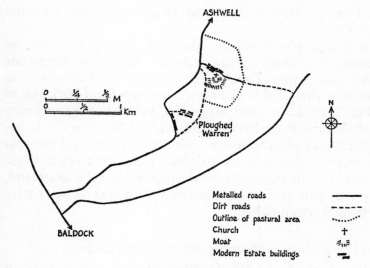

Fig. 11. Bygrave.

church was *outside* the central pair of moats. There are some indications that the southern and eastern sides of an outer moat may have been more extensive. It seems possible that the whole village street, its houses and the church may have been enclosed within a bank and ditch.

Field paths, slight banks and sunken ways mark out the area of pasture land which surrounded the village nucleus. This pasture land sloped down from the village, with a dip and rise to a crest on the east. Only to the west of the Ashwell road is it no longer possible to identify the inner core of pasture, but there are banks and field roads which could mark such an area. Walking around Bygrave village the suspicion grows that the first settlement may have been for stock farming with a boundary bank round the village nucleus and something like a ring fence around a much larger area of surrounding pasture land. When arable farming developed on the land still further out, the clearly marked, central rectangle of pasture land remained. Could the fortified area of Therfield village represent a similar beginning?

Northern Hertfordshire, the Vale of Baldock or, as Chauncy described it, "the Vale of Ringtale or Wringtale which lyes North of the great Ledge of Hills crossing the Northern Part of this County (extending from Barkway to Offley)", contains some suggestive evidence for continuity of settlement from Roman and even earlier times.[14] It has a typically English landscape, yet there are strong hints that this may not always be the original landscape. Even in those areas where the English were the first to clear the woodland, they may not at first have created nucleated villages with large arable open-fields.

East Hertfordshire: Edwinstree and Braughing Hundreds

Although north-east Hertfordshire as a whole is marked off from the centre and west in so many respects, it consists of two quite different landscapes. Chauncy appreciated this; he lived just where Odsey, Edwinstree and Braughing Hundreds met, in Ardeley (Plate 23). In contrast to the 'champion' countryside of Odsey, and north Edwinstree, the southern part of Edwinstree and Braughing Hundreds were 'enclosed'.[14] Professor W. G. Hoskins chose a map of this southern area to illustrate the theme of 'Saxon Villages and Medieval Dispersion', drawing attention to 'the tangle of narrow lanes and paths winding from one isolated farmstead

[14] Chauncy, I, pp. 2 and 189, which continues, "where the Soil is mixd with a white Marle, yields the choicest Wheat and Barley, such as makes the best Mault that serves the King's Court, or the City of London, which caused Queen Elizabeth often to boast of her Hitchin Grape". See p. 182 below.

to another'.[15] Ermine Street cuts directly across this country from north to south. The English arrived early but not necessarily from the same direction as in the northern parts of Hertfordshire. They probably came up the Thames and the Lea and its tributaries, the Stort, the Ash, the Rib, the Quin and the Beane; or they may have left the Thames before reaching the Lea and come through the Essex forests.

Braughing is the most interesting area in which to consider what may have happened. The Roman town (Fig. 6) was sited at the junction of the Rivers Rib and Quin and became the focus for a remarkable number of Roman roads. The present villages of Braughing and Standon (Plates 7 and 8) are both well outside the area of the Roman town and away from the road junctions. Standon is on the Rib; Braughing is on its tributary the Quin, nestling attractively in the valley below the Roman road to Great Chesterford, an important Roman settlement. Were the villages so sited because the area of the Roman town was still occupied or because it was abandoned and feared? What is important is that Braughing, which was an extremely important early English centre, is so oddly sited. It could only have been reached across fords; the main road to the north is still barred by a ford. Yet Braughing was the head of a hundred and a deanery; the church in the tenth century was a minster; and the area may have been a royal domain. The Domesday Book description of Braughing strongly suggests an area which had long been settled and was already cultivated nearly to the margin by 1086. Domesday Book figures cannot easily be translated into modern acreages but there could have been some 2400 acres under the plough in 1086 as compared with about 3000 in 1905. An important Saxon centre grew up very close to a vital Roman one, but on a significantly different site. Very likely this happened quite early in the English settlement, though it is no longer

[15] *The Making of the English Landscape*, Fig. 8 (Hodder and Stoughton, 1955, p. 74, Penguin, 1970, p. 92).

possible to argue that the name of Braughing, the people of Br(e)ahha, itself suggests early settlement. The only explanation which seems to make sense of Braughing's importance as a centre of English church administration and local government is that, for a long time after the English arrival, the site of the Roman town was not deserted and that the new English settlements were deliberately sited to the north and south of the Roman town. One can speculate that as the Romano-British town site decayed and Braughing flourished something of the town's prestige was transferred to Braughing.

The way in which the Roman road network may have helped the English settlement to spread from a centre like Braughing can be seen in the topography of the remote little village of Meesden. Meesden is a parish of 1008 acres, in the centre of countryside typical of north-east Hertfordshire and north-west Essex. The undulating plateaux are broken by many small streams; the country is wooded and attractive in a low key. This was one of the areas in which it was suggested that London's third airport might have been sited. Nuthampstead neighbours Meesden on the northwest. The centre of Meesden is heavy clay falling away on all sides. On the north and north-east it slopes down to the infant River Stort and a tributary stream; the soil is mixed and lighter here. To the south are the headwaters of the River Ash. The Roman road from Braughing to Chesterford ran through the south-eastern part of the parish. The area was, in fact, much more accessible to English settlers than it is to modern travellers. They could have worked their way up the valleys of the Stort or Ash, or along the Roman road from Braughing. What is interesting is how the landscape was changed once the English reached the area.

There are three areas of settlement (Fig. 12). Meesden (Upper Green) is in the highest part of the parish, above the 137 metres contour line. The ground is flat and wet; Meesden (*Measdun*) means bog hill. Trees would not have

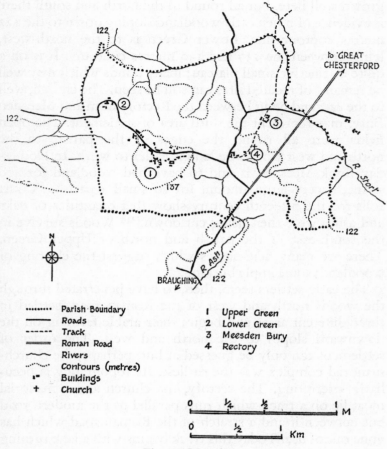

to GREAT
CHESTERFORD

R Stort

R Ash

BRAUGHING

122

N

.... Parish Boundary
——— Roads
- - - - Track
═══ Roman Road
~~~ Rivers
.... Contours (metres)
▪▪ Buildings
✝ Church

1 Upper Green
2 Lower Green
3 Meesden Bury
4 Rectory

0   ¼   ½   1 M
0   ½   1 Km

Fig. 12. Meesden.

79

grown well here, but all round to the north and south there is evidence of much early woodland sloping down to the 122 metres contour line. Lower Green is to the north-west, lying between the 137 and 130 metres contours. It is on a quite distinctive small plateau; many ponds which may well be remains of moated sites can still be seen. The church, well to the east and lying between the Rectory farm and Meesden Bury, may represent the third area of settlement. The open fields were all round the edges of the parish, to the north and west where the land is easier to work. In Domesday Book Meesden is said to have had woodland for 400 swine, a very large amount for so small a parish. "Court rolls for the fifteenth century show that quantities of oaks and ashes were then being cut down."[16] Woods survive in the south-east of the parish and north of Upper Green. There are many field-names which suggest the clearing of woodland; some imply burning.

The early settlers seem, then, to have penetrated through the woods north and west of the Roman road, settled in three different areas and begun their arable farming on the downward slopes to the north and west. The order of settlement can only be guessed at but, perhaps, the church-manorial complex was the earliest. Its topography is peculiarly interesting. The rectory, the church and a manorial moat lie on a track which runs parallel to the modern road but between it and a stretch of the Roman road which has gone out of use. Today this track begins with a lane turning off the modern road at Rectory Farm; it is continued north of the Bury by a footpath to a ford across the Stort. The map shows nothing south of the rectory but there is, in fact, a most obvious piece of overgrown road between the rectory and the Roman road. It does look as though the first English settlers turned off the Roman road one kilometre south of where it crossed the Stort and made their own track to a

[16] V.C.H., IV, p. 88. I owe much of this interpretation of Meesden to the Hon. Baron Dimsdale of Barkway.

different crossing place further upstream. In a second phase of settlement the local farmers worked uphill towards Upper Green and on to Lower Green, burning and uprooting the trees on their way. In time Upper Green became the dominant site, giving its name to the parish. A considerable number of footpaths and field roads converge on Upper Green today; three old farmhouses and farmsteads still stand on the green.

The area to the south-east of Braughing, in the bend of the River Stort, has been too little investigated, archaeologically or topographically. It has certain interesting features which Peter Richards' current study is bringing out. Many churches, e.g. at Eastwick, Hunsdon and Stanstead Abbots, adjoin Roman sites. Those at Hunsdon and Stanstead, as well as the churches at Widford and Little Hadham, are not at the centres of present settlements. These facts suggest early settlement by the English at Roman sites, settlement in isolated farms and hamlets, with nucleated villages only emerging later. The road from Stanstead to Sawbridgeworth (A414) has only recently been straightened; the marked bend to the north, to take in the Romano-British site at Eastwick, is most revealing of the antiquity and continuity of settlement in this area. The site of Stanstead village, so far from the old church-manorial centre and by a river crossing, the bridge of Thele, is a good example of how when growth occurred it was not necessarily in the same place as the early settlement site.

The growth of Stanstead Abbots across the river and the consequent creation of Stanstead St Margarets, is paralleled in two larger places in east Hertfordshire, Sawbridgeworth and Bishop's Stortford, which have similar lay-outs. William Page pointed out their significance in 1917:

all the important trading towns which have grown up at fords and bridges over the Lea and Stort have their bridge-heads. This is particularly pronounced at Sawbridgeworth and Bishop's Stortford, where the county boundary follows the River Stort except where the east and west roads through these towns cross the river, and here the county boundary projects by a tongue of land into the east or Essex side of the river. The object is the protection of the bridge or ford and the enforcement of the payment of tolls. Both these towns have similar characteristics. The market-place, now built over, at each town was square, and is placed in relation to the crossing of the river and not to the road.[17]

Close examination of the two places suggests what may be significant differences between them. At Bishop's Stortford the Roman Stane Street crosses the Stort at a ford over 600 metres north of the present and medieval river crossing. The Bishop of London's castle, built soon after the Norman Conquest, was sited so as to control this new river crossing. Stane Street went out of use in the area of the Stort crossing and new roads developed to the south, to the new ford. The market place is a rectangular area between these roads with the church on its southern side. The tongue of land across the river, Hockerill, covers both fords. Page's description fits Stortford perfectly. But Stortford has the appearance of a purely English site with very little relationship to earlier Roman settlements, of which many have been found in the area, unless it is, like Withington in Gloucestershire, a deliberate early English settlement across the river from the Roman 'town'.

Sawbridgeworth fits Page's description less tidily. There are no major Roman roads in the area, but substantial evidence of Roman settlement along the Stort, most of it on the eastern or Essex side. The 'east and west road', which crosses the Stort into Essex, is the county boundary. It was not protected by the tongue of Hertfordshire which projects into

[17] 'The Origins and Forms of Hertfordshire Towns and Villages' in *Archaeologia* Vol. LXIX, 1917, Second Series, Vol. 19, 1920, p. 53.

Essex. What this tongue did contain was the manor of Hyde Hall, "an estate which has remained in the same family from the date of its first appearance until the present day", that is from the thirteenth to the early twentieth century.[18] But this area may have had a much longer history as a unified holding; it could be the two hides (*c.* 240 acres) held by a sokeman in 1066 and might even have begun as the farmland of a Roman villa just to the north.[19] By 1066 Sawbridgeworth was the most valuable estate in Hertfordshire, because it was intensely cultivated. In so far as Domesday Book statements can be turned into reliable measurements it would seem probable that almost as much of the parish was under the plough in 1086 as in 1838, about two-thirds. But there was no market grant until 1222. Sawbridgeworth belonged to Asgar the staller and passed to Geoffrey de Mandeville. Its importance and its boundaries may be due to the agricultural wealth it produced rather than to any commercial advantage brought by the site. Indeed the 'east-west' road, which formed the northern side of the market square where it crossed A11, meanders to the west through the local countryside and does not look like an important communication route.

Central and West Hertfordshire

Whatever may prove to have been the history of the Catuvellauni in their latter days, whenever the English reached West Hertfordshire, there is little evidence for continuity of settlement here. Intensive study of Harpenden has produced indications of considerable scattered Roman and earlier Iron Age occupation related to the comprehensive road system which the Viatores uncovered as well as to subsidiary roads. But almost none of these sites were occupied later. Their relationship to medieval settlement is quite different from the pattern in Wymondley and Reed. The

[18] V.C.H. III, 1912, p. 340.
[19] Lionel M. Munby, ed., *The Story of Sawbridgeworth*, W.E.A., 1966.

sites of farms and other buildings, the field shapes and even most of the road pattern of Harpenden have little connection with the lay-out of Roman settlement. The Roman sites in Harpenden have become fields, many of them called black or grove: "the dark debris resulting from fires and the decay of vegetable matter such as thatch and wattle can cause dark patches in lighter-coloured soil and this can lead to such names as Blacklands or Black Acre being given to the field".[20] In Harpenden grove seems to have been used by the English to distinguish an overgrown, abandoned settlement site from a wood proper.[21] The northern part of Hatfield, now Welwyn Garden City, was the area chosen for settlement in the Iron Age but it was not an area of English settlement.[22] Whatever Roman settlement there was in the centre and west of the county seems to have decayed and the forest returned. All the evidence is that "except in the extreme north (Hertfordshire) was thickly wooded when the Anglo Saxon settlement began".[23] The author of the *Gesta Abbatum* claimed that the Chilterns were impenetrable forests, full of wild animals, until Abbot Leofstan cleared the area south of Watling Street in the eleventh century and made the roads safe. Miss Levett believed that he cleared 'the country round Cassiobury, Watford, Croxley, Rickmansworth, Sarratt, Langley, Aldenham, Elstree and Barnet'.[24]

Wheathampstead, which included Harpenden, was granted to Westminster Abbey by King Edward the Confessor in 1060, as "ten hides of common land . . . its fields, meadows, pastures and thickets of wood".[25] There are nineteen Ends and eighteen Greens in the area of Wheathampstead-Harpenden. These are the hamlets created by the abbey of Westminster's piecemeal clearing of the woodland over many

[20] *Field Archaeology in Great Britain*, H.M.S.O., 1973, p. 19.
[21] *Wheathampstead and Harpenden*, pp. 15 and 22.
[22] *Hatfield*, pp. 24–27.
[23] *Place-Names*, p. XIV.
[24] A. E. Levett, *Studies in Manorial History*, 1938, pp. 180–1.
[25] *Wheathampstead and Harpenden*, op. cit., p. i.

centuries, working outwards from the early nucleus in Wheathampstead village. Hatfield was settled in a similar way. It was granted to the abbey of Ely by King Edgar in about 970 'because, since the country is wooded, the brethren can find timber for the fabric of their church, and wood sufficient for other purposes'.[26] Here too there are many greens and a great many hide place-names. A hide was a family holding, of approximately 120 acres. However the Domesday Book entries are interpreted, they suggest a very different situation from that in Braughing or Sawbridgeworth. At the most less than a quarter of Wheathampstead's later arable acreage and less than a half of Hatfield's was ploughed in 1086.

This kind of settlement explains why the authors of *The Place-Names of Hertfordshire* could claim that 'it is not the village, but the hamlet or the single farmstead, which dominates the map of Hertfordshire'.[27] The historical parishes west of the River Lea, in Cashio and Dacorum Hundreds, average nearly 4500 acres; while the parishes in Odsey and Edwinstree Hundreds, in the north-east, average just under 2000 acres. As we have seen, Miss Campbell's mapping of the information in Domesday Book (Figs. 3 and 4) makes it clear that east of the Hitchin gap, east and north of a line from Hitchin to Hertford to Stanstead Abbots, the eleventh century population density and density of settlements was greatest, as was the extent of cultivated arable. The Chiltern edge, west of the Hitchin gap, and the southern Hertfordshire plateau had the lowest population density and the largest area of woodland.

West and central Hertfordshire may have been an area of 'dispersed or hamleted' settlement, but it contains substantial nucleated villages. The original core of Wheathampstead was just such "an early nucleated settlement off the line of the Roman road (where) remains of a Saxon burial were found

[26] *Hatfield*, op. cit., p. 24.
[27] *Place-Names*, op. cit., p. XIV.

... to which the probable date of 628-634 has been attributed".[28]

Markyate is, perhaps, the best surviving example of a nucleated, street village in Hertfordshire; unlike Wheathampstead it straddles a Roman road, Watling Street. Before the by-pass was built one drove north from St Albans through sixteenth and seventeenth century houses along a street so narrow that there was a 15 m.p.h. speed limit. The houses cling to the sides of a long street, most of them end on to the road. Narrow gardens run back behind them. An air photograph (Plate 6) taken before the by-pass was built makes the arrangement very clear. You can see the sites of medieval farmsteads, in their tofts, with their crofts behind them, and at their ends the hedge which marks the boundary where the arable open fields once began. The by-pass has slashed through this landscape but it has closed one end of Markyate's street, so that today you can walk in relative peace and look at the village.

One of the most attractive street villages in Hertfordshire, Walkern, is well to the east of Markyate, almost in Odsey Hundred. The same pattern of house plots, as in Markyate, can be seen stretching away from the street along its west side. The Georgian manor house with a seventeenth century, octagonal brick dovecot is on this side of the street too. There are many other buildings worth looking at, although it is the ensemble which really gives Walkern its quality. The isolated situation of the church, across the tiny River Beane and off the main road at Church End to the north, immediately raises the question whether some older form may have preceded the pattern of street settlement. The name Walkern means a fulling mill; the church is on the east

---

[28] Page, pp. 47-8 and 58. It is extraordinary that Page, a remarkable pioneer of landscape history, should have been so blinded by the orthodoxies of his day as to have stated (p. 47) that "the scattered, dispersed or hamleted settlement, is, as regards this country, Celtic in origin and no example of it occurs in Hertfordshire".

of the River Beane by a ford; a later mill straddles the river far to the south; Finche's End lies at the southern end of the street. East of this settlement area is a tangle of lanes and greens and an impressive motte and bailey. Perhaps the street settlement grew from north to south, joining Church End and Finche's End, along the road which follows the Beane valley.

Quite different in appearance from the street villages are the few, surviving, green villages of Hertfordshire, 'settlements formed round an open or enclosed area, or ring fence' as Page described them. Bygrave, and perhaps Therfield, began like this. Joscelyne Finberg believes that 'in Hertfordshire a triangular shape is more common' than a rectangle.[29] Cottered, the next parish to Walkern but one, and further east, has such a triangular green. It lies where two roads fork, but the area of green is much larger than the triangle produced by the road junction; the building line is a long way back from the road. The church at the base of the green has an aisleless nave, very light and spacious, with a large wall painting of St Christopher facing the south porch entrance. St Christopher, the travellers' saint, is shown by a river and a medieval road; there is no river at Cottered, but the village is on the Buntingford-Baldock road. Cottered Lordship, a charming, moated fifteenth century house is near the western end of the southern side of the triangle, near to the church. Walkern might have had a green like Cottered's, before it developed as a street settlement, with the church at the base and the street forming one side of the triangle. A footpath west of the Beane or a road east of it may mark the other side of the original triangle. Only one cottage remains on this road.

Joscelyne Finberg pointed out that villages like Northaw and Aldbury, which have the triangular plan, 'are in country where dense forest had to be cleared before any

---

[29] Joscelyne Finberg, *Exploring Villages*, 1958, p. 8.

settlement could be made . . . we seem to see traces of an enclosure to protect cattle from wild beasts'.[30] Two Cottered place-names are suggestive: Stocking Hill, a clearing of stumps, and Row Mead, rough meadow. Northaw is in the south of the county, on its boundary with Middlesex. Its name, significantly, means north enclosure or enclosed wood. The English Place-Name Society volume comments "all this area was part of the dense forest on the Middlesex border and is still well wooded". There was a 'wood called Bereueuue' in 1370, Barvin Park today; the Great Wood was 'probably the North Hall woode of 1611'. Aldbury, in the north-west of the county, is full of wood names: Stocks, Old Copse, The Scrubs, Walk Wood, Turlhanger's Wood; the latter contains the element *hangra* meaning a slope, which may also be present in The Hangings, Hangingrove in 1432.[31] Standing in Aldbury (Plate 9) looking up at Ashridge woods which pour over the hilltop from Little Gaddesden one can well understand this name.

Aldbury with its pond and stocks in the middle of the green and surviving houses round it is one of the most attractive villages in Hertfordshire. Northaw is more revealing: the houses back onto the triangular green and their gardens run out into it. While Aldbury faces its green, Northaw turns its back on it. The church at Northaw is at the apex of the green. At Aldbury it is off to one side, west of the base of the green. Was there any typical lay-out of such villages? It is unlikely. Hertfordshire has a great many greens but the vast majority of them were never the centre of a nucleated village.

The appearance of a village today is not always the best evidence for its early history, at least if it is not analysed critically. Redbourn has one of the most beautiful and impressive greens in Hertfordshire, but it also clings to both sides of Watling Street, very much like Markyate a little to

---

[30] Joscelyne Finberg, op. cit., p. 8.
[31] *Place-Names*, pp. 113–14 and 26–7.

its north. The Tithe Map of 1841 (Fig. 13) shows a parish peppered with scattered clusters of houses from Norrington End in the north to South End in the south, from Beeson End in the east to Holsmer End and Wood End in the west. The main manorial site, Redbournbury, with its mill is two kilometres south-east of Church End and nearly as far from the main street. Only half the houses listed in the Hearth Tax return of 1663 (38) were in 'Street End', the significant name given to the settlement on Watling Street. Only four houses were at Church End, which is at the western apex of Redbourn's common; the eastern base is Watling Street. In 1663 Wood End in the extreme west of the parish had eight houses; Revel End, in the north-west, seven. The other Ends had fewer, but all of them had several middle-sized houses, with three, four or five hearths, as well as some larger houses. We are left with the impression that settlement began in Redbourn in many different small clearings in the woodland, that a church was built at one end of a central clearing around a green, and that later still the main road attracted the largest concentration of dwellings.

Hertford and St Albans

The English not only determined very much of the basic shape of Hertfordshire's village settlements but they also fixed the sites of the county's two chief towns. There is no evidence for Iron Age or Roman occupation in the centre of Hertford. Ermine Street crossed the River Lea much nearer Ware than Hertford and most of the Iron Age and Roman occupation sites in the neighbourhood were on the heights above the Lea valley, to the south towards Hertford Heath, or to the east in and around Ware. Mrs Matthews has suggested that, when the Roman bridge across the Lea collapsed, it was natural that travellers should choose the ford at Hertford where 'the river is considerably smaller' in preference to that at Ware. "The name of Hertford tells us

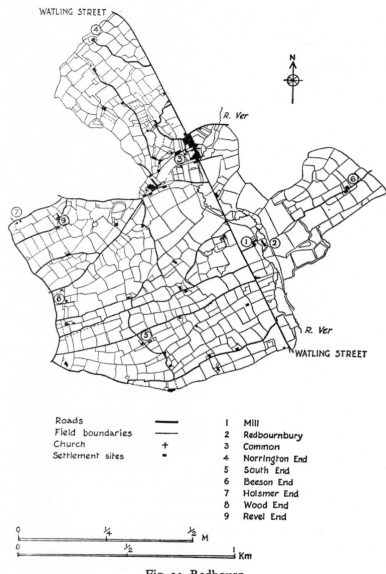

WATLING STREET

R. Ver

R. Ver

WATLING STREET

Roads	——	1	Mill
Field boundaries	—	2	Redbournbury
Church	+	3	Common
Settlement sites	▪	4	Norrington End
		5	South End
		6	Beeson End
		7	Holsmer End
		8	Wood End
		9	Revel End

0   ¼   ½   M

0   ½   1   Km

Fig. 13. Redbourn.

that it was as a ford that it was first distinguished."[32] What is in dispute is when any considerable settlement developed here. There is no archaeological evidence for early Saxon settlement at Hertford. But the county 'capital' claims that it must have been an early settlement, because it was here that the first synod of the English church met in 673. The synod met at 'Heorutford' which local sentiment has identified with Hertford and, indeed, there have been two local commemorative celebrations during this century. But William Page and his V.C.H. team challenged this identification on both ecclesiastical and topographical grounds, suggesting Hartford, Hunts. as a more likely location for the synod. Unpopular as it may be, locally, to say so, his argument has never been properly answered.

Briefly it is that the Bishop of London, in whose diocese the Hertford area then was, was not present at the synod; while the Bishop of Dunwich (Suffolk), in whose diocese Hartford, Hunts. lay, actually presided. The topographical evidence is that

> A settlement like Hertford on an old road does not generally belong to any ancient Saxon type. The more ordinary Teutonic form of settlement would be at Hertingfordbury . . . besides the relation between the two places suggested by their names, the position of Hertingfordbury village, which extends into the parish of St Andrew, Hertford, may point to a time when Hertingfordbury and Hertford were comprised in one territorial unit, in which case Hertingfordbury may have been the original settlement.[33]

Hertingfordbury, on a spur between the Lea and the Mimram rivers, has all the appearance of an old settlement site, indeed it could be a place in which settlement has been con-

[32] C. M. Matthews, *Haileybury since Roman times*, 1959, pp. 8–10 and 195.
[33] V.C.H. III, p. 492 n. 27 and 493 n. 28.

tinuous since the Iron Age. The 'bury' in its name may imply that there had been an Iron Age stronghold here, as at Arbury and Wilbury in the north of the county. The name of Epcombs, in Hertingfordbury, reinforces this suggestion for the last syllable comes from the rare Old English word 'camp' which can be used of a fortified open space. Perhaps it would be wisest to suspend judgment over the meeting place of the synod of 'Heorutford'. But if it did meet here, it seems likely that the meeting was in open country by a ford and that there was no considerable settlement in existence then.

Hertford owes its existence as a town to King Edward, Alfred's son; it was the base from which he began the reconquest of the Danelaw. The Anglo-Saxon Chronicle reports that:

> After Martinmas this year (912), King Edward had the northern fortress at Hertford built, between the Maran (Mimram) and the Beane and the Lea. Then afterwards, the summer after (913), between Rogation days and Midsummer, King Edward went with part of his forces to Maldon in Essex, . . . Another part of his forces built the fortress at Hertford on the southern bank of the Lea.[34]

Around these fortresses there developed a double town with two market places (Plate 10): the northern town was centred on the Old Cross with a church, St Mary the Less, on the site where the public library is now; the southern town was centred on the market place by the Shire Hall with a church, St Nicholas, in Maidenhead Street where Woolworths is now. The town had its own reeve and a royal mint. It became the centre of government for the new shire. It was well sited from a military point of view but not with regard to local communications and trade routes. Hertford was at its most prosperous in Saxon times and in the early Middle

[34] *Anglo-Saxon Chronicle*, pp. 96–7.

Ages was to fall behind its neighbours.

The Danish wars which had led to the royal foundation of Hertford must have affected the neighbourhood severely. Under the treaty of Wedmore (878) the boundary between Wessex and the Danelaw was defined as 'up on the Thames, then up on the Lea unto its source'. In 894–5 the Danes

> pulled their ships up . . . the Lea (and) built a fort by the Lea, twenty miles above the City of London . . . the following autumn the king (Alfred) encamped in the neighbourhood of the fortress while the corn was being reaped, . . . the king . . . made two forts on the two sides of the river, but when they had just begun that operation . . . , the host (the Danes) . . . abandoned (their ships) and went across country

to Bridgnorth on the Severn.[35] The Danish camp is reputed to have been on Widbury Hill south of Ware. If it was, Alfred's two forts must have been still further south. Hertford is never mentioned during the Danish wars and it does not seem likely that much of a settlement could have flourished in these frontier conditions. The town's constricted centre and odd shape reveal quite clearly the dominating importance of the castle site.

St Albans has a more peaceful history, one that reflects domestic discord rather than invasion. There have been four 'towns' (Fig. 14) along the little River Ver, just to the north of where it bends sharply from east to south. The valley of the Ver comes down from the gap in the Chilterns, taken by Watling Street. Near St Albans the valley bottom is alluvium with a belt of gravel on each side of it. To the east and south there is a marked change in the contour and the soil. The ground falls away and boulder clay takes the place of the gravel. The first local site, developed by the Catuvellauni, was at Prae Wood about 120 metres above sea level and west

[35] Ibid. pp. 88–9.

of the river. Verulamium, the Roman town, was much lower down but on the same southern and western side of the river, on riverside alluvium and gravel. The first Saxon town, Kingsbury, was on the other side of the river, on a spur of glacial gravel, facing Verulamium. St Albans lies on

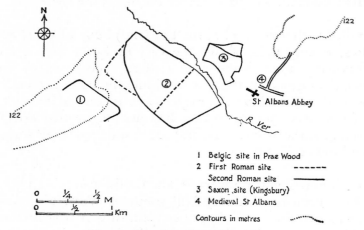

Fig. 14. The four sites of St Albans.

the same side of the river as Kingsbury but at a substantially higher site and solidly founded on glacial gravels. Human intrigue seems to have played a more important part than geography in determining the location of St Albans.

Verulamium was certainly still inhabited, as a functioning town, in the late fifth century. People probably lived on the site for very much longer; it was not deserted, but neither did it become an English town like Canterbury, Chester, Lincoln or York. Kingsbury "arose on the north of the lake or pool that protected the northern side of the Roman city" as "a castle or fortified village" and became "a Saxon town of considerable size, protected by earthen ramparts on all sides ... it was a royal town governed by the king's officers independently of the abbey".[36] Offa may well have settled

[36] V.C.H. II, pp. 123–4 and 475–6.

the town when he founded the Benedictine monastery higher up the hill on the supposed site of St Alban's martyrdom. John Shrimpton's seventeenth century account of what followed is worth quoting. Wulsin was abbot in the middle of the tenth century: "in his time a village with a few houses being erected nere to the Monastery, he called together people of other villages therein to inhabite and procured a Market to be Kept there". Abbots Ealdred and Eadmer carried out the levelling of what remained of Verulamium. Shrimpton describes how Ealdred "stopt up all the passages underground . . . for they were the lurking holes of whores and theeves". Eadmer "out of these remains of Verulam . . . new built the most part of his Church and Monastery . . . In this Abbat's time Verulamium was for ever layd in her grave."[37]

Kingsbury was the next target. Wulsin's successor, Alfric, bought the great fishpool, which was the principal source of the livelihood of the inhabitants of Kingsbury, and drained it. Fishpool Street remains as witness. Aelfric bought Kingsbury from Aethelraed the Unraed and later levelled as much of it as he could, but the king retained a small bulwark near the monastery. It was not until 1152 that King Stephen was persuaded to allow this bulwark to go: "the last remains of the town were levelled and the site ploughed and sown".[38] But St Albans had won its battle before the Conquest and the forty-six burgesses mentioned in Domesday Book were the abbot's, not the king's, tenants. St Alban's town was to grow around the market site north of, and uphill from, the abbey, the site which the abbots had selected before the Norman Conquest.

[37] John Shrimpton, *The Antiquities of Verulam and St Albans*, ed. Carson I. A. Ritchie, 1966, pp. 26–7.
[38] V.C.H. II, p. 476.

SELECT BIBLIOGRAPHY

Gover, J. E. B., Mawer, Allen and Stenton, F. M. *The Place-Names of Hertfordshire* (1938).

Seebohm, Frederic *The English Village Community* (1883).

Finberg, H. P. R. (Ed.) *The Agrarian History of England and Wales*, Vol. I Part II A.D. 43–1042 (1972).

Page, William 'The Origins and Forms of Hertfordshire Towns and Villages' in *Archaeologia* Vol. LXIX (1917), Second Series Vol. 19 (1920).

Reid, R. H. 'Reed: a topographical problem' in *Hertfordshire Past and Present* No. 3 (1962–3).

4. The medieval expansion

The growth of towns. Rural expansion. The homes of the wealthy.

The growth of towns

FOR SOME TWO hundred and fifty years after the Norman Conquest the population of Britain was increasing. All the evidence from Hertfordshire is of expansion and development. This was the period when towns took root. So great was the economic expansion that new towns were created by local landlords to bring them some of the profit. The shapes of the inner parts of many Hertfordshire towns reflect, even today, the ways in which they began their growth. Royston is the most noteworthy of the new towns. It did not exist when Domesday Book was made. A priory was founded near the cross roads formed by the Icknield Way and Ermine Street, about a century after the Conquest, and in 1189 the priory was granted the right to hold a market. By 1307 Royston was thought of as a distinct 'vill' though it lay within five parishes, three of them in Hertfordshire and two in Cambridgeshire. Most of Royston was in Barkway and the town did not become a separate parish until 1540.

At first people may have been drawn to the cross roads by the religious aura of the priory, or of Rohesia's Cross, which gave its name to the town though Rohesia's identity is not known for certain, or of Royston cave, a beehive shaped hole cut in the chalk below the Icknield Way which is carved with rough figures from the high Middle Ages and which may have been used as a hermitage; Sylvia Beamon believes it was, at one time, a place of worship used by the Knights Templars. While sanctity may have surrounded the beginnings of Royston, it was the market charter which led to its growth. That the old butter market, directly above the hermit's cave and in the middle of the Icknield Way, was to prove more attractive than the cave is symbolic. All that remains of Rohesia's cross is a lump of millstone grit by the crossroads, the socket in which is supposed once to have held the cross. Royston grew along the four roads which met here, more particularly north and south along Ermine Street. The street was then much wider and contained the main market place. As the stalls became permanent and shops replaced them there was infilling; two parallel streets were created which can still be seen north and south of the crossing of the Icknield Way.

Royston grew up around the priory with encouragement: Baldock bears all the appearance of having been planted by the Knights Templars in the twelfth century. But there had been intensive Iron Age and Roman settlement in the area, though this was not appreciated until recent excavations revealed the evidence (Fig. 8). Two Roman roads met just south of the Icknield Way and joining, crossed it. The area around the junction and crossing was granted to the Knights Templars about 1140. In 1189 Richard I confirmed an earlier grant of a market. We have no idea how much occupation of the area there was when the Templars took over. It may have been completely abandoned for many centuries or there may have been people living here. What is certain is that the Templars made a new town alongside the old site. "The centre of the medieval settlement was well to the west of that of its predecessor, and its interesting zig-zag plan, based on two main market-streets meeting at right angles, seems to have been devised to skirt the Roman settlement."[1] Centuries later the road diversions of this medieval new town were a major obstacle to motorists on the A1 and a consequent nuisance to the people of Baldock, until the modern by-pass was built. The Roman road from the south, forming the boundary between Weston and Willian, was

[1] Ian Stead, 'Baldock', in *Small Towns*, p. 125.

deflected from its junction with the Roman road from Braughing, Pesthouse Lane. The new road ran parallel with Pesthouse Lane, turned at a right angle to the north-east, and crossed Pesthouse Lane in 250 metres, joining the Icknield Way in another 250 metres (Fig. 8). Baldock's medieval market place, now narrowed by infilling, was in the middle piece of the dogleg, the 250 metres between the new road and Pesthouse Lane. A church was built at the widest end, just west of where the new road turned north-east. To the south the deflected road remained open, providing a splendid second market area, which may have been used only in more modern times. Most of the street line survives without infilling, though some of the best buildings have been destroyed since the Second World War (Plate 11). As early as 1185 Baldock contained a "blacksmith, ironmonger, tailor, shoemaker, tanner, mason, cook, carpenter, mercer, weaver, saddler, goldsmith, merchant and vintner". In 1334 it was assessed for tax at 177 shillings as compared with Royston's seventy shillings.[2]

Chipping Barnet, in the south of Hertfordshire, also grew around the widening of a deflected road, following the grant of a market to the abbey of St Albans in 1199. There was no Roman road here but this road also became part of A1.[3] The Great North Road, linking up pieces of Roman roads, was to run through these market places. It seems most likely that this famous English trunk road was in the process of creation when Baldock and Barnet became market centres.

Less than eight kilometres south of Baldock and eight hundred metres east of the Great North Road is St Nicholas' church, once the centre of the large parish of Stevenage. Stevenage was an area of scattered settlement; there may never have been any considerable village nucleus by the church and the Bury. Yesterday they were off the beaten

[2] Maurice Beresford, *New Towns of the Middle Ages*, 1967, pp. 195, 261 and 452–3.
[3] Ibid, p. 453.

track though today the New Town is engulfing them. Within two centuries of Domesday Book the centre of Stevenage had moved from the church to the road. In 1281 the abbot of Westminster, who was lord of the manor of most of Stevenage, obtained a grant of a market and fair. Robert Trow-Smith, Stevenage's historian, has described the growth of alehouses to serve travellers, which followed the move to the road. "By the fourteenth century this new Stevenage at the road junction was a flourishing little town which completely overshadowed the old settlement." Even in the nineteenth century the wide High Street, with water running down it and packed with horses at fair time, must have resembled its medieval predecessor. But long before this there had been the same kind of infilling as at Royston. The market and fair had been restricted and "were held in and about the market cross which stood at the north end of Middle Row, that little conclave of shops and houses which sits in the centre of the High Street".⁴ Trow-Smith's description makes it clear that at one time the open High Street had continued much further south.

A similar move to the main road occurred between six and eleven kilometres south of Royston, along Ermine Street. We can follow the process at work quite clearly because there were two failures before success came with the creation of Buntingford. In 1252 the lord of the manor of Pope's Hall in Buckland had a grant of a Friday market and a three days' fair. These were held at 'the New Cheping', Chipping on A10; *cieping* meant market. In 1258 the lord of the main manor of Buckland obtained the grant of a market on Tuesdays and a three days' fair just north of Chipping, in Buckland village proper, which bestrides A10. Neither Chipping nor Buckland markets prospered notably. All that remains are two little hamlets strung along Ermine Street. Success came when in 1360 Elizabeth de Burgh, lady of the manor of Pope's Hall, transferred the market from Chipping

⁴ Robert Trow-Smith, *The History of Stevenage*, 1958, pp. 12 and 28–9.

to the place where Ermine Street falls gently to cross the River Rib, originally at a ford. Some of the land here, in Layston parish, belonged to the manor of Pope's Hall. The area got its name from the ford. Buntingford was carved out of the parishes of Layston, Throcking, Aspenden and Wyddial (Fig. 15). In this it resembles Royston. The first reference to Buntingford by name is in the Templars' records in 1185; it does not appear in Domesday Book. In 1288 it is described as a hamlet; by 1292 there was a chapel of St John the Baptist, belonging to Throcking Manor, on the site where St Peter's now stands. About 1333 the rector of Aspenden built an oratory near Ermine Street. Clearly the hamlet was growing as traffic on the main road increased. Elizabeth de Burgh chose a good site, not only because of the ford, but also because the road from the Pelhams to Baldock crosses Ermine Street here. The main road was widened in a triangle, between its junction with these two roads, to make the marketplace.

Here the town of Buntingford was successfully established . . . we have the lay-out of a fourteenth century market town . . . It will be noticed that the road from the east joins the Ermine Street at the south end of the marketplace, thus compelling all cross-country traffic going east or west to pass through the marketplace and pay toll.[5]

Another ford around which a town grew was Watford, the ford used by hunters; although land in the area was granted by will in 944–6, it was listed under Cashio in Domesday Book. "The town of Watford . . . springs into existence as a market-town in the reign of Henry II without any earlier reference."[6] The marketplace was still evident on the first edition of the six-inch Ordnance Survey map; this

[5] Page, p. 53.
[6] W. G. Hoskins, 'The Origin and Rise of Market Harborough' in *Provincial England*, 1963, p. 57.

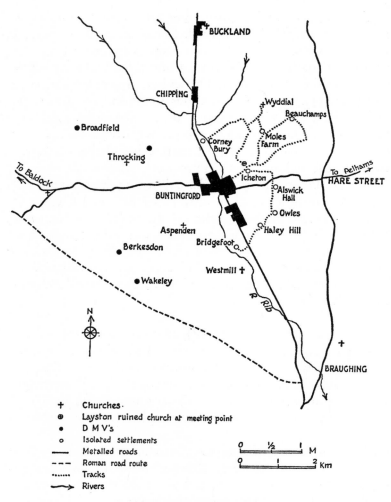

Fig. 15. The area around Buntingford.

"shows the church half a mile north of the bridge with the characteristic widening of the main road to form a market-place; a distinct kink in the frontages suggests where the marketplace terminated".[7] In 1334 Watford was assessed at 135 shillings and Buntingford at forty-four shillings, as compared with Baldock's 177 shillings and Royston's seventy shillings. This assessment, incidentally, was *before* Buntingford had acquired a market.

The growth of new towns could affect existing towns. While St Albans prospered in the early Middle Ages, Hertford decayed because of the challenge from neighbouring Ware. Hertford had 164 burgesses in 1086, St Albans only forty-six; Hertford's three mills were worth ten pounds, St Albans' three worth only two pounds. But by 1290 St Albans had more taxpayers and they were richer and by 1338 the taxable value of Hertford was only half that of Ware. At the time of the Norman Conquest Ware was only a village, though wealthy and populated. However it was much better situated than Hertford, "beside the ford on the Roman road (where) there was a fall in the river . . . and, probably, a natural division into two channels, one of which could be turned to account as the mill stream".[8] Fuller observed, correctly, that "Weare is the proper name of that town (so called anciently from the stoppages which there obstruct the river . . .)".[9] Old people still pronounced it 'Weir' between the World Wars. The people of Ware and their lords, the Earls of Leicester and Winchester, made the most of their advantages to Hertford's detriment.

A bitter fight for control of the traffic on the River Lea raged from 1191, when Hertford people broke down the bridge at Ware, until 1274 when the bailiffs of Ware "neglected the weirs, so that no boats can pass".[10] Hertford is

---

[7] Beresford, p. 455.
[8] Edith M. Hunt, *The History of Ware*, pp. 1 and 16.
[9] Thomas Fuller, *The Worthies of England*, ed. John Freeman, 1952, p. 231.
[10] Hunt, p. 17.

upstream from Ware and so its London traffic was at the mercy of Ware's inhabitants. In fact Hertford's position was challenged not only by Ware but also by Cheshunt, Chipping Barnet and Hatfield, as well as by London merchants. In 1247–8 the Londoners built their own granary at the Bridge of Thele, in Stanstead St Margarets, from which they transported corn to London in their own boats. Ware obtained a weekly market in 1199 and an annual fair in 1254. By the last quarter of the thirteenth century "Hertford had lost to Ware the passage of the Lea and the possession of the main road". Traffic had reverted to the neighbourhood of the old Roman crossing of the Lea and Hertford decayed through the fourteenth and fifteenth centuries. "It seemed rather a village than a borough."[11] Meanwhile Ware acquired the beginnings of an industrial population, such as Hertford had never had: "Before the Barons War (there were) no dyers, weavers or tanners in (the) vill of Ware, but after there were dyers and weavers but no tanners."[12] The main wealth of Ware, however, has always come from corn and malt and their transport to London by water. The triangular marketplace with its base at the church had its most important houses on the south side backing onto the river. The best way to view Ware is from the River Lea and the best views of Ware are from some of the roof tops in the High Street (Plates 13 and 14).

The post-Conquest prosperity of St Albans produced physical changes which are well documented. They must serve as an example of the way in which the centres of many Hertfordshire towns were moulded into a pattern that survived in the twentieth century. The marketplace which Abbot Wulsin had created about 950, north of the abbey, was transformed after the Conquest. It covered the ground from St Peter's church to the High Street, along which Watling Street had been deflected, and from Chequer Street

11 V.C.H. III, pp. 499 and 500. See also pp. 380–3.
12 Hunt, p. 4.

to French Row (Plates 15 and 16). This huge, triangular open space was gradually filled in. The market area was first divided up between the different trades, each of which had a row of stalls. Shambles originally meant a stall and the separate shambles of flesh, fish, leather, and pudding sellers are mentioned in contemporary documents, as are the malt, wheat and wool markets, and a cordwainers' and cobblers' row. The stalls had become permanent shops and houses by the early fourteenth century: conveyances of property refer to stalls in the early thirteenth century but to shops by the fourteenth century. So "the houses and courts and alleys between Chequer Street" and "Market Place were gradually formed". French Row, earlier known as Cobblers Row, was built before 1335.[13]

Middle Row in Stevenage was created by a similar process of infilling, as was the centre of Ware and Hitchin. Land Row, Middle Row and Water Row developed inside Ware's triangular marketplace and then disappeared, leaving the High Street with a much smaller open marketplace. Bancroft in Hitchin used to widen out as it went southwards (Plate 12). The original open marketplace at the centre of the township was framed by High Street and Bucklersbury on the west and by the churchyard, the River Hiz and Sun Lane on the east. Infilling has obscured the shape of the original centre of Hitchin, except when looked at from the air or in plan. Two separate blocks of shops are divided by the small surviving marketplace, now a car park, where the original breadth of the widening triangle can be seen. The open market ended, as at St Albans, on a through road, Tilehouse and Bridge Streets, and to complete the parallel on the other side of this road was Hitchin Priory founded in 1317. The market must have been long established by that date. Hitchin had a fair in 1221 and by 1268 the borough was farmed to the burgesses. Perhaps the founding of the priory restricted the expansion of the market. Permanent stalls

[13] V.C.H. II, p. 470.

probably appeared in the late thirteenth century; continuous tenure was taken for granted by 1470. Whether or not the infilling can be dated, narrow streets or passages like Middle Row in Stevenage, Bucklersbury in Hitchin, and French Row in St Albans should lead the enquiring eye into a study of the whole central town plan. There is, for example, just such a passage north of the church and east of the main road in Berkhamsted. Back Lane probably marks the original outer boundary of the market area which would have been an oval bulge in the main street next to the church.

Rural expansion

The growth and prosperity which led to town development did not leave the countryside unaffected. Just as people moved to the main roads in Stevenage and Buntingford so they did in the villages. Whitwell developed at the expense of its mother settlement, St Paul's Walden and, as we shall see, Puckeridge grew out of Braughing and Standon. Codicote moved from a site around the church, east of the Hitchin-Hertford road, onto that road perhaps after Henry III granted a market and fair to St Albans Abbey, the lord of the manor. Redbourn's similar move can be, tentatively, dated to some time around 1178 when St Albans Abbey enlarged its small chapel and grange at Redbourn, to honour the newly discovered relics of the mythical St Amphibalus. The priory, as it became, was close to Watling Street and its enlargement entailed encroachment on the Heath, Redbourn Common, which had stretched from Church End to Watling Street and possibly beyond. By the sixteenth century, and perhaps long before, the centre of Redbourn looked like a street village. Only the situation of the church, eight hundred metres to the south-west, and the huge common between suggested a different origin.

Movement to the main road was one consequence of economic and population growth, more general was further clearing of woodland and new settlement. Even in the more densely settled north-east of the county there were some parishes which in 1086 still had much woodland. One was Pelham where Domesday Book records sufficient wood to graze 316 swine. The area known as Pelham in 1086 later became three separate parishes. Stocking Pelham was the Pelham in which the land was covered with *stoccen* or stumps of trees. Brent Pelham was the Pelham which had been cleared of trees by a great fire. The Barnets were cleared by burning parts of the woodland belt which covered south Hertfordshire, as the name suggests. The three Barnets, Chipping or High, East, and Friern Barnet, were post-Conquest settlements. Woodland clearing and new settlement continued for two hundred years after the making of Domesday Book. Miss Levett commented of St Albans' estates that "while many of the villages were of ancient origin, the greater part of the arable land was in the thirteenth century of comparatively recent enclosure and cultivation".[14]

This post-Conquest clearing and new settlement was, for the most part, piecemeal. As population pressure increased in the twelfth and thirteenth centuries manorial lords permitted assarting within their manors and this produced some dispersal of settlement from the original nucleus. This might be quite localised; but, where the manorial estate was large and very little clearing of woodland had taken place, post-Conquest assarting could produce a considerable landscape of dispersed or hamleted settlements. The three Pelhams, which lie south of Meesden on the eastern border of the county, are covered with small settlements, 'ends' and 'greens' and scattered moated sites. Anstey, north-west of Brent Pelham, has four 'ends'—Daw's, Pain's, Puttock's and Snow—and two manorial sites with moats, Bandons and Hale Farm; Hale Farm has a castle mound as well as its moat. The church and the hall lie on the southern rim of a second,

[14] Levett, p. 181.

larger castle site. Every one of these seven settlement sites is separated from the rest. There is no 'true village'. Yet this is intensive settlement for a parish of only 2150 acres, with a population of some 230 in 1676 and 387 in 1801.

Anstey, like its neighbour Meesden, does have a village centre of a kind today; it is between the church and the Knoll in Anstey and at Upper Green in Meesden. Layston, to the west of Anstey, has no nucleus, unless the new town of Buntingford can be thought of as one. Layston church is a ruin to the east of Buntingford and above it; the site is seven hundred metres from the River Rib and nearly a kilometre from Ermine Street. There is no observable evidence of an abandoned village near the church, although old tracks which converge here lead to Wyddial, Beauchamps, the Hare Street—Barkway road, Alswick Hall, and down to the ford (Fig. 15). There is only a moat, south of the church, which could be the Icheton of Domesday Book, Echington in 1411, which "may well have been the original name for the chief manor of the parish, Layston being at first merely the name of the church".[15] The rest of the old parish contains only scattered settlement sites, none of them even hamlets. Haley Hill in the south was the home of Juliana de Hayle in 1294. Owles and Alswick Hall lie north-north-east of Haley Hill; both are moated and Alswick Hall had its own chapel. Beauchamps, two kilometres further north, has an impressive moat. It is now in Wyddial parish. Moles Farm lies a kilometre south-west from Beauchamps; Bridgefoot, the home of Walter ate Bruge in 1294, was much further south-west on the River Rib. And this is all of Layston, save for a lost site, Gibcrack, recorded in 1537. Since the modern word gimcrack comes from the medieval gibecracke, it is hardly surprising that this building has gone and the site has been lost.

Codicote in the centre of the county, like Redbourn in the west, appears to have had a similar beginning as an area of

[15] *Place-Names*, p. 182.

scattered settlements before it coagulated around its church, and then moved to the main road. The east of the parish has a group of hamlets—Driver's End, Nup End, Plummer's, Rabley Heath, and Potter's Heath. At the beginning of this century each of them except Potter's Heath, consisted of one farm and two or three cottages. While it is quite easy to identify the landscape of dispersed or hamleted settlements in many parts of Hertfordshire, it is difficult to distinguish between areas which were assarted from a nearby, existing parent nucleus and areas which began purely as hamleted settlements. Where Domesday Book lists several distinct holdings in one parish, as in Stevenage and Hertingfordbury for example, there can be no doubt about the age of the dispersed settlement. Professor W. G. Hoskins mentioned 'Roxford (in the parish of Hertingfordbury) and Epcombe', in his classic *The Making of the English Landscape*, as farms "which Domesday Book shows were cultivated on their own, quite outside the cooperative agriculture of the village fields".[16] At Hertingfordbury, and perhaps at Stevenage, one of the original hamlets, containing the parish church, may have grown into a nucleated village. If this happened at Stevenage the church site soon lost its attraction to that of the main road; and at Hertingfordbury the scattered settlements survive while the nucleus was never very considerable.

I have implied (p. 89) that the pattern of settlement sites in Redbourn indicates this type of development; and, while most of Redbourn, like all of Codicote, belonged to the abbey of St Albans in 1086, there were two small subsidiary holdings. But the field shapes revealed in the 1841 Tithe map are evidence that most of the parish was once open field (Fig. 13). They have the sinuous shape left by piecemeal enclosure of furlongs. The homestead sites at a number of Redbourn's Ends, some of them early in date, look as though they were taken out of open field strips; they do not look

[16] Hoskins, *Landscape*, 1970, p. 55.

like primary settlements in the woodland. Redbourn's field system, then, suggests that the first clearing was made from a nucleated settlement creating an open field parish, but that there was early pressure for consolidation of remote holdings, to make them workable. Gradually compact fields and farms would emerge within the open fields and a new farm house be built near each newly consolidated holding. The general impression conveyed by St Albans' estates is that the abbey favoured the expansion of its own manors, from nucleated village centres, rather than subletting assarts to free tenants. At the same time within this structure there was "the beginning of a process of exchange in order to secure compact holdings and separate closes, the planting of hedges . . . (which) was in full swing by 1300, and can be traced back to 1250 or 1240".[17] The later appearance of Codicote and Redbourn, both St Albans' estates, is deceptive: it may well be due to this process of enclosure rather than to the way in which these parishes were first cleared.

The abbeys of Ely and Westminster, undoubtedly, settled their great estates in Hertfordshire by granting out assarts, many of which became sub-manors. Ely owned Hatfield. In Domesday Book half of the cultivated arable was in demesne; by 1251, when a survey was made, the villein (peasant) land was nearly double the demesne acreage. There were fifty-three tenants of all kinds in 1086, 122 in 1221, and 128 in 1251. There had been considerable territorial expansion in the twelfth and thirteenth centuries, which seems to have reached nearly its peak in 1251. This took place on two parallel lines. The manor in the centre of the parish was expanded, hence the increase in villein arable. At the same time outlying uncultivated land was granted out to free sub-tenants. Eighty more acres of assart are described in 1251 than in 1221. By 1251 there were nearly seventy small free tenements, ranging from a mere rood (a quarter of an acre) to one and a half virgates (sixty acres in Hatfield). The total

[17] Levett, p. 185.

acreage of these free tenements in 1251 was about 750 acres, about the same as the demesne, 765 acres. In addition there were ten large free tenements, often with the status of sub-manors. Seven were hides (120 acres) and three half hides. These sub-manors and hides were distributed all round the edges of the parish, mostly in the north, leaving a central core of manorial open field around Hatfield township. Many of the hide names survive today: Cromer Hyde, Symonds-hyde, Hatfield Hyde, and Handside in Welwyn Garden City. Perhaps one reason for this survival is that these new settlements created by assarting continued for many centuries to be fundamental to the working of local government and local law enforcement. The 1487 Court Rolls contain a typical entry: "John Archer and William Couper are chosen and sworn as constables for Lodewikhide. Thomas Colyn and William Hilton for Bokenwickhide."

The abbey of Westminster settled the joint parish of Wheathampstead and Harpenden in the same way. There were two abbey manors: one was Wheathampstead which controlled the open fields on each side of the River Lea, cultivated from the nucleus in Wheathampstead village; the other was Kinsbourne or Harpenden which controlled another group of open fields in the west of Harpenden, cultivated from Harpendenbury Farm. There is a magnificent, ancient barn here, and the Victorian exterior of the house conceals a splendid, late medieval roof with the suggestion of an interior of importance. The site is on the River Ver by a ford and a track which leads from Watling Street in Redbourn to Kinsbourne Green in the extreme north-west of Harpenden. The area between these two manors, around the valley which gave its name to Harpenden, and the northern part of Wheathampstead proper, east of the Lea, were granted out by the thirteenth century if not before, in 120 acre parcels of freehold land. A survey of 1528 records twenty-seven such holdings. The nucleus of Harpenden almost certainly began as just such an assart. The parish church is first referred to in 1221 and there is no evidence for the existence of any township here before the church was built.

Two of the processes which I have been describing can be seen taking place in Braughing and Standon, though the church had no part in them. The nucleated Saxon village centres were away from the road in river valleys, but by the twelfth century new, market settlements had appeared along Ermine Street, while the main clearances produced sub-manors on the valley slopes and the crests of the hills. These two neighbouring parishes stretch for eleven kilometres along Ermine Street; Standon, at its widest, is seven kilometres from east to west. The parishes are shaped like elongated bowls (Fig. 16) and this can be seen from two roads, one at each end of the area. Leaving A10 for Hay Street, just where the northern end of the dual carriageway, Puckeridge by-pass begins, there is a lovely view of the site of Roman Braughing to the south. The ground slopes downwards and the vista is framed by woods. Then the road rises over the watershed between the Rib and Quin rivers and Saxon Braughing can be seen, nestling half-hidden in a hollow, by the Quin (Plate 7); its open ploughlands cover the plateau beyond the river. The Quin joins the Rib in the southern part of Braughing parish and the enlarged Rib meanders south through Standon. There is a superb view up this Rib valley from the road which leaves Ermine Street for Much Hadham, at Wadesmill. The road winds round the hillside on the southern and eastern bank of the Rib, giving a view of Youngsbury Park and then, from near Swangle's Farm, the Rib valley can be seen opening up to the north.

To the east of Standon and Braughing there is quite a sharp rise to a plateau; to the west there is a more gentle slope which continues beyond Ermine Street. The one point where the western rise is steeper has the significant name of Hangingwood. Here the road along the river through farm land is suddenly threatened by woods. The slopes on both

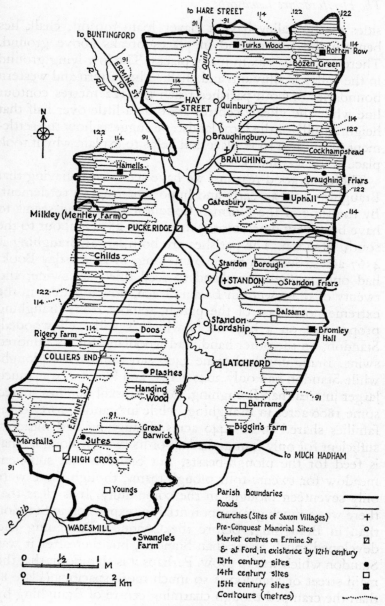

to HARE STREET

to BUNTINGFORD

N

■ Turks Wood
Bozen Green

Rotten Row

HAY STREET
Quinbury

Braughingbury
+ BRAUGHING
Cockhampstead

Braughing Friars
■ Uphall

Hamells

Milkley (Mentley Farm) ○
PUCKERIDGE ☒

Gatesbury

Childs

Standon 'Borough'
+ STANDON
Standon Friars

Balsams
Standon Lordship
■ Bromley Hall

Rigery Farm ■
COLLIERS END ☒

Doos

LATCHFORD ☒

Plashes

Hanging Wood

Bartrams

Great Barwick

Biggin's farm

to MUCH HADHAM

Marshalls
Sutes
HIGH CROSS

□ Youngs

WADESMILL

Swangle's Farm

R Rib

Parish Boundaries	
Roads	
Churches (Sites of Saxon Villages)	+
Pre-Conquest Manorial Sites	○
Market centres on Ermine St	☒
& at Ford, in existence by 12th century	
13th century sites	●
14th century sites	□
15th century sites	■
Contours (metres)	

0   ½   1 M
0   1   2 Km

Fig. 16. Braughing and Standon.

sides of the valley have a clayey loam topsoil; chalk lies beneath the surface and in places breaks above ground. There are chalk pits in many places. The low-lying ground in the valley is alluvium and chalk. The eastern and western boundaries of both parishes reach the 122 metres contour line while the village centres are only a little over half that height. Study of the local landscape suggests how the settlement of the area took place and helps to explain why it took place in the way it did.

There are good reasons, we have seen, for believing that Braughing was an early and important English settlement. By the time of the Norman Conquest Braughing seems to have been very much more settled than its neighbour to the south, Standon. The parishes are both large: Braughing is 4367 acres, Standon 7746. Braughing, in Domesday Book, had only enough woodland to feed thirty-six swine, and twenty of these were in Bozen Green, now a hamlet in the extreme north-east of the parish, remote from Braughing proper and on a high table which is still well wooded. Standon, on the other hand, had woodland for six hundred swine. Braughing had some 2400 acres under the plough, while Standon had only 2040 acres; and Standon was much larger in area than Braughing. Forty peasant families shared some 1800 acres in Braughing, while in Standon forty-eight families shared some 1440 acres. Braughing had meadow sufficient for only four and a half of its twenty ploughs, that is feed for the plough-beasts. But Standon had sufficient meadow for twenty-four plough-teams, though there were only seventeen ploughs in the community. It is clear that there was a much greater potential for expansion in Standon than in Braughing. Before the Conquest Braughing had developed much faster than Standon, but thereafter it was Standon which was to grow. Perhaps it is significant that the main street of Standon is so much more spacious (Plate 8) than the cramped though charming centre of Braughing by the church.

Most of the important settlement sites in Braughing and in the north of Standon, many of them manors or sub-manors, were in existence by the eleventh century. Some of these sub-manors began to establish manorial markets on Ermine Street, which ran through the western side of Standon. Thus Puckeridge developed from Milkley (Mentley Farm). The manor was first mentioned in the twelfth century. There was a Roman villa here. The moated site of the medieval manor, next to the later farm, lies in rolling wooded countryside above and to the west of Ermine Street. In 1311 Robert de Milkley received a grant 'of a market on Thursday and a fair' on August 29th at his manor of Puckeridge. The settlement of Puckeridge had grown up where two Roman roads met, and given a new name to the manor of Milkley. The manor of Standon Friars, across the Rib to the east and on the edge of the plateau looking down on Standon village, had a grange at a place called Popeshall (Papwell) also on Ermine Street but further south. By 1295 there was a market here which may have been the beginning of Collier's End.

While this was happening in the north of Standon, new grants of land were being made in the south. The land here seems to have been cleared and settled in a wave-like motion which spread south down the valley and then up the slopes, in stages. Six grants of land, which became sub-manors, had probably been made before Standon passed from the de Clares, who held it from 1086 to 1314 (Fig. 16). Another group of manors, which seem to date from later in the fourteenth century, are sited significantly on the southern parts of the eastern and western plateaux. They swing round in a curve from Balsams to Marshalls. Balsams lies snugly at the head of a little valley which opens up to the south-east; it may have been the site of a manorial fruit and herb garden mentioned in an extent of 1262. Marshalls is on the slopes west of High Cross on Ermine Street. Another of these new sites was Latchford, by a ford over the Rib, halfway between

Standon village and the next ford to the south, the romantic-
ally sited and appropriately named Great Barwick. Berewic
was the name given to an outlying part of an estate. Further
new sites appear in the fifteenth century records. They are
small and remote, infilling round the boundaries of the two
parishes. Examples are Bromley Hall on the eastern boundary of Standon, Biggin's Farm in the south, and Rigery Farm
in the extreme west. At the same period new settlements seem
to have taken place in the extreme north of Braughing at
Turks Wood and Rotten Row. All these places are high up
and remote.

The many scattered hamlets and farms in Braughing and
Standon parishes are the result of localised assarting undertaken from two large nucleated villages, which were the
original centres of settlement. What is fascinating is that so
many of these later settlement sites are today so inaccessible.
Where there have once been hard surfaces and even metalled
roads today there are often only bridle paths. Braughing and
Standon are full of roads to nowhere; this is ideal walkers'
country.

The homes of the wealthy

The impression of expansion which analysis of town and
village landscapes has produced is confirmed by the study of
the homes of the wealthy. Hertfordshire had two main kinds
of Norman castles: strategic ones and those with merely
local importance. The royal castles, at Berkhamsted and
Hertford, and the Bishop of London's castle at Bishop's
Stortford, Waytemore, "formed a defensive screen on each
of the principal Roman roads, about twenty miles from
London".[18] Benington and Walkern, on the other hand,
were centres of Hertfordshire baronies and held by partisans
of Geoffrey de Mandeville as western outliers of his Essex
holdings. The castle at South Mimms, just outside the old

[18] Renn, p. 15 and 25.

county boundary, may have been built by Geoffrey de Mandeville in 1142–3. Other Hertfordshire castles, Anstey, Barkway (Periwinkle), Pirton and Great Wymondley could have been built to protect local property during the anarchy of Stephen and Matilda's reign, as Therfield (Tuthill) certainly was by the abbey of Ramsey. At Anstey, Pirton, Therfield and Wymondley there is evidence that "the castle was associated with a rectangular village enclosure"—'an early village fortification', though at Therfield and Wymondley, I have suggested, the village enclosures may antedate the Norman mottes.[19]

What remains of these castles today suggests their different purposes. Berkhamsted Castle (Plate 17) is low lying, almost in the marsh which made the building of the railway line running along one side of it so difficult. The perimeter wall stands in places surrounding a large area, the bailey, which once contained many buildings. Members of the royal family were born and died in this royal castle. The Black Prince lived here and kept John, King of France, as his prisoner. At different times Thomas Becket and Geoffrey Chaucer were responsible for the castle's upkeep. A wide moat still surrounds it and in the north-east corner is the motte, on which there once stood a shell keep. Berkhamsted Castle, impressive even in decay and almost inside a market town, contrasts sharply with Walkern Castle. This earthwork is deep in the countryside on the plateau east of Walkern village. An oval shaped bailey is marked by a deep ditch and bank. The motte is a mound in the garden of Walkern Bury Farm whose cattle graze around the bailey. The view over the Beane valley, from the farm, is delightful suggesting that Hamo de St Clare, a supporter of Geoffrey de Mandeville, who built the earth and wood castle, wanted to dominate his immediate surroundings. They were the lands of his chief manor, but the site has no wider strategic significance.

Anstey Castle is also in remote countryside and on a

[19] Renn, op. cit., p. 5 and 25.

plateau, but the view is much more restricted than at Walkern. The castle site lies alongside the church and the Hall. The fine motte is overgrown but the deep moats are still filled with water. Anstey Castle had a stone keep, unlike Walkern, and survived in use much longer than Walkern. The site, the ensemble with the church and its lychgate, is most attractive; but like Walkern it can only have been chosen with local domination in mind, though Geoffrey de Mandeville did acquire it from King Stephen in 1141. Anstey and Walkern are in situations which emphasise the difference between their builders' horizons and those of the kings who sited Berkhamsted, Bishop's Stortford and Hertford Castles to dominate key fords and routes up valleys.

It may be a strategic accident that so many castles are in the north-east of the county. But it cannot be for this reason, that the 150 identified moated sites are so densely concentrated in this area (Fig. 17); in fact the north-west of the county contains scarcely a site. Derek Renn sugges 's that it is in the north-east that 'a group of sites . . . may contain important evidence of the transition from the earthen (castle) mound to the moated enclosure, which still has to be worked out'.[20] These moats are evidence for the continuing predominance of the north-east of the county into the high Middle Ages. Most moats surrounded the homes of lesser gentry and aspiring freemen, though a great variety of medieval sites might be moated. The reasons for building a moat round one's dwelling place were many: as drainage, to provide a water supply, for use as a fishpond, for defence, and because they became fashionable giving evidence that their possessor was successful and wealthy. There has been little systematic study of the Hertfordshire sites but it is observable that most of them are no longer occupied. Most moated sites are to be found in outlying parts of parishes, often in woods. There are suggestive parallels. Their situation is reminiscent of that of the Victorian farmhouses built

[20] Renn, op. cit., p. 1.

in the outlying parts of parishes after parliamentary enclosure and abandoned in the mid-twentieth century, as
personal transport improved. The woods which have grown
over the forsaken sites are reminiscent of the Roman and
Belgic sites in Harpenden which the English, appropriately,
called groves. One example of a moated site which is still

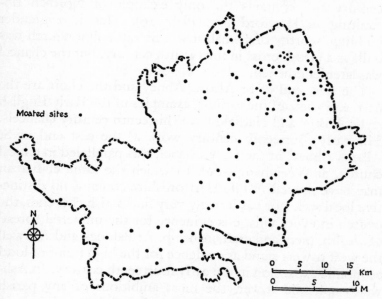

Fig. 17. Distribution of moated sites.

occupied and which contains a magnificent fifteenth century
house is worth mentioning, Cottered Lordship. Sutes in
Standon is a century and a half older. There are other
occupied moated sites, with buildings from different dates:
examples, at random, are Moat Farm in Much Hadham,
Pirton Grange, and Salisbury Hall in Shenley.

The most outstanding impact on the landscape made by
man's building during the early Middle Ages was in the
churches. St Albans Abbey, in spite of the nineteenth
century restorations by Lord Grimthorpe, still conveys the

grandeur of its early Norman building, in the crossing and in the eastern parts of the nave. There are several Norman parish churches with their apses surviving, at Bengeo, Great Amwell and Great Wymondley; all three of them vividly convey the feel of a Norman village church. Hemel Hempstead's parish church is almost completely of the late twelfth century and contains the only example of Norman rib-vaulting in Hertfordshire (Plate 19). This is a grander building, worthy of a small town. Sarratt's flint church was built as a Greek cross in the twelfth century, but the chancel was later lengthened.

The west end of St Albans Abbey and the choir are the best, and some of the earliest, examples of the Early English style. Anstey and Hatfield have thirteenth century chancels. The early fourteenth century work at the east end of St Albans Abbey, in the Lady Chapel, was paralleled in a local church, at Wheathampstead, to which the same craftsman may have moved. While Hertfordshire contains no distinctive local style nor has it many very fine parish churches, the church in every village is evidence for the universal spread of wealth, piety and craftsmanship. At Baldock and Ashwell the west towers stand as evidence for the high point of local economic expansion in the early fourteenth century. In Ashwell's splendid tower, the most ambitious of any parish church in Hertfordshire in Pevsner's opinion and now in grave danger of collapsing, famous graffiti record the end of the days of expansion; in translation they read: 1350. wretched, wild, distracted—the dregs of the mob alone survive to tell the tale—at the end of the second (plague epidemic) was a mighty wind. St Maurus thunders in all the world!

SELECT BIBLIOGRAPHY

Beresford, Maurice *New Towns of the Middle Ages* (1967).
Trow-Smith, Robert *The History of Stevenage* (1958).
Hunt, Edith M. *The History of Ware* (1946, 1949).
Renn, Derek *Medieval Castles in Hertfordshire* (1971).
Appropriate parish histories in the *Victoria County History*.

5. Late medieval decline

Deserted medieval villages. Hunting parks.

THE CHANGES WHICH occurred in Hertfordshire between
the early fourteenth century and the early sixteenth century
are complex and only half understood. There is no doubt
that there was a substantial population decline in the fourteenth century, beginning before the Black Death of 1348–9,
and that this decline affected the settlement pattern and the
appearance of the landscape. There were changes in the way
of life of manorial lords which produced new areas of woodland. But there is evidence also for growing prosperity,
especially perhaps in the fifteenth century. The prosperity of
the better off peasants not only changed the field patterns
but it can be seen in the house building and rebuilding which
has given Hertfordshire a rich endowment of late medieval
timber frame houses that is only now being properly
appreciated. In this chapter I shall only describe the landscape changes which are related to population decline.
Peasant affluence continued through the sixteenth into the
seventeenth century, and its effects will be described in a
separate chapter.

Deserted medieval villages

The decline of Hertford in the fourteenth and fifteenth
centuries was only the most extreme example of a process
which affected other market towns, but it made little lasting
physical impact on their appearance for any decay was more
than repaired in later prosperous times. It was in the countryside that this period made its biggest mark, for there was a
substantial abandonment of small sites which had been

settled earlier. The study of deserted medieval villages in Hertfordshire by K. Rutherford Davis makes three important points. Abandoned sites are far more common in the north and east of the county than elsewhere. They tend to be the smaller settlements on the fringes of villages, those settled late and at the margin of cultivation. Many so-called deserted villages were never more than hamlets. The deserted sites group significantly around surviving prosperous centres, Buntingford, Stevenage, St Albans and Tring; almost all the abandoned sites in the south and west of the county are grouped round these last two places.

Although Hertfordshire is not one of the classic counties of deserted sites like Norfolk or Warwickshire, it contains far more than any neighbouring county except Buckinghamshire. Bedfordshire, Cambridgeshire and Essex together have fewer abandoned settlements than has Hertfordshire. It is significant that eleven out of seventeen identifiable sites in Bedfordshire and six out of fifteen identifiable sites in Cambridgeshire cluster round the Hertfordshire border. They are in the upper valleys of the Ivel, the Hiz and the Cam rivers. Of fifty-nine identifiable Hertfordshire sites listed in 1973, thirty-seven are in the north-east quarter of the county (Fig. 18), near the headwaters of those rivers which drain the southern slopes of the same chalk ridge drained to the north by the Cam, Hiz and Ivel.[1] This area on the county boundary, around the Icknield Way, had been intensively and continuously settled since early Iron Age times at least. The clustering of shrunken and deserted sites in the region may mark the reversal of a two thousand year old process; it seems probable that abandonment of marginal settlements had begun in the early fourteenth century; it may

[1] I have not included 'shrunken' sites in the total and have accepted the emendations (published in *Medieval Research Group Report* No. 22, 1974, pp. 57–9) to the lists in the county gazetteer printed in Maurice Beresford and John G. Hurst *Deserted Medieval Villages*, 1971, pp. 183–4, 187 and 190. K. Rutherford Davis *The Deserted Medieval Villages of Hertfordshire*, 1973 is responsible for many of the emendations.

have been intensified by the Black Death. Perhaps it is no accident that it is in Ashwell church tower, in this border region, that an anonymous contemporary bemoaned the change. Many fascinating, if often inaccessible, pieces of the county's landscape remain as witnesses—'survive to tell the tale', in the words cut into Ashwell church tower.

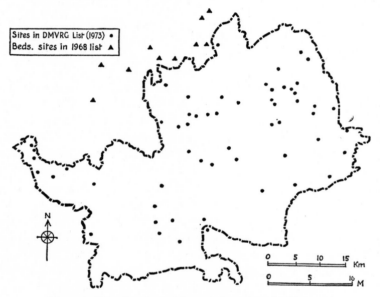

Fig. 18. Distribution of deserted medieval villages.

There are ruins of churches still to be seen at Chesfield, Layston, Minsden, and Thundridge, though the latter may never have been a village or hamlet. Church sites may be guessed at among the mounds which mark sites like Wakeley in Aspenden. The foundations of the church at Broadfield in Cottered could be seen in the 1930s, but they vanished soon after. In 1965 the site was excavated by Philip Rahtz, one of only two Hertfordshire deserted medieval village sites to have been excavated. This excavation revealed that the church had been built about 1220 and that the building and its cemetery had been deliberately planted on a site previously occupied by three houses. One of these was a house of superior construction which may have been a simple manor house. Broadfield Hall, a seventeenth century house rebuilt in the nineteenth century, stands on the site probably occupied by the new manor house which replaced the one

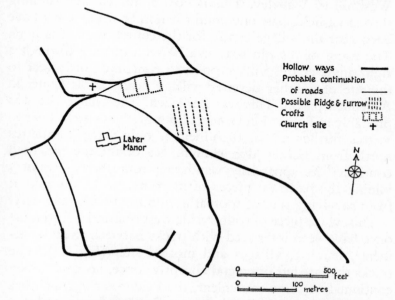

Hollow ways
Probable continuation of roads
Possible Ridge & Furrow
Crofts
Church site

N

Fig. 19. Broadfield deserted village. Based on *Broadfield Deserted Medieval Village* (Fig. 2) by Eric C. Klingelhöfer.

destroyed in 1220. The church itself was dismantled and accidentally burnt down about 1450.[2]

The long term result of the building of the church and the movement of the manor house was to produce changes in the village's street plan (Fig. 19); one hollow way silted up. The street plan, the lay-out of Broadfield, can be partially reconstructed from air photographs taken before the excavation and the subsequent ploughing up of the area. It

[2] Eric C. Klingelhöfer, *Broadfield Deserted Medieval Village*, 1974.

suggests an irregular grouping around a junction of local roads. This is different from the apparent lay-out of Wakeley, much of which can still be seen in fields to the east of Arden Farm house. Wakeley seems to have been a street village. House platforms can be clearly seen along the south side of the old route of the track from Cherry Green in Westmill to Wakeley. This is now a sunken way running through a field, past one pond to another which must have been near the village centre for the church mound is here. The route of the old road can be seen turning through a right angle at this village pond to continue north-west to the site of another deserted village near Tannis Court in Aspenden parish. This was Berkeden. The village site was probably at Berkesdon Green, although the church was 700 metres further north. Broadfield is only three kilometres north from Berke(s)don church. No doubt the old road continued its apparently wandering route across country joining the parishes; pieces of its route can be guessed at from surviving tracks, footpaths, and the parish boundary.

This whole piece of countryside west of Buntingford must once have been interlaced with tracks between small settlements, hamlets, villages and moated sites (Fig. 15). The tracks that are left often end abruptly; once, no doubt, they continued to some settlement, the evidence for which has vanished. The area lies between Ermine Street and the Roman road from Braughing to Baldock (Plate 5) which itself has gone out of use between Cherry Green and Hare Street. Anyone wishing to make their own voyage of exploration into the kind of countryside produced by scattered settlement and assarting from Roman roads could hardly choose a better area than the two sides of Ermine Street between Royston and Braughing.

Throcking provides a good example. This is not a completely deserted site: the church, rectory, Throcking Hall and other houses are grouped around a rough rectangle of roads. There was an earlier street settlement between Middle and Lower Farms, however. The only evidence for this on the current sheet of the $2\frac{1}{2}''$ (1:25,000) Ordnance Survey map is that the hedgeline to the north-east of Lower Farm, on which the farm is sited, continues in a straight line to the south-west, cutting off the bend in the road which passes Middle Farm. The hedge and the road make a 350 metres long, narrow triangle. Inspection shows that this contains house platforms; the hedgeline is that of the original village street which followed an almost straight line from the church to Lower Farm site. With the abandonment of the Lower Farm end of the village, Middle Farm was sited on what may have been the Back Lane and this became the through road, while the village street became a hedgerow.

Guy Beresford's excavation of Caldecote, north of Baldock, is producing evidence about the farm houses and barns of a medieval Hertfordshire village. This "settlement, dating from the late Saxon period, was deserted before 1428; a few peasants remained in occupation until the late sixteenth century . . . During the fifteenth and sixteenth centuries many of the crofts were amalgamated and a new metalled road, constructed on built up ground, gave access to the crofts to the west of the old sunken road." Buildings of 'cob, primitive framed and timber framed' have been found; 'the timber houses . . . built on chalk block sills . . . overlay earlier structures".[3]

While many of the small places in the north-east of the county ceased to exist as communities, the larger parishes in the centre and west seem to have survived the appalling losses brought by the Black Death in 1349. Codicote had twenty-four tenants in 1086; in 1349 sixty-five people, about half of the then tenants, died. Barnet in the south of the county and Park in St Stephen's parish, St Albans each lost

---

[3] *Medieval Village Research Group Reports* No. 20/21, 1972–3, pp. 30–31, No. 22, 1974, pp. 22–3; 'Medieval Britain in 1973: II. Post-Conquest' compiled by John Cherry in *Medieval Archaeology* Vol. XVIII, 1974, pp. 216–17.

eighty-five tenants in 1349, while Abbots Langley which had only nineteen tenants in 1086 lost eighty-two in 1349. Yet none of these St Albans' manors experienced desertion. Miss Levett has calculated that more than 900 acres of arable land in Abbots Langley lost their tenants; the arable acreage in 1905 was 2267. Yet new tenants were found for almost all the empty holdings.[4] The villages which St Albans' Abbey controlled seem to have been large enough communities to have had sufficient reserves of manpower, often woman-power as Miss Levett makes clear, to withstand the shock. Significantly, in the late thirteenth and early fourteenth centuries, before the plague, the abbots were able to make excellent bargains with newcomers seeking to take up land in the area. There must have been room for expansion and opportunities for advancement in the communities into which these *adventitii* were admitted.

There were abandoned sites in the west of the county. Tiscot near Tring was discovered by air photography (Plate 18). Perhaps it is significant both that the air photograph shows very clearly a triangular village grouped in rectangular blocks on each side of a street with three ponds, two at points of the triangle and the third in the middle of one side, and also that Tiscot is near Tring. If the original site was a green village like Aldbury on the other side of Tring, which the air photograph suggests but does not prove, then it may have been an early pastoral settlement which decayed with later clearing and the extension of arable. The growth of Tring would have attracted the inhabitants of a decaying Tiscot. In contrast Pendley, an arable village near Tring, had to be forcibly cleared to make a park in the mid-fifteenth century (see pp. 133–4 below).

Enforced desertion seems to have been rare in Hertford-shire; apart from Pendley there are only two clear cases. In

[4] Levett, Table II, pp. 284–5, 253–4, and 191–2. Mr Davis uses the Victoria County History figure of eighty-four tenants for Codicote. I have accepted Miss Levett's. They do not affect the argument.

one sheep farming was the villain of the piece: the prior of Royston kept his demesne lands at Cockenach in Barkway for folding 200 sheep. Kitts End in South Mimms, now in Hertfordshire, was diminished by eighteenth century emparkment and lost its life blood when Telford diverted the Holyhead road in 1826. With these three exceptions the county's deserted sites can, probably, all be explained as the result of the abandonment of areas of marginal cultivation, because of the attraction of a neighbouring centre sited on a main road. Not surprisingly this happened most often in the region where the pressure of population on resources had produced intensive settlement before the fourteenth century. Air photography has revealed that many Ends and Greens in the north-east of the county, where deserted sites are most prolific, shrank at the edges. In fact the distinction made by the specialists between 'shrunken' and deserted sites is too fine a one given the scattered nature of much of Hertfordshire settlement. But this does not affect the general argument that it was the north-east which was most affected.

It was here that climatic change, which began in the fourteenth century, the beginning of what geologists have called the 'Little Ice Age', had its most serious and long lasting effects. There were disastrously rainy summers between 1314 and 1325. Bad harvests and animal epidemics, leading to famine, followed. Erratic weather conditions continued. Cattle disease, and then a drought, had a dramatic effect in 1341. A large part of the arable

lay unploughed at Hatfield, Totteridge, Datchworth and Welwyn, and in the north-east at Barkway, Barley, Reed, Cottered, Buckland, Wyddial, 'Alfladewyk' (Beauchamps in Wyddial), Great and Little Hormead and Meesden. At Braughing, Royston and Therfield the fields were in the same condition. Ware and Hertford and their neighbourhood seem to have escaped, but Benington, Westmill, Aspenden, Walkern, Wakeley, Rushden and Wallington were all half desolate. So, too, were Sandon, Ashwell, By-grave and Clothall.[5]

The lay subsidies which provide this evidence are illegible in part and this may explain the absence of any place in the west of the county, but the centre and south were obviously much less affected than the north and east. Virtually every parish in the north-east quarter of the county, marked out by a line south from Ashwell to Benington and eastwards to Braughing, is mentioned as agriculturally blighted in 1341.

It is hardly surprising that the effects of overpopulation, pressing on resources to produce starvation, disease and death, should have been more marked in the north and east of the county than elsewhere. In the smaller communities in the north and east of the county there were fewer human reserves and the local population may well have been nearer the margin of subsistence even before the plague came. Unfortunately we do not have any figures for plague deaths from this area from which we could judge the immediate, local effect of the Black Death. While we do not yet know when most of the abandoned sites in Hertfordshire finally ceased to be occupied, Mr Davis suggests that a great many of the deserted sites in the north-east, particularly those around Buntingford, may have begun to decline before 1334, for they are omitted from the tax assessment, for tenths and fifteenths, of that year. The predominance of the north-east of the county which had been so marked from such early times may have vanished during the fourteenth century.

Hunting parks

Hollow ways, the mounds of house platforms, and over-grown moats are the visible evidence in the landscape for the fate which overtook many Hertfordshire peasants and lesser lords in the late Middle Ages. The abandonment of marginal

[5] V.C.H. IV, p. 187.

farming land made it easier for the greater lords to follow their taste and create hunting parks. The process of woodland clearing to make agricultural land available, which had continued since Belgic times, was overtaken by the desire to recreate woodland. Hertfordshire is a county of parks, but only three, at Benington, St Albans and Ware, were mentioned in Domesday Book. There may, of course, have been more. Certainly many new parks were made during the Middle Ages. By 1485, when the first Tudor became king, there were about forty hunting parks or game preserves in the county.[6] They were regarded as the proper acquisitions of people of status. Sometimes they have left behind them evidence of their existence in the names of farms or woods. Park Farm in Nuthampstead was formerly the home of Cecil ate Park who is listed in the 1296 Subsidy Rolls. Park Wood in Bramfield was the home of Richard de Park in 1294, while Park Green in Ardeley may have been associated with Stephen le Parker who was also listed in the 1294 Subsidy Rolls. There is still a park round Ardeley Bury and a small one at neighbouring Walkern, the 1324 accounts for which survive. It cost thirteen shillings and fourpence a year to cut the hedges round the park. This reminds us that a hunting park was not all woodland; indeed much of it could be open space. It was an enclosed game preserve and hunting ground.

The distribution of these parks is significantly different from that of the moats and castles of the early Middle Ages (Fig. 20). There are far more parks, and the larger ones too, in the south and west, than in the north-east of the county. This may have been partly because the west had more woodland still available but that cannot have been the only reason, for much of the woodland in these parks was clearly

[6] J. E. Harting, 'Hertfordshire Deer-Parks' in *Transactions of the Hertfordshire Natural History Society*, II, 1881–3, pp. 97–111 lists thirty-four old deer parks. The volumes of the *Victoria County History* give medieval references for thirty-eight; there were probably more. The examples which follow, unless otherwise indicated, come from the parish histories in the V.C.H.

planted on land which had earlier been cleared and settled for farming.

In 1290 King's Langley is described as having a new park "containing eight acres of meadow, which used to be mowed before deer were placed therein . . . And one hundred and twenty acres of land which were arable." There is a reference

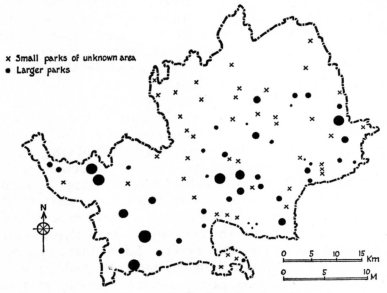

x Small parks of unknown area
• Larger parks

N

0   5   10   15 Km

0   5   10 M

Fig. 20. Distribution of parks.

in the Close Rolls for 1397 to "the late king's time (when) about 160 acres of arable land . . . were enclosed to enlarge the king's park . . . and by reason of the enclosure . . . tithes are lost".[7] The park was steadily enlarged by taking in more farm land until it reached a maximum size of some 950 acres. The southern boundary of the park can still be clearly identified; it follows the parish boundary and is marked by a footpath. The fields to the north were once part of the royal park; it is an interesting reversal in land use that what were

[7] Lionel M. Munby, ed., *The History of King's Langley*, 1963, pp. 16 and 142.

once arable fields to the south of the footpath are now wooded. Hertingfordbury park was first mentioned in 1285. In 1359–60 the keeper paid for three men, who worked for five days at threepence a day, cutting wood and enclosing the park. John Norbury obtained a licence in 1406 to enclose 800 acres of arable land and wood, 'of his own soil' and adjoining his manors of Bedwell and Little Berkhamsted, in order to make a park. The abbot of St Albans persuaded his copyhold tenants in Tyttenhanger, in 1427–8, to give up their share of the manorial meadow and pasture, in return for compensation, so that he could make a deer park. The abbot, however, did clear Tyttenhanger Heath and, while he took half of this too for his park, he turned the other half into fertile pasture land.

The most outstanding example in Hertfordshire, of turning arable and pasture land into a park, is at Pendley near Tring. Dorian Williams' nineteenth century house, a well known adult education college, and its garden stands on the site of a medieval village. In 1440 Sir Robert and Agnes Whittingham were granted rights of free warren in their manor of Pendley and given a licence to enclose 200 acres in the parish to make a park. By 1448 the tenants were prevented from exercising their common grazing rights over eighty acres. Sir Robert Whittingham was a Lancastrian and on Edward IV's accession in 1461 he was attainted for treason; in 1462 Pendley was granted to the Bishop of Exeter. It was, therefore, probably before 1461 that Sir Robert had completed his 'take-over'. What had happened was described in 1506: Pendley had been

a great town, . . . At that time there was no great mansion house there, but there were in the town above thirteen plows besides divers handicraft men, as tailors, shoemakers and cardmakers with divers others. The town was afterwards cast down and laid to pasture by Sir Robert Whittingham, who built the said place at the west end there as the town sometimes stood, for the town was in the east and south part of the same place.

As late as 1491–2 traces of earlier hedges could still be seen.[8] Peter Richards has been able to define the old boundaries of the three great parks in Hunsdon from old maps, documents and field work, although much of the ground has been covered by a wartime airfield. It is perhaps typical of Hertfordshire that where a medieval hunting park has not been transformed into a later park, the ground has been radically altered by modern construction. The Old Park at Hunsdon was in existence by 1124; in 1296 a commission was appointed to deal with "the persons who entered the park of John Engayne at Hunsdon, hunted therein, and carried away deer". Poaching was an inevitable and frequent corollary of preserving game. Parks increased in Hunsdon. Richard Duke of York was allowed in 1445 to enclose "a way called Jermynslane" which was sixteen feet wide and a hundred virgates long in his park at Hunsdon, provided he made another road to the south of the park. This was part of the process of creating "Goodmanneshyde" park. In 1503 Hunsdon was granted for life to the Countess of Richmond and parkland was mentioned in the grant. Three parks were named in 1529; 'New' park had been recently constructed by Henry VIII. In 1532 the King killed two stags in Wyntrey Park, which may well have been another name for one of the three.[9]

The way in which parks could grow and fill much of a parish can be illustrated from Sawbridgeworth. There were many manors in the parish; they represent 'an unusually complete example of the process of subinfeudation'. Three of these manors acquired substantial parks. The parent manor, of Sayesbury, had a park by 1237 when William de Say acquired ten buck deer from the royal forest of Essex. In

[8] Quoted in V.C.H. II, p. 285.
[9] V.C.H. III, p. 329.

1245 William got a licence for free warren, that is the right to hunt hares, rabbits, partridges and pheasants on his land. Such a licence was itself a status symbol but it was far better to get a licence to enclose land for a deer park. William obtained this too, and in 1283 poachers broke into the park, 'hunted therein and carried away deer'. An inventory made at the death of William de Say, son of the William who was granted free warren, in 1295, included 'forty acres of wood in which there are wild animals'. When Geoffrey de Say died in 1359 there was a park of sixty acres with great trees and deer in it. When Geoffrey's son, William, died in 1375 there were 100 acres of wood.

Pishiobury was an early sub-manor which became almost independent of Sayesbury. In 1248 the de Says granted Pishiobury the right of free hunting with dogs, birds or nets, on its own land, and free fishing in the river, in return for the de Says obtaining rights of free warren over all Sawbridgeworth, including Pishiobury. A rental of 1294 lists 156 acres called the park, in Pishiobury estate. In 1337 there is a complaint of people breaking into Pishiobury park, hunting there and stealing deer. The estate was temporarily divided in 1343 and the document refers to the park of Gedelesho (Gilston) and Gedelesho Wood. The park keeper is mentioned and a house within the second gate, which suggests a boundary bank or ditch to the park. An extent of the manor in 1534 describes a park with a perimeter of nearly two miles, which means that it must have contained some 260 acres, with a lodge on one side for the keeper and a moated house within the park. The park was well wooded, with game, deer and rabbits.

Shinglehall was produced by the fusion of two subinfeudated manors about 1301. In 1414 the estate came to the Leventhorpes and in 1439 John Leventhorpe got a grant of free warren in Sawbridgeworth, Thorley and Bishop's Stortford. In 1447 he obtained a licence to enclose 400 acres of arable, forty acres of meadow, and eighty acres of wood in Sawbridgeworth and Thorley to make himself a hunting park. This meant that something like 900 acres, mostly in Sawbridgeworth, was hunting park by the end of the Middle Ages. Some of the land was in Gilston and some in Thorley. Sawbridgeworth contained 6639 acres; the three parishes together 9160 acres. Though not all of a park was woodland there was a considerable enlargement of woodland entailed in emparking so much of the parish.[10]

One of the dilemmas which the landscape historian meets in a county of rapid change can be illustrated from Sawbridgeworth. The county maps of the seventeenth and eighteenth centuries show Hunsdon's three parks and parks at Gilston and Thorley, but Sawbridgeworth has only one rather diminutive park at Pishiobury which is still in existence. A considerable area of medieval parkland must have been disparked quite early, leaving very little trace on the landscape, save in the woods and coppices which survive more generally in the upland High Wych than in Sawbridgeworth proper. North-west of Sayes Park Farm, Sayes Coppice and Golden Grove may well be remnants of Sayesbury Park. In some of these remoter parts of the parish one can well imagine what the landscape looked like when parkland, but there is no unmistakable evidence on the ground.

The two processes of change described in this chapter were, to a degree, complementary. They are the background against which the developments discussed in the next two chapters need to be seen.

SELECT BIBLIOGRAPHY

Davis, K. Rutherford *The Deserted Medieval Villages of Hertfordshire* (1973).

Klingelhöfer, Eric C. *Broadfield Deserted Medieval Village* (1974).

[10] V.C.H. III, pp. 335, 337–8, 340; and *Sawbridgeworth*, pp. 13–17.

Levett, A. E. *Studies in Manorial History* (1938).
Munby, Lionel M. (ed.) *The History of King's Langley* (1963).
Munby, Lionel M. (ed.) *The Story of Sawbridgeworth: I. From Prehistory to the Present* (1966).

6. The impact of the gentry

Newcomers. Country houses. Landscaped parks. Follies and tombs.

Newcomers

THE SIXTEENTH AND the early seventeenth centuries were a time of rapid inflation and sensational growth of population and national wealth, in which there were many opportunities to make a fortune. The proximity of London affected Hertfordshire in two ways: its rapid growth produced an insatiable market for almost anything the county could produce; and people who made their fortune in London often settled in Hertfordshire, bringing their wealth into the countryside. The Fanshawe family had acquired Ware Park in the 1570s out of the profits made from the post of Queen's Remembrancer in the Exchequer. In 1630 Sir Richard Fanshawe wrote 'An Ode, upon occasion of His Majesties Proclamation . . . Commanding the Gentry to reside upon their Estates in the Countrey':

> Nor let the Gentry grudge to go
> Into those places whence they grew,
> But think them blest they may do so.
>   Who would pursue
>
> The smoky glory of the Town,
> That may go till his native Earth,
> And by the shining Fire sit down
>   Of his own hearth
>
>   . . . .

The Countrey too ev'n chops for rain:
You that exhale it by your power,
Let the fat drops fall down again
In a full shower.

The continuing two-way relationship between the City and the 'country'—remember in the seventeenth century one's county was one's country—succoured Hertfordshire with many 'fat drops' over centuries. The processes which were set at work in Elizabeth's reign had transformed the economy of Hertfordshire by the nineteenth century, with substantial effects on the landscape. The gentry and the peasant farmers were the human agents of change. Although they will be treated separately, it must be appreciated that there was no iron wall between the gentry and yeomen farmers, any more than there was between the peers and the gentry. The Capel Earls of Essex and the Earls of Verulam were descended from peasant stock, in the direct male line. No one could draw a sharp line, on one side of which were all the minor gentry and on the other yeomen or husbandmen, but in general terms there are clear distinctions between the substantial, manorial, estate owning families and the local farmers. This chapter is concerned with the former group.

From the sixteenth century onwards Hertfordshire experienced a considerable influx of new rich families, seeking homes and landed estates. Fuller in the seventeenth century made the witty claim that 'such who buy a house in Hertfordshire pay two year's purchase for the air'.[1] Of 395 manors or similar estates, whose successive owners can be traced through the county histories, 168 (42·5%) were in the hands of the Crown in 1540. By 1550 only twelve of these 168 properties remained in the hands of the Crown. This enormous dispersal of land provided opportunities for new families to build up estates. Manors changed hands fast in the 1540s. The disposal of Crown property, much of it

[1] *Worthies*, p. 229.

once church land, is only half of the story. The astonishing
fact is that of these 395 properties only forty-two belonged
to the same family or institution in 1700 as in 1540; and
seventeen of these were institutionally owned. The average
Hertfordshire manor changed hands at least two or three
times in this period of 160 years. So private property was
coming on the market frequently and new families could
easily buy estates in the open market. My own calculations
have been confirmed by those of others. C. A. Holmes has
shown that only ten per cent of the leading county gentry
who took sides in the seventeenth century civil war belonged
to families who had settled in the county before 1485, while
nearly forty-three per cent had arrived since 1603. Lawrence
and Jeanne Stone have shown that the families of only two
out of sixty-three identifiable owners of landed estates in
Cashio and Dacorum Hundreds in 1663 had owned their
estates before 1500, while twenty-four had obtained possession between 1600 and 1649.[2]

While London merchants were prominent among seventeenth century newcomers, the bulk of the Crown land dis-
posed of in the sixteenth century went to people with Court
connections, from the Lord Chancellor, Sir Thomas Audley,
down to three royal doctors. Courtiers also bought estates
from private sellers. Sir William Cecil bought Theobalds in
Cheshunt from Robert Burbage and Sir Nicholas Bacon
bought Gorhambury from the grandson of the Ralph Row-
latt who had acquired it from the Crown on the dissolution
of St Albans Abbey. William Ibgrave, Henry VIII's em-
broiderer, acquired land in Abbots and King's Langley.
Benington and other Hertfordshire property was bought by
the Caesar family in 1614. The founder of the family in
England was a foreign doctor, a royal physician; his three

---

[2] Clive Holmes, *The Eastern Association in the English Civil War*, 1974, pp.
12–14 and App. 3, p. 231; Lawrence Stone and Jeanne C. Fawtier Stone,
'Country Houses and their Owners in Hertfordshire, 1540–1879' in *The
Dimensions of Quantitative Research in History*, ed. W. O. Aydelotte, A. C. Bogue
and R. W. Fogel, 1972, p. 94.

sons became, respectively, a judge who was James I's Chancellor of the Exchequer and Master of the Rolls, a Dean of Ely, and an Exchequer Baron. The Fanshawes were a Derbyshire yeoman family who rose by their own merits and bought the manor of Ware from the Countess of Huntingdon.

Country houses

Such people wanted houses which would reveal their achievements, houses worthy in themselves and set in an appropriate landscape. Nikolaus Pevsner has commented on the wealth of Elizabethan and Jacobean houses in Hertfordshire, while Lawrence and Jeanne Stone reckoned that the major phase in country house building in Hertfordshire was over by 1580. All of them attributed the county's popularity with successful statesmen, lawyers and merchants to its nearness to London. London "provided a perpetual source of recruitment of new personnel and a perpetual fountain of wealth for new building", in the Stones' words. By the late seventeenth century Hertfordshire had a very high proportion of houses per acre in comparison with many parts of Britain. There were something like 'ninety rich squires' in the county at any one time.

The houses which they built were of very different sizes. There were a few giants, more enormous houses, and many much smaller among the 151 occupied at some time or other between 1540 and 1879, "which offered visible proof of their (occupiers') political and social preeminence". Ashridge, Hatfield House and Theobalds 'were more like palaces than houses'.[3] Of these Theobalds, on which Lord Burghley and James I lavished so much, has vanished as a result of the Civil War. Fuller described how it was "taken down to the ground (for the better partage among the soldiery) anno 1651; and, from the seat of a monarch, it is now become a

[3] Unless otherwise indicated the quotations are from the Stones' article, pp. 56–123.

little commonwealth; so may entire tenements, like splinters, have flown out of the materials thereof. Thus our fathers saw it built, we behold it unbuilt".[4] Fuller's poetic description might apply, with minor amendments, to many later houses. Cassiobury, rebuilt by James Wyatt at the beginning of the nineteenth century, went in 1927. It had been built between 1545 and 1556 and rebuilt for the first time at the Restoration. Panshanger, built by a pupil of James Wyatt's before 1808, was pulled down in the 1950s.

Country house building took place in waves. There was a great increase in the stock of large houses before 1580, a renewed spurt in the 1640s and 1650s, and between 1680 and 1720 much refacing and rebuilding which did not greatly increase either the number of houses or their size. Another building boom took place between 1750 and 1820. The fashionable site for a country house changed. Sir Ralph Sadleir's Standon Lordship, built in 1546, some parts of which remain in the present house, was sited 7–800 metres downstream and away from the village. It is still a secluded site, though not in parkland. Sir Nicholas Bacon's Gorhambury, built between 1563 and 1568, was uphill from the abbots' old manor house and still further away from the site of Verulamium and from St Albans. It became fashionable to live remote from social inferiors, "protected against the intrusion of the outside world by extensive grounds and parks, surrounded by high walls, and guarded by gates and lodge keepers". Fashions in eighteenth century landscaping made water popular so that, for example, four substantial houses were strung along the Mimram valley within four kilometres of one another. Two have gone: Panshanger and Tewin House which was "rebuilt in a magnificent manner by General Joseph Sabine" sometime in the early eighteenth century, and pulled down by the Cowpers after they had acquired it in 1804. Two houses survive: Marden Hill was built between 1785 and 1790 and altered by Sir John Soane

[4] *Worthies*, p. 230.

in 1819; his treatment of the interior led Pevsner to describe "the composition" of a first floor room as "one of his masterpieces, . . . so original as to be almost perverse, but the effect, although complex, is not at all confusing". Tewin Water was built by Henry Cowper before 1806, when it was described as 'new and handsome'. Its strict classical appearance and gleaming white colour still strike the eye of the passerby (Plate 20).[5]

The expenditure of the new rich on their houses, in the first great wave of building, was phenomenal. Sir Nicholas Bacon's Gorhambury, in its simple, first form a single courtyard house, cost £3,177 11s 9¼d; it was modestly appropriate for a man whose motto was *Mediocria Firma*, a motto which he inscribed on the tiles and a chimney piece in his house. Later a long gallery was added and Francis Bacon built a second courtyard, as well as a completely new house in the valley near the Ver, which cost some £10,000. Francis' attitudes were typical of many of the second or third generation new rich. "When his lordship was at his country house at Gorhambery, St Albans seemed as if the court were there, so nobly did he live . . . None of his servants durst appeare before him without Spanish leather bootes; for he would smell the neates-leather, which offended him." By the 1770s the brickwork of Nicholas Bacon's house was in a bad condition so that it had to be abandoned. The present Gorhambury House was built between 1777 and 1784 and cost £16,829 6s 6d. It has a grand Corinthian portico and Corinthian columns on the other, garden front. The house rises abruptly from the lovely park, looking almost too urban for its surroundings (Plate 21).[6]

Lord Burghley, Sir Nicholas' brother-in-law, began building his palace at Theobalds in 1564; it was almost complete

---

[5] *The Beauties of England and Wales: Hertfordshire*, Vol. VII, 1806, pp. 271 and 272. The references to Pevsner can be found under the particular houses.

[6] John Aubrey, *Brief Lives*, 1949, pp. 189–90; V.C.H. II, p. 396; *Gorhambury*, anon., 1938, pp. 4 and 8.

in 1585. The building costs were at least £12,000; altogether Burghley spent £25,000 on his house and estate. Theobalds, in the opinion of John Summerson, was the most influential of all Elizabethan houses.[7] Between 1607 and 1612 Robert Cecil, Burghley's son, spent nearly £40,000 on building Hatfield House and improving its surrounds (Plate 2). The plan and elevation of Hatfield House were based on Theobalds, but changes were made during the building operations. The result has many unique features. While most of the house is, like Theobalds, in red brick with stone dressings, 'a deliberate study in colour contrast', the south front was 'redesigned as a solid stone façade'. Professor Lawrence Stone has given reasons for suggesting that the new plan is 'the first known architectural achievement of Inigo Jones'. The unique features on the south front, which were designed when the change was made, are the pilasters between the windows and the 'projecting corbelled sills and flattened mullions and transoms' of the windows. The 'elegant simplicity' of the clock tower may be another of Inigo Jones' contributions. The main design was by Robert Liming, carpenter, with the collaboration of two others and Robert Cecil himself; Cecil chose the site. One of the changes made in Liming's design led to the unusual plan of Hatfield House. The basic structure "consists of two high square blocks at either end, linked by a lower section in the centre and with wings running out at right angles".[8] The ends of the wings were expanded into blocks three rooms deep, jutting out of the east and west façades, to meet the needs of a change in internal function.

Hatfield House must stand for the buildings of this first boom phase though it was put up long after the main wave of newcomers had reached the county and looked forward,

[7] J. Summerson, 'The Building of Theobalds, 1564–85' in *Archaeologia*, 1959; Conyers Read, *Lord Burghley and Queen Elizabeth*, 1960, pp. 122–3, and 556; and 'Lord Burghley's Household Accounts' in *The Economic History Review*, Second Series, Vol. IX, 2, 1956, p. 344.

[8] Lawrence Stone, 'The Building of Hatfield House' in *Family and Fortune*, 1973, pp. 74, 78–80.

Plate 11 Baldock

Plate 12 Hitchin

Plates 13 and 14 Ware, Views over Rooftops

Plate 15 St Albans, Clock House at Bottom End of Medieval Market Place

Plate 16 St Albans, Medieval Inn in French Row

Plate 17 Berkhamsted Castle

Plate 18 Tiscot, Deserted Medieval Village

Plate 19 Hemel Hempstead, Norman interior of Parish Church

Plate 20 Tewin Water House

Plate 21 Gorhambury

Plate 22 Rothamsted Manor House

in some of its architecture, to a later age. The renewed spurt of building in the 1640s and 1650s, to meet the demand from another wave of newcomers, was in a different style, or rather styles. Two outstanding large houses, Balls Park of *c.* 1640 and Tyttenhanger of *c.* 1654–60, are associated with the architect Peter Mills. They are plain, brick houses, so formal and classical that they might be early Georgian. Balls Park has an unusual, central hall which may have been an open courtyard. Pevsner claims that Tyttenhanger's 'magnificent staircase . . . with a balustrade of sumptuous openwork foliage scrolls' is one of the earliest of its kind in the country.

Most of the middle-sized country houses, built or rebuilt in the middle of the seventeenth century, were in the Dutch gable style and show much less of a break with Elizabethan-Jacobean buildings. Rothamsted is a good example (Plate 22). Sir John Wittewronge, its new owner, carried out considerable alterations and additions between 1639 and 1680. "Curvilinear gables were superimposed on the plain pointed ones, whose outlines are still traceable in the brickwork. The clock-tower was added about 1650, and in 1659 a loggia at the south-west corner, . . . The cluster of moulded chimneys above the dining-room is dated 1654." There are entries for payments to builders in Sir John Wittewronge's accounts, but no record of the full cost. Sir John Wittewronge's grandfather had emigrated from Flanders in the early 1560s in a 'hott time of persecution' of Calvinists. Sir John, though a parliamentarian, was 'ever a lover of pictures'. During the Civil War he not only persuaded the Committee for Delinquents to surrender the sequestered pictures of his royalist relative, Sir Richard Price, but he also bought "several pictures that were his Majesty's . . . they cost me near £300". Rothamsted was rebuilt after Sir John's third marriage to the daughter of a London merchant, perhaps to house the pictures as well as the new bride.[9] In 1662 Thomas Fuller

[9] D. H. Boalch, *The Manor of Rothamsted*, 1953, pp. 4 and 38–9; the Wittewronge papers are in the Hertford County Record Office; Memoir of

commented on the impact which the building of the previous century and a half had made on the county: "Surely no county can show so fair a bunch of berries; for they so term the fair habitations of gentlemen of remark, which are called places, courts, halls and manors in other shires."[10]

Building, or casing older houses in brick, was common in the late seventeenth and early eighteenth centuries. Sir Henry Chauncy has left us a pen picture of a family who lived near him and whose neutrality contrasts with Sir John Wittewronge's involvement with parliament during the Civil War. It was families like this who built or redesigned so many "pleasant, simple, comfortably proportioned" Hertfordshire houses in the styles fashionable from the reigns of William and Mary to George I. Ralph Freeman of Aspenden, son of a London merchant,

> in the time of Rebellion did quit all public Imployments, affected a retired Life, and pleased himself with the Conversation of his Children. He made his House neat, his Gardens pleasant, his Groves delicious, his Children chearful, his Servants easie, and kept excellent Order in his Family: He had a general insight in Architecture and Husbandry.

Ralph Freeman, his son, 'cased and adorned this Mannor House with Brick, beautified the Gardens with delicious Greens, the Grove with pleasant Walks, and made all things neat and curious to the Spectator.'[11] The original Aspenden Hall had been built at the beginning of the seventeenth century and stones from the churches of the deserted villages of Berkeden and Wakeley may have been used. It was pulled down in about 1850.

---

the Wittewronge family, printed by Robert Clutterbuck in *History of Hertford*, Vol. 1, 1815, p. 408; *Report on the Manuscripts of the Earl of Verulam*, 1906, p. 64.

10 *Worthies*, p. 229.
11 Chauncy, Vol. I, pp. 248–9.

Houses which survive from this period are Benington Lordship, Aldenham (*c.* 1700), Beechwood's north-east façade (1702), the Golden Parsonage (1705), Fanhams Hall at Ware which has been so altered as to be unrecognisable, Lockleys at Welwyn (1717), the original Hamels at Braughing (*c.* 1720) which was 'made sham Elizabethan in the nineteenth century', John Scott's house at Amwell (*c.* 1730), Much Hadham Hall (1735), and Wyddial Hall built after a fire of 1733. Robert Morden reacted to the changes taking place, rewording Fuller's description of Hertfordshire with a new emphasis:

This County has an incredible number of Pallaces and fair Structures of the Gentry and Nobility. From Totteridge where the County begins, and East-Barnet to Ware, are so many Beautiful Houses, that one may look upon it almost as a continual Street. The rich Soil and wholesome Air, and the excellence of the County, have drawn hither the Wealthiest Citizens of London.[12]

Perhaps Morden noticed the first significant shift of settlement from the north-east to the south-west of the county. The Stones have shown how the siting of country houses changed. In 1599 twenty-nine per cent of the houses in their sample were in the north-eastern quarter and only thirteen per cent in the south-west quarter of the county, while by 1879 the respective percentages were sixteen and twenty-six per cent.

Many of the houses which Morden noted have gone, in the great destruction of 1790 to 1829, as well as more recently. But one really outstanding house survives from the early eighteenth century, "Leoni's Moor Park, a stone mansion with (a) splendid giant Corinthian portico and a hall with paintings by Annigoni". The Duke of Monmouth's house, built in 1670, was "entirely new-cased and fronted with Port-

12 R. Morden, *The New Description and State of England*, 2nd ed., 1704, p. 71.

land stone" in the 1720s for Benjamin Styles, a merchant who made a fortune out of the South Sea Bubble. The interior was almost rebuilt. The oval dome may have been added in Lord Anson's time (1755–62) when the house was further improved.[13]

A group of ten houses illustrate the high point of Georgian rebuilding and new building, roughly between 1750 and 1780. They are Youngsbury near Wadesmill (1745) which had the top storey removed and a portico added in 1948–50; Brocket Hall (1755–80); the Grove at Watford (1756, enlarged in 1780 and *c.* 1850); Wormleybury (1767–9); Theobalds Park (1768); James Wyatt's Gaddesden Place (1768–83); Hitchin Priory (1770–1); Woodhall Park (1777); Gorhambury (1777); Woolmers (*c.* 1800); and Hunsdon (1804–5). Lord David Cecil's affectionate words about Brocket cannot be bettered: "that perfect example of the smaller country house of the period, with its rosy, grey-pilastered façade, its urbane sunny sitting-rooms, its charming park like a landscape by Wilson."[14] Pevsner's description of Hitchin Priory makes a pointed contrast: "a mansion of stone with a noble Palladian south front with small central semicircular porch and two projecting wings, each turning a large Venetian window towards the garden." Brocket was built by the son of a self-made Nottinghamshire attorney, Hitchin Priory by a family of prosperous Turkey merchants.

Hunsdon, home of the Calverts who were successful brewers, provides a perfect illustration of the difficulties in 'dating' the often rebuilt country houses of Hertfordshire. The wife of the owner, Nicholson Calvert M.P., kept a diary:

6 August 1805

We find building the new house so dreadfully expensive a job, that we meditate giving the matter up, though we have completed cellars, etc. We think of adding to, and

[13] Pevsner, pp. 24 and 170–1 and *Beauties*, pp. 311–14.
[14] Lord David Cecil, *Melbourne*, 1965, p. 28.

repairing the old house instead, which we fortunately as yet, have not pulled down. It will cost half as much, perhaps only a quarter as much as a new house would.

16 April 1806

I hear there is hardly a bit of old Hunsdon House left standing, so it is merely the name of adding to it—it will be nearly a new house.

Yet the Royal Commission on Historical Monuments claimed that "only the outer walls remain, the interior being entirely the work of 1804", while Pevsner described much of the core of the house as though it were of early sixteenth century date.[15]

The country house building boom of 1750 to 1820 climaxed in the Gothic revival. In 1782 James Wyatt remodelled the late Tudor mansion of Pishiobury, south of Sawbridgeworth, 'mildly medievalising'. About 1795 his son, Sir Jeffry Wyatville, built Hilfield at Bushey; it is a 'castellated, turreted, and cemented house with a gatehouse, complete with portcullis', originally known as Sly's Castle. Wall Hall, Aldenham, was built and Hertford Castle gatehouse much altered about 1800 in typical Gothic styles. The climax came in 1808 with Panshanger and Ashridge. Ashridge remains; a 'romantic Gothic palace' built by the Wyatts on the foundations of a medieval monastery, it is one of the more striking sights in Hertfordshire, both inside and out. The towers, turrets and spire which surmount the drive up through the wooded parkland are an appropriate introduction to the immense heights of the staircase hall, the entrance hall and the chapel tower.

In 1815–20 the early Tudor courtyard house at Knebworth was refashioned. Three sides were pulled down; the Great Hall was left; on the east front only the details were

---

[15] Mrs Warenne Blake (ed.), *An Irish Beauty of the Regency, Mes Souvenirs— the journals of Mrs Calvert*, 1911, pp. 49 and 66. Cp. R.C.H.M., p. 128; V.C.H. III, p. 325; Pevsner, pp. 141–2.

altered. A new west front was built in the fashionable idiom. The stucco cement which was used to imitate stone has not weathered well, and its appearance today gives the great house a peculiarly dreary and drab look. James Lees-Milne called Knebworth 'undeniably hideous'. Almost contemporary with the changes at Knebworth was the transformation of Sir Henry Chauncy's home at Ardeley Bury into "an enchanted castle" (Plate 23). The "fanciful architect . . . added a circular flint tower, two polygonal brick turrets, divers pinnacles, . . . made the windows Gothic, erected a baronial hall with a big fireplace, a minstrel's gallery and a plastered timber roof, and inserted Gothic vaulting in other rooms".[16]

Landscaped parks

'Buildings and Pallaces are but Grosse Handy-works' without gardens, wrote Francis Bacon.[17] The gentry of Hertfordshire were pioneer gardeners. Robert Cecil embellished the surrounds of Hatfield House with a garden and vineyard which Evelyn, who saw it in 1643, regarded as 'the most considerable rarity besides the house'. Cecil employed three gardeners; one, the elder John Tradescant, to import trees and plants from Flanders and France. Cecil's cousin, Francis Bacon, laid out an extraordinary garden at the Pondyards in Gorhambury Park, the formal pattern of which can still be seen. Sir Henry Wotton saw in the garden at Ware Park 'a delicate and diligent curiosity', the work of Sir Henry Fanshawe. Sir William Temple so admired the garden at Moor Park in 1655 that he called his own house Moor Park. It was "the perfectest Figure of a Garden I ever saw . . . the sweetest Place".[18]

[16] Pevsner, pp. 24, 78, 158–60, 151–2 and 39–40.

[17] Francis Bacon, *Essays*, 1937–66, p. 187.

[18] *The Diary of John Evelyn*, ed. E. S. de Beer, 1959, p. 46; Sir Henry Wotton, *Reliquiae Wottonianae*, 2nd ed., 1654, pp. 270–1; Sir William Temple, 'Upon the Gardens of Epicurus; or of Gardening in the Year 1685' in *Miscellanea: the second part*, 3rd ed., 1692, pp. 127–30.

The garden was an antechamber to the park. The whole landscape became a frame for the house and a status symbol. Norden commented in his 1590 survey that Hertfordshire "at this day is . . . much replete with parkes, woodes and rivers".[19] The early county maps show some of the parks. The most astonishing piece of park making which still survives is at Hatfield. Robert Cecil rearranged the whole landscape around his new house, to give himself more privacy. The open fields of Hatfield lay north of Fore Street and came close to the old Palace. The woodland and park which lies between the railway station and the house was in 1604 all arable land. Cecil bought out his own copyhold tenants, paying them nearly £10 an acre. In 1614 alone, £2995 was spent in this way. The arable fields were then turned into the woodland and park of today. At the same time Hatfield Wood, a hunting park of nearly 2000 acres which stretched from Millwards Park to Newgate Street, was divided between the Earl and forty-four commoners who surrendered their rights. 560 of the Earl's 1000 acres were made into New Park, while the remainder and the commoners' 883 acres were cleared and cultivated. Woodland and arable were switched around on a scale only matched by twentieth century developers.[20]

Before looking at other great parks which survive, it is necessary to make a point which underlines the significance of the process taking place in the sixteenth and seventeenth centuries. Norden claimed that there had been more parks in Hertfordshire 'heretofore' and this was because he witnessed disparking. The opportunities for profitable farming in Hertfordshire were such that medieval parkland was ploughed up where no one chose to live on the estate. Typical of what happened is the licence given by Queen

[19] John Norden, *A Description of Hertfordshire*, 1598, reprinted 1903, p. 2.
[20] Barbara Hutton, *Hertfordshire Local History Council News Sheet*, No. 13, 1956. Professor Lawrence Stone (*Family and Fortune*, pp. 41–2) has only seen the financial implications of these sales and purchases.

Elizabeth I, in 1589, to a Watford tenant to turn part of Oxhey park into tillage. Though at least six old parks were enlarged and twelve new ones made between 1485 and 1700, eight were disparked. The parks that have gone left their marks on the landscape, as at King's Langley and Little Hadham, and even in places at Theobalds.

The Tudors abandoned the royal palace at King's Langley and a 1558 survey recommended that the 'park may well be disparked', though nothing happened for some time. In 1652 some ten tenants were leasing 'land in the park'. By the eighteenth century two large farms took up the whole area of former parkland. Their fields were and are rectangular and large, like those produced by parliamentary enclosure, and quite unlike the neighbouring fields which are smaller and have the sinuous edges which suggest piecemeal enclosure of the open field furlongs. King's Langley park illustrates, in miniature, the many changes through which the Hertfordshire countryside has gone. This piece of land, once wooded, was cleared for farming, returned to open woodland as a deer park, and was in the seventeenth century once again cleared and ploughed for the farmland, which it still is—but for how long? It is well suited to 'development'.[21]

So rapid was the speed of change that new parks were made and disparked within a generation. In 1635 Sir Arthur Capel obtained a licence to add some 500 acres of Wickham Hall farmland to his existing 240 acre park around Hadham Hall. His son, the first Capel Earl of Essex, moved to Cassiobury and by 1686 the whole of the enlarged park was 'broken up into three main farms'. Sir Arthur had married Elizabeth, only child of Sir Charles Morrison of Cassiobury. This marriage made Sir Arthur one of the richest commoners of his day, adding the Morrison estates to the existing Capel wealth. Sir Arthur made many 'additions and embellishments' to his property. Cornelius Janssen's family group

[21] *King's Langley*, pp. 51 and 58–9.

shows his formal garden seen from the new Banqueting Hall. The picture was, no doubt, intended as a "representation of the great works with which he had embellished" what was then the family seat.[22] Ironically in the year in which it was painted, 1640, Arthur Capel as county member stood up in the House of Commons "to represent the grievances of this country". In the next year, however, he was made a peer for his support of Charles I and he died on the scaffold shortly after his king. Perhaps Arthur Capel's heir found that Hadham was too closely associated with an unhappy childhood. Sir Arthur's works were rapidly effaced by neglect, but the landscape bears the marks of his emparkment to this day.

The fields within the old park area, like those in King's Langley park, are large and the hedgelines straight. North and south the landscape is markedly different from this. Albury parish, to the north, has no nucleus and the nucleus of Little Hadham, to the west and around an important cross roads and ford, is a late development as the site of the church suggests. Both these parishes have the irregularly shaped road and field pattern, suggestive of scattered settlement. This can be seen in the hedges south of the winding, sunken road which passes Upwick and Level's Greens, though the fields here are larger than they once were. The Roman road (A120) was the boundary of the old park on the south. In places along the southern side of this road the fields have rectangular shapes; though they were not in the park they were once part of the estate farm. Further south, however, the landscape has the same irregular pattern as between Upwick Green and the northern park boundary. The old park boundary, incidentally, can still be traced in hedges and tracks.

One of the greatest of Hertfordshire's parks came and went only a little less quickly. William Cecil spent as much on the park and gardens as on the house at Theobalds. He

[22] William Minet, *Hadham Hall*, 1914, pp. 31, 11 and 58.

"greatlie delighted in making gardens, fountaines and walkes; which at Theobalds were perfected most costly, bewtyfully, and pleasantly".[23] Horace Walpole commented on Hentzner's description of Theobalds, listing the 'obelisks, pyramids, and circular porticos, with cisterns of lead for bathing' and 'a labyrinth', for good measure.[24] James I added 320 acres between 1607 and 1608 and spent £11,000 in 1612 in buying still more land. Between 1620 and 1622 a nine mile wall was built round the park. When Michael Drayton commented on the changing landscape in the Lea valley in 1613, he may have had Theobalds as well as Waltham Forest in mind.

Where daintie Summer Bowers, and Arborets are made,
Cut out of Busshy thicks, for coolenesse of the shade.

. . . .

The Ridge and Furrow shewes, that once the crooked Plow,
Turn'd up the grassy turfe, where Okes are rooted now:
And at this houre we see, the Share and Coulter teare
The full corne-bearing gleabe, where sometimes forests were.[25]

Though buildings cover much of the area today, more recent splinters than those of which Fuller wrote, some of the woodland remains, fragments of the park walls, and significantly named farms—Oldpark, Woodgreen Park, and Theobalds Park. The site of Theobalds House is today covered by the Cedars public park.

The pressure on land which this ploughing up and building represents makes the survival of so many parks in Hertfordshire all the more significant. Gorhambury, Cassiobury, Moor Park and Ashridge are among the most impressive of

[23] Peek, quoted in V.C.H., III, pp. 448-9.
[24] Horace Walpole, *On Modern Gardening* (1780) 1975 ed. p. 7.
[25] Michael Drayton, *Polyolbion*, 1613, 1622, second part p. 2.

the survivors, each significantly with a different type of owner today. Parks were not all woodland; like medieval royal forests they included farmland, as Gorhambury always has. A plot of 1634 and an undated seventeenth century sketch and survey take us back to the park much as Francis Bacon left it. "The park is enclosed with a very fair new pale, such as is seldom seen about any other park". Its bounds are suggested by the gates marked on the sketch; they coincide almost exactly with the area of park shown on an estate map of 1768. The modern area of grassland is slightly larger to the north and substantially so to the east. Within this park area, while there was a 'deare house', "a good part of the ground is mowable and very good pasture" but some was 'excellent ground for wheat', according to the seventeenth century survey. The fields may have been recently made, for "the yongar hedges . . . are very manie and good".

Francis Bacon may have been responsible for developing this area. He certainly was responsible for "the waulk through Pray wood and the stand thear on the hill for prospect", which can still be seen. The view is downhill, past the wall of Verulamium, towards the site of St Mary de Prae and the valley of the Ver. "The tarase grounde, newly set with rows of trees, from the park gate at Windmill Hill to Verulam House", of the survey survives in the main, though it has lost the full glory of Francis Bacon's design. Aubrey described the 'three parallel walkes', of different species of trees of the same size, looking like 'works in Irish stitch'. Verulam House, Bacon's own child, and 'the delicious parke' near it have gone; the park was all 'plowed up and spoil'd' by 1656. Some of the oak woods around old Gorhambury House survive with the ruins. 'Under every tree' of this wood Bacon had 'planted some fine flower . . . paeonies, tulips' and some were still there thirty years after his death when Aubrey saw them.[26]

[26] *Report on the Manuscripts of the Earl of Verulam*, 1906, pp. 184–5; J. C.

The most remarkable of seventeenth century Hertfordshire parks, Cassiobury, was transformed in the eighteenth century. The Earl of Essex altered the mid-sixteenth century hunting park, after the Restoration, laying out gardens and grounds in the formal style associated with Versailles. Moses Cook, who had been gardener at Hadham Hall, was responsible, although a late edition of Defoe's *Travels*, perhaps in snobbery, gave the credit for the large wood-walks to Louis XVI's gardener, Le Notre.[27] Le Notre may have landscaped St Paul's Waldenbury Park, however. During the eighteenth century formal gardens went out of fashion. Charles Bridgeman, creator of Gobions in North Mimms, was one of those responsible. Horace Walpole "observed in the garden of Gubbins . . . many detached thoughts, that strongly indicate the dawn of modern taste".[28]

Lancelot (Capability) Brown remodelled existing parks to create what he believed were the natural curves of the English landscape. He had a hand in landscaping nine Hertfordshire parks: Ashridge, Beechwood, Cole Green, Digswell, The Hoo in St Paul's Walden, Littlegrove in East Barnet, Moor Park in Rickmansworth, Pishiobury, and Youngsbury near Wadesmill. Digswell and Littlegrove have gone; only the lake at Pishiobury is attributed to Brown; and what he did at The Hoo is not clear. Cole Green was absorbed into Panshanger. At Beechwood "Brown's task was to thin out rather than to plant on any extensive scale". Brown worked at Ashridge between 1759 and 1768. "The park, and particularly that area of it which is known as the Golden Valley, remains much as Brown left it with fine plantations and

---

Rogers, 'The Manor and Houses of Gorhambury' in *St Albans and Hertfordshire Architectural and Archaeological Society Transactions*, Vol. IV new series, pp. 35–112 quotes Aubrey at length and reproduces 1634 and 1768 maps. The sketch is H.C.R.O., I.B.10.

[27] V.C.H. II, p. 454; iv. pp. 277–80; the 8th ed. of Defoe's *Travels*, 1775, Vol. II, p. 140.

[28] Walpole, p. 21.

open glades." Youngsbury, too, remains very little altered save for massive tree planting on the edge of the park, to hide a planned by-pass road. Brown remarked of Youngsbury "that Nature had done so much little was wanting, but enlarging the River", which he did. It is a comment on the Hertfordshire landscape that Brown found it so much to his taste.[29]

Moor Park, now a golf course, was one of Brown's masterpieces. There had been some landscaping when Styles' built his house. A hill was removed to improve the view, an action which Alexander Pope condemned because it 'let in the north wind':

> Or cut wide views through mountains to the plain,
> You'll wish your hill a sheltered seat again.

In fact the action opened up an attractive view over the Chess valley. Brown has been credited with this but he was about ten at the time; what he did was to take away more earth from the existing gap. Hills had been removed before: Moses Cook cut through one at Cassiobury. Brown worked for Lord Anson who spent £80,000 between 1755 and 1760. A series of undulations and hillocks capped with plantations, and a small lake with an Ionic temple beyond it, were Brown's main contributions. Dr Samuel Johnson commented:

> A grateful mind I praise! All to the winds he owed
> And so upon the winds a Temple he bestowed.

Lord Anson was an admiral who had sailed round the world. The gardens which Sir William Temple loved were transformed at this time.

Moor Park has been operated on three times, but much of the landscaping survives on the golf course. Other parts of

[29] Dorothy Stroud, *Capability Brown*, 1975, pp. 71, 102 and 246.

the park have been built upon. One of the houses on this exclusive estate, built in 1937, drew from Pevsner the comment that it was "in the typical International Modern style . . . The curved outer staircases and the curved canopies should be noted. With the general rectangularity of blocks and windows they form the sort of contrast which abstract painters and sculptors of the twenties and thirties relished and which Le Corbusier introduced into architecture."[30]

Bayfordbury, near Hertford, was bought by Sir William Baker in 1758. In the next four years he built himself a most elegant house, and then laid out what became a famous garden in his 270 acre park. Some of the cedars were planted in 1756 and the ha ha was dug by 1766; it is shown clearly on Dury and Andrews' map of that year. This innovation was hailed by Walpole as a "capital stroke . . . the destruction of walls for boundaries . . . the invention of fosses . . . so astonishing that the common people called them Ha! Has!"[31]

The last of the great landscape gardeners was Humphry Repton. He worked on eleven Hertfordshire parks: Ashridge, Brookmans in North Mimms, Cassiobury, Lamer in Wheathampstead, Little Court at Buntingford, Organ Hall and Wall Hall near Aldenham, Panshanger, Tewin Water, Wood Hill and Wyddial Hall. Two of these did not amount to much: the plans for Wood Hill, probably the Wood Hill in Hatfield, were never completed; and whatever was done at Little Court cannot have been very extensive. At Wall Hall Repton only advised on garden improvements: it is now a College of Education. Organ Hall has vanished under Borehamwood's expanding estate. Brookmans is today a golf course. While the house at Lamer has been rebuilt and the woodland is rather run down and much of the estate simply farmland, "the remains of a good park survive". Wyddial Hall still "presents a late eighteenth century appearance which combines with a thickly wooded background

[30] Pevsner, p. 171 and W. Branch Johnson, *Hertfordshire*, 1970, pp. 121–2.
[31] Walpole, p. 21; Pevsner, pp. 54–5.

and sloping lawns to make a Reptonian scene of considerable charm". Of the larger parks, Repton's most ambitious scheme has been most desecrated in recent years. Lord Cowper asked Repton, in 1799, to redesign all his four estates in the Mimram valley, Cole Green, Panshanger, Tewin Water and Digswell. While Digswell was left out of Repton's plans, the other three were treated as a unit. Capability Brown's Cole Green was absorbed into a grand scheme. In his Red Book Repton wrote of 'the whole of the beautiful valley from Welwin to Hertford'; 'to each of these places' Repton proposed to give "a degree of extent and consequence which it could not boast exclusive of the others . . . their united lawns will, by extending thro' the whole valley enrich the general face of the country". Dorothy Stroud has described how Repton widened the Mimram, making small lakes opposite Tewin Water and Panshanger houses, and planted 'both sides of the valley . . . on a vast scale'. Thanks to Repton the valley of the Mimram is still a beautiful place, but Panshanger park has been damaged since the house was pulled down in 1953. In 1975 a motorway type by-pass was constructed through the area, from which the sweep of the surviving woodland can be seen. But who knows how much will remain for the future of, what Pevsner called, 'one of Repton's most perfect schemes': "the view from the house past the groups of trees down to the lake created by a widening of the River Mimram is superb" (Plate 24).[32]

The formal, Versailles appearance of Cassiobury vanished under Repton's attentions, though the avenue of limes planted by Moses Cook in 1672 which crosses the golf course to Whippendell Wood remains. Part of the park has been built on and much of the area is a public recreation ground in which many of the avenues and clumps of trees, planted by Repton and others can be seen. Repton's land-

[32] Dorothy Stroud, *Humphry Repton*, 1962, pp. 54, 50 and 108; Pevsner, p. 185; Hugh Prince, 'The Changing Landscape of Panshanger' in *E.H.A.S. Transactions*, Vol. XIV, Part 1, pp. 42–58.

scaping of the waters of the River Gade remains the centre-piece of the local landscape. Ashridge is the largest and most varied park in Hertfordshire; it goes back to the Middle Ages and was enlarged by John, Earl of Bridgewater in Charles II's reign. It is still possible to walk among the "lofty groves of trees, so thick set together that the like is scarce anywhere else to be seen" and to see the deer, both remarked on by a visitor in 1681. Repton worked mainly on the gardens at the end of his life. He called Ashridge 'the youngest favourite, the child of my age and declining powers'. The monastic history of Ashridge may have inspired Repton's cloistered monks' garden, rose and rock gardens, and dell with a grotto, but they lead directly into Victorian garden making.[33]

Follies and tombs

Linking the house with its landscaped park were the follies of which eighteenth century taste made so much. The Folly Arch at Brookmans Park, Potters Bar, all that remains of Gobions, was put up about 1750. It is evidence for the beginning of a new fashion for things medieval. Wall Hall had a Gothic revival front added in 1802, and a sham ruin, parts of which came from Aldenham church: it became, for a time, Aldenham Abbey! Bulwer Lytton, the novelist and first Baron, added to the 'romantic paraphrase of the Gothic palace', which Knebworth House had become, 'a tiny, almost ivy-obscured folly representing the choir of a church with two very good gothic revival windows'. An open shell-lined grotto at Benington Lordship, made by a Hertfordshire landscape gardener, was built in 1832 in the walls of the Norman castle with mock medieval knights' heads, a Greek

[33] Thomas Baskerville quoted in V.C.H. II, p. 210; Hugh Prince, 'Parkland in the English Landscape' in *The Amateur Historian*, Vol. III, pp. 332–49 and IV. pp. 23–5 and 33–4; and 'Parkland in the Chilterns' in *The Geographical Review*, Vol. XLIX, No. 1, 1959, pp. 18–31; Stroud, p. 160.

inscription, and a statue of the Buddha.[34] It is sad that this is the only surviving Benington folly, for Mary Caesar of Benington Place, a member of the Freeman family of Aspenden, was one of the great folly builders and gardeners. At the centre of a literary circle, which included Pope, Swift and the Harleys of Wimpole in Cambridgeshire, she and her husband received many sets of verses to their 'chapel', 'bower', 'grotto', 'religious building' and, from Pope, 'folly'.[35]

Hertfordshire has two outstanding, surviving follies, one hidden underground, one in full view and public use. John Scott, the Quaker poet, built himself a grotto at Amwell, cut into a hill, with several rooms and passages decorated with shells, and crowned with an octagonal summerhouse Dr Johnson called it "Fairy Hall; none but a poet could have made such a garden", but Barbara Jones sees Scott's work as unconsciously morbid, "working towards the full exploitation of horror".[36] In sharp contrast to Scott's grotto is what must be very nearly the most perfect folly in England, Nicholas Revett's Greek cross church at Ayot St Lawrence, of 1778–9 (Plate 25). Sir Lionel Lyde, a London tobacconist and director of the Bank of England, was able to slight the village church and build a new one, sited as an eye-catcher at the end of an avenue from Ayot House. This 'religious building' was no ruin, though the sides and back were left in unfinished brick, not stone covered like the façade facing the house. It was used by worshippers, though "the unfortunate villagers had to make a wide detour, approaching the building from the back and entering by a side door so as not to spoil the view from the House". This extraordinary piece of evidence for landlord power in the eighteenth cen-

[34] Barbara Jones, *Follies and Grottoes*, 1974, pp. 343–5; Pevsner, pp. 96–7, 151–2 and 58.
[35] Manuscript letterbooks in the possession of T. Cottrell Dormer of Rousham House, Steeple Aston, Oxon. Charles Caesar's eldest granddaughter, Jane, married Sir Charles Cottrell Dormer. There are eight letterbooks, A–H.
[36] Jones, pp. 169–71.

tury has met with different reactions at different periods. Cussans indulged in a typical Victorian outburst: "Sir Lyonel Lyde, having ... more money than wit, made a public exhibition of his wealth and folly by building in his park ... a heathen temple." Sir William Beach Thomas wrote, in 1950, of 'the Byzantine horror'. George Bernard Shaw, who lived in Ayot, seems to have shared this aesthetic judgment, but Pevsner, in 1953, described the ground plan as 'remarkably original'. The church, which is Greek not Byzantine, is not only a unique piece of architectural and social history but has its own beauties.[37]

Follies were for the living. After death the gentry left other monuments. The tombs and tablets which commemorate them in so many Hertfordshire churches reveal their origins and connections; they were the last visible impact the gentry could make on the landscape. The finest tombs in the country are in St Albans Abbey, the late medieval brass of Abbot de la Mare and the chantry chapels of two other abbots and of Humphrey, Duke of Gloucester. Another royal tomb, that of Edmund of Langley, first Duke of York, in King's Langley church provides a splendid display of medieval heraldry. But these are exceptional; it is the tombs and brasses of the gentry which fill the parish churches. A few churches, at diagonally opposite ends of the county, taken as examples, will serve to remind the reader that a church is not merely an empty shell.

Sawbridgeworth, 'a veritable storehouse of monuments', contains late medieval brasses and seventeenth century tombs of the Hewet, Mildmay, and Leventhorpe families. There is a brick-built chapel of 1730 in Great Gaddesden church with a fine collection of eighteenth century Halsey tombs. This is an excellent place to visit: the contrast between the elegant formality of the sculptures and the

[37] J. P. F. Broad, 'The building of the new church of Ayot St Lawrence' in *Hertfordshire Past and Present*, No. 4, 1964, pp. 27–35; Beach Thomas, pp. 64–5; Pevsner, pp. 45–6.

charm of the simple, rural landscape around Great Gaddesden is symbolic of the life style of the eighteenth century
rich. Barkway has a variety of monuments in its church:
Sir John Jennings by Rysbrack is outstanding. Watford,
like Sawbridgeworth, is rich in brasses and tombs: those in
the Morrison Chapel, which include two monuments by
Nicholas Stone, commemorate the owners of Cassiobury.

For a full appreciation of the impact on the landscape of
five centuries of the county gentry, their tombs, their
follies, their houses and their parks should be taken together.
Sir Henry Chauncy believed that it was the "clear, sweet and
very wholesome" air which induced "many of the Nobility
and Gentry to build stately Pallaces and Fabricks, pleasant
Dwellings and delicious Seats in this County".[38] Whatever
their motives, we can today enjoy much that remains of their
handiwork.

SELECT BIBLIOGRAPHY

Stone, L. & J. 'Country Houses and their Owners in Hertford-
    shire, 1540–1879' in *The Dimensions of Quantitative Research*
    (1972).
Stone, L. 'The Building of Hatfield House' in *Family and Fortune*
    (1973).
Summerson, J. 'The Building of Theobalds 1564–85' in *Archaeo-
    logia* (1959).
Boalch, D. H. *The Manor of Rothamsted* (1953).
Minet, William *Hadham Hall* (1914).
Rogers, J. C. 'The Manor and Houses of Gorhambury' in *St
    Albans and Hertfordshire Architectural and Archaeological
    Society Transactions* (1933–5).
Johnson, W. Branch *Hertfordshire* (1970).
Stroud, Dorothy *Capability Brown* (1950, 1957, 1975).
Stroud, Dorothy *Humphry Repton* (1962).
Jones, Barbara *Follies and Grottoes* (1953, 1974).
Chauncy, Sir Henry *The Historical Antiquities of Hertfordshire*
    (1700, 1826, 1975).

[38] Chauncy, Vol. I, p. 12.

7. Farmers and the changing landscape

Piecemeal enclosure. The garden of England. Smaller domestic buildings. Parliamentary enclosure.

Piecemeal Enclosure

THE SURVIVING PARKS are among the most beautiful places in Hertfordshire. They are a fit setting for some of the finest buildings in the county, but very much more of the county's acreage bears the coarser marks of the farmer. The 1/25,000 Ordnance Survey map shows field boundaries. If one puts together the sheets which cover the centre of West Hertfordshire from Bovingdon and Sarratt in the west to the Waldens and Hitchin in the north the overriding impression is of a constant snake-like pattern. The reversed S shape of the open field furlongs survives in today's field boundaries, although they are chopped up at right angles by short, straight hedges. These hedges may be of all ages. Miss Levett wrote that the early "break up of the virgate as the normal holding" on St Albans' estates, the securing of "compact holdings and separate closes . . . can be traced back to 1250 or 1240. Some of the earliest entries are concerned with hedges."[1] Piecemeal enclosure continued into the twentieth century when Manland and Westfield Commons in Harpenden were enclosed. This latter day enclosure left its own mark: remnants of the furlong boundaries can be traced in a few roads, Sauncey Avenue for example, and in some of the property boundaries.

The landscape of piecemeal enclosure can be studied in many parts of the county. In spite of all the housebuilding, for a rapidly rising population, over sixty-seven per cent of

[1] Levett, p. 185.

the county's acreage in 1960-1 was still used for agricultural purposes; over much of this land the furlong boundary reigns supreme. Let us look at some examples. Bovingdon must be one of the best parishes for such a study: the roads and the field boundaries flow in a wave-like formation over most of the parish from south-west to north-east. This flow used to continue through the south-eastern part of Hemel Hempstead towards Bennett's End and Leverstock Green until this piece of countryside was transformed into a New Town neighbourhood. Even now the two old roads which define the area, Chambersbury Lane and St Albans Hill, formerly Bennetts End Lane, preserve the curves of the furlongs. Some of the first, new roads inside the area, Belmont and Great Elms, have been constructed along the lines of the furlongs.

A manorial survey of 1523 which is based on an older description, possibly of the early fourteenth century, refers to some 1000 acres in Bovingdon and Flaunden and 2000 acres in Hemel Hempstead as already enclosed. The survey covers some 7000 acres, of which 3000 seem to be in small unhedged pieces. The surviving open field areas were largely on the chalk slopes and pebble gravel; these were the least fertile areas but the earliest cultivated. By the end of the seventeenth century another survey shows that most of the surviving open fields had gone; the few that remained were on the chalk slopes. Some hint of what the fields looked like is conveyed by the hedges growing on what were balks in an area on the north side of Picott's End Lane, just to the west of Grovehill woods. The spreading New Town has not quite touched these fields, yet! There is another similar area in Bovingdon.

The land that was enclosed earliest was on the heavy clay of the uplands, good corn land. Grazing was provided by wide greens along the lanes. A dispute about rights of pasture under the hedges of Redbourn Road, Hemel Hempstead was recorded in 1380. The old hedgelines can still be seen

165

in many places in spite of building and road widening. In contrast to the section of the road in Redbourn parish, which was narrow, the road in Hemel Hempstead widens substantially. Little roadside greens can be seen, especially near Cupid Green. The road turns through a right angle here, becoming High Street Green, and runs through west Hemel Hempstead to Leverstock Green. Roadside greens can just be made out in places along High Street Green; the hedgelines are not easy to follow though many of the old trees have been left in the very pleasant development of this long road.

Dorothy Cromarty, on whose work these paragraphs are based, is not sure that all of this part of Hertfordshire was ever open, common field. It is not always easy in the Chilterns to fit early field systems into a simple dichotomy of common open fields and fields held in severalty which were individually cleared from the woodland. What is clear is that the landscape is deeply marked with the furlong pattern and this is quite different from the landscape north of the Waldens, in Pirton for example, or the quite different landscape around the Hadhams.[2]

There is a charming piece of almost secret countryside to the north of commuter Harpenden and to the east of Luton airport in which the complexities of the landscape can be studied. They can be seen best by taking a winding route along narrow lanes through places with evocative names. The route is shown in Fig. 21. This is based on the 1:25,000 Ordnance Survey sheets TL11 and 12, but reduced in scale, so it is advisable to take the relevant Ordnance Survey sheets along on any exploration of the route. Starting at Cold Harbour, now in Harpenden, one drives north through Bower Heath, past Hill Farm and Great and Little Plummers to Peter's Green in Kimpton parish. Perry Green is only 200 metres to the east of the complex road junction which makes up Peter's Green. The road to the north-east passes Law-

[2] Dorothy Cromarty, 'Topography and Settlement' in *History of Hemel Hempstead*, ed. Susan Yaxley, 1973, pp. 12–14.

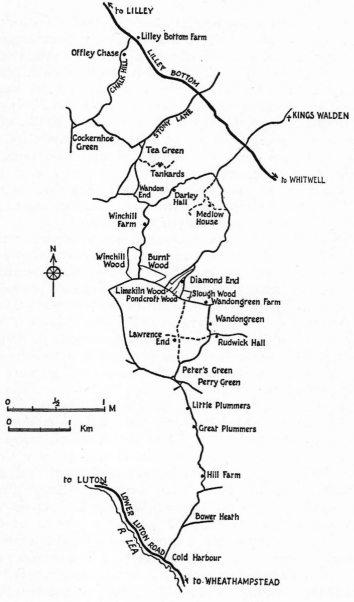

Fig. 21. From Harpenden to King's Walden.

167

rence End in its park on the left, Rudwick Hall and Wandon-green on the right. There is a T junction at Wandongreen Farm; the road to the left leads to the enchanting little woods which surround Diamond End; their names, Slough, Pond-croft and Limekiln Woods, are as suggestive as are Burnt Wood and Winchill Wood further along the road. Between these last two woods the road turns north to Winchill Farm and Wandon End on the Offley parish boundary. At Tea Green, just north of Wandon End, there is a choice of route. North-east, straight down Stony Lane, leads im-mediately to Lilley Bottom; a less direct route is north-west to Cockernhoe Green and then down the winding Chalk Hill, past Offley Chase to Lilleybottom Farm.

The essential clues to the landscape through which this journey is made lie in the narrow, winding lanes, often with high hedges, and in the many Ends and Greens. These are of all shapes and sizes: Cockernhoe Green is huge and not much built up, save at one end by modern housing; Peter's Green is surrounded by a mixture of old and new houses. Tea Green is on a high plateau with an open view of Luton air-port and the surrounding country; Diamond End is buried in woodland in a combe. There are other small greens with only one or two farms beside them. The field pattern on either side of this route is much more complex than in Bovingdon and made more difficult to interpret by modern ploughing out of hedges. There are substantial areas of open landscape in which the hedges have gone, as in Law-rence End park and in the fields around Rudwick Hall and Wandongreen. In other places, between Winchill Farm and Medlow House and between Wandon End, Darleyhall and Tankards, surviving field boundaries hint at ancient furlongs and strip farming, intermixed with the irregular shapes suggestive of individual clearings. The evidence for open field furlongs becomes more obvious along Chalk Hill and Stony Lane and in the field boundaries across the valley sloping up through King's Walden to Preston. There are

long, curving hedges and alongside Chalk Hill, where the
hedges have been removed, some high hedge banks survive.
On a route like this, and particularly between Winchill
Farm and Tea Green, it is foolish not to stop and get out of
the car. It may be difficult to visualise this piece of landscape
from such a compressed description; it is a truism that landscape has to be looked at as well as read about and studied
from maps. This description is given to encourage and help
the reader to go and look.

The men and women who made much of this type of
Hertfordshire landscape are anonymous for the most part,
but every so often a family emerges from the records. In
Knebworth a peasant family called Deards built up a local
estate during the later Middle Ages. They were one of
several families who were busy exchanging their open field
strips in order to acquire compact holdings for hedging,
but they did not neglect the acquisition of existing small
fields, orchards and gardens. Ralph Dardres is mentioned in
1349; other Deards follow; so successful were they that in
1489 a clerk, recording the transfer of the estate to the
Lyttons, actually listed a manor of Dardes. There was no
such manor but presumably the family holding was so impressive that the error occurred through an excess of lawyer's caution. John Dardres was acquiring more pieces of
land in the early sixteenth century and by 1605 a part of
Knebworth was known as Dardes End. The Deards were
now a yeoman family; in 1627 John Dards gave a bell to the
parish church, the earliest of the surviving bells, and an interesting example of the varied ways in which people who
had made their fortunes established their respectability in the
community.[3]

At least ten fields called Deards are shown on an estate
map of 1731 and the same boundaries can be seen on the
early 25″ Ordnance Survey map. The majority have obviously once been furlongs; they are in the triangle formed

[3] Lionel M. Munby (ed.), *Knebworth*, 1953, pp. 11–12.

by the Broadwater-Watton road, B197 between Broadwater and new Knebworth which used to be A1, and the road from Knebworth to Broom Barns. The Cuffley-Stevenage loop line, opened in 1920, cut right across this triangle. The area west of the railway line and behind the new houses along B197 has become one large field. But the old field boundaries remain in the area between the railway line and the Broadwater-Watton road, as does one old road now a footpath. The Deards' enclosures can be pieced together from such fragments. There is an additional interest to the area. The Broadwater-Watton road crosses what seems to be a tiny stream, barely a ditch, which has been given a considerable, and at first sight unnecessary, cement culvert. This is Broadwater, the meeting place of the medieval hundred, and notices in the Deards' roadside fields explain that the area is still 'liable to flooding'.

Families like the Deards must have flourished in many parts of Hertfordshire. Only occasionally has the family and its holding been identified. Long Tag's Field and Lamb's Croft, in King's Langley, get their names from families whose names have been found in fourteenth century Court Rolls. The Armigers began collecting crofts on the south side of Langley Hill at this time. The site of Armiger's Place can be identified on the ground, thanks to a Tudor survey. King's Langley, like its neighbour Bovingdon, has many fields with the reversed S shape. Their creation by piecemeal enclosure can be followed in three surveys, of 1556, 1591 and 1619. King's Langley proper was not only more completely enclosed than its upland hamlet, Chipperfield, but it had fewer and larger farms. Enclosure had gone a long way by 1556 and it was still continuing but not finished by 1619. Typical of the new farmers was the King family; leading figures in the community by the seventeenth century, they were millers, reeves of the royal manor, and tenants of the demesne and other farms.[4]

[4] *King's Langley*, especially pp. 26–8, 41–2, 47–78.

The Garden of England

It is people like the Deards of Knebworth, the Kings of King's Langley, and the Neales of Harpenden who have given much of the county 'its family face', to abuse Thomas Hardy's verse:

> Flesh perishes, I live on,
> Projecting trait and trace
> Through time to times anon.

The constant application of the description 'garden' to Hertfordshire is more than plagiarism of a literary turn of phrase. The farmers of Hertfordshire, who worked their way upward from serfdom to yeoman status over the centuries, had turned their fields into gardens in comparison with the open landscape to the north. Perhaps it was Fuller who first coined the memorable phrase that Hertfordshire was 'the garden of England for delight'. Defoe plagiarised it in recording how 'two foreign gentlemen' passing over Bushey Heath 'were surprised at the beauty of this prospect' and one said "That England was not like other countries, but it was all a planted garden". The phrase was reproduced by Peter Kalm in 1748, Joseph Spence in 1752 and in *The Gentleman's Magazine* in 1806. In 1822 William Cobbett, riding between Hemel Hempstead and Redbourn, summed it up: "Talk of pleasure grounds indeed! What that man ever invented, under the name of pleasure-grounds, can equal these fields in Hertfordshire?" An anonymous *Journal of a Tour to Scarborough* of 1798 comments, of "the inclosures at the foot of" Oliver's Mount, that "even these will fail with a man who has seen Hertfordshire".

What made the Hertfordshire fields so attractive was their hedges. Sir John Parnell described the countryside around St Albans and North Mimms in 1769 and called it 'a most exquisitely Beautifull cultivated Hedgerow'd Country'.

171

I know of no part of England more beautifull in its stile than Hertfordshire: thro' out the oak and Elm hedgerows Appear Rather the work of Nature than Plantation, generally Extending thirty or forty feet Broad, growing Irregularly in these stripes, and giving the fields the air of being Reclaimed from a general tract of woodland . . . I am Apt to believe sevral of these stripes of hertfordshire from their Irregular but most Beautifull swells are pieces of Natural wood left when the Rest was cleared for the Purposes of agriculture.[5]

Sir John Parnell was an acute observer. If he had noticed the plants which grew in such hedges he would have delighted Dr Max Hooper and Dr Pollard who suggest that hedges that originate as 'pieces of Natural wood' contain dog's mercury, bluebells and wood anemone which are woodland plants. Barnes Lane in King's Langley, from the parish boundary with Hemel Hempstead at least to Barnes Farm, has dog's mercury in both hedges and even where the hedge has been destroyed dog's mercury grows in the grass. This is a fascinatingly narrow, winding lane of great age. At the very beginning of the route from Harpenden to King's Walden (Fig. 21), between Hill Farm and Great Plummers, the road cuts through a hedge which may mark the boundary of an Anglo-Saxon estate.[6] The hedgeline to the east, along an overgrown track to Bishey Wood, is full of bluebells and dog's mercury.

Hertfordshire hedges were carefully tended by the farmers and regularly layered; plashing it was called. Arthur Young

---

[5] *Worthies*, p. 229; Daniel Defoe, *A Tour through England and Wales*, 1724–6, Everyman Edition Vol. 2, pp. 8–9; William Cobbett, *Rural Rides*, Everyman Vol. 1, p. 86; B.M. 10358 e3; London School of Economics: Misc Coll. 38. I am indebted to Mr M. Tomkins for these and other references. See his articles 'The Hertfordshire seen by Defoe and de Saussure' and 'Hertfordshire: the Garden of England' in *Hertfordshire Countryside*, Vol. 24, No. 133, pp. 44–6 and Vol. 29, No. 177, pp. 18–20.

[6] *Wheathampstead and Harpenden*, p. 8.

believed that this was "the county where the plashing system is carried on to the greatest extent . . . it has been universally practised here from time immemorial". Plashing, which Arthur Young described, was undertaken every twelve years and the considerable cuttings were used for domestic fuel. The economic justification for keeping "oak, ash, sallow . . ., plants more generally calculated for fuel than fences", in the hedges was that "they form a material object in the rural economy". Whether holly, which adorns so many hedges in West Hertfordshire, was used for fuel seems doubtful, but it must have contributed to making the hedges 'good fences . . . without the aid of any ditches'.[7] Along the sides of the roads, north and south of King's Walden, the holly has been shaped like stone balls on pillars. This unusual topiary work has given the public highway the formalised appearance of a landscaped entrance to a private park or garden.

Smaller Domestic Buildings

The Hertfordshire famers who prospered in the later Middle Ages and through the sixteenth and seventeenth centuries not only left their mark on the county's fields and hedge-rows, their houses bear their imprint too. There was a building boom to match the population explosion and this sometimes led to conflict with the authorities. John Wood, carpenter of Wormley, who was in trouble with Quarter Sessions in 1634, was one of many. He had built a house 'overthwarte' a common footway. Squatting is not a modern discovery. At Colney Heath, between St Albans and Hatfield and to the south, there are some houses which look as though they had been built on land taken from the Heath, the waste. They are on the south side of the road between

[7] Arthur Young, *General View of the Agriculture of Hertfordshire*, 1804, 1813 (reprint 1971), pp. 49–53.

Colney Heath and the church. Such building was dubiously legal.[8]

Hertfordshire is full of timber-framed houses, many of which are masked by later fronts or concealed by substantial rebuilding. In describing Lombard House in Hertford, Harry Forrester commented on "the peculiar adaptability of timber-framed building to additions, alterations, and re-fashionings, the ultimate outcome perhaps bearing little resemblance to the design originally conceived and appearing only to deceive".[9] Because the R.C.H.M. *Inventory* and the *Victoria County History* volumes were published before the First World War, when smaller domestic buildings were not properly studied, Hertfordshire's wealth of houses has not been adequately appreciated. Thanks to the work of local people like Graham Bailey, Barbara Hutton and Gordon Moodey a great deal of information has been accumulated and the county's smaller houses are now receiving the attention of one of the Royal Commission's Investigators, Mr J. T. Smith. This is not the place to attempt a serious study, however brief, of the new evidence but it is important that the rich stock of smaller houses should be appreciated by anyone looking at the county's scenery. There may be as many as 6000 houses in the county which were built before the nineteenth century. Some understanding of the different types of houses which survive is necessary for any appreciation of the landscape.

Improving an existing house or building a new one can be undertaken for different reasons. It may be to keep up with fashion, to display success, or to gain more comfort and more privacy. Whatever the mixture of motives, it was the increasing wealth, which came from improved farming and the successful exploitation of the growing London market, that made it possible for so many Hertfordshire husbandmen,

[8] M. Tomkins, 'The Story of Colney Heath' in *Hertfordshire Countryside*, 1970, Vol. 25, Nos. 138, 139, 140.
[9] Harry Forrester, *Timber-framed Building in Hertford and Ware*, 1965, p. 16.

yeomen and minor gentry to build themselves better houses. The oldest surviving type of house in Hertfordshire, not many of which are left, is the aisled hall. The earliest in the county may be Almshoe Bury in Ippollitts; houses like this were built from the thirteenth century onwards.[10] The simplest kind of house which survives, very common in the late Middle Ages, was one room wide and open to the roof. Such 'hall houses' are usually between sixteen and eighteen feet deep and consist of three parts: a central hall; a solar or parlour, a private bed-sitting room for the head of the household and his wife, at one end; and service rooms, for storing and preparing food and drink, at the other end. Between the hall and the service end was a passage into which both the front and back doors opened; the passage was shut off from the hall by a screen. Raisins in Wheathampstead is such "a small sixteenth century hall house . . . the home of a poor family . . . The service end and open hall survive." These timber-frame houses were fashioned by a carpenter and the parts brought to the site and assembled. "The timber frame was raised into position by props, and it is still possible to see the notches in the woodwork in the front (of Raisins) into which the props were fitted."[11] The central hall of houses like this might be of one or two bays, each bay being the section between two wallposts; so a two bay hall would have a truss spanning the width of the hall, the truss being supported by substantial wallposts and braces. Charles Lamb's Button Snap in Westmill is a three-bay hall house, the hall having one bay; there is also a four bay hall house in Westmill, the hall having two bays. There is a good example of a hall house, still thatched, in Great Hormead and three more at Snow End in Anstey (Plates 26 and 27).

This simple hall house developed two, rather more elaborate variants. One or both of the ends were enlarged into

[10] Almost all the houses mentioned in this section have been drawn to my attention by Mr Graham Bailey.

[11] Kathleen Foreman, *About Wheathampstead*, 1974, pp. 37 and 51.

wings with overhanging jettied fronts accommodating an upper floor. Harry Forrester noted the popularity of, what he called, the L shape in Hertford and Ware "particularly for simpler buildings. Does it represent one half of the courtyard house?", which was the shape adopted for contemporary large country houses. This shape "was eminently suitable for restricted spaces in the streets of flourishing towns, since the longer of the wings could be made to point rearwards". He argued that it "seems to occur more frequently in old country towns than the hall and cross-wings type, which is more appropriate to the open countryside or the village". Single cross-wing houses can be seen along St Andrew's Street and Fore Street in Hertford and in West Street and Crib Street in Ware. The Old Cross Cottage and Old Cross Post Office in Hertford and 15 West Street, Ware, with 'the only known surviving corner post in Hertford or Ware', are among examples of this type of house which Harry Forrester has described.[12] However these single cross-wing houses, with the solar in the wing, are just as common in the countryside. Among examples which Graham Bailey has studied are Luffenhall Farm in Clothall, the Oak Cottage tea-place at Hare Street (Plates 28 and 29), and several along Watton-at-Stone High Street.

Cromer Farm in Ardeley is a good example of the type of double cross-wing house which is fairly common in the county's countryside. Cross Farm near the boundary between Wheathampstead and Harpenden is another (Plate 30). Such houses had a central hall, open to the roof, with two-storeyed wings projecting forwards. The roofs of the hall and of the two wings had separate ridges, running at right angles to one another. A variant form of this double cross-wing house was fashionable by the fifteenth century among the emerging yeomen and minor gentry. This was the Wealden house, so called from its frequency in the Weald

12 Forrester, pp. 13–14, 10–12, and 41–2.

of Kent. In these houses a common roof ridge covered the whole length of the house, with the roof sloping to the front and back. Since the wings projected, this meant that the eaves overhung the hall section at the front. There is a Wealden house at Caldecote, but its roof elevation has been altered. Fabdens in Thundridge (Plate 31), Southend Farm in Stevenage, and Oak Beam in Walkern are other examples; there are suggestive remnants of what may have been Wealden houses in Hertford. A rather unusual, and quite differently arranged, house is the Chapel Farm at Woodend in Ardeley. It has a continuous jetty or overhang with the hall on the first floor; there is a running vine pattern on the bressumer plate. The bressumer is the beam which supports the joists of the overhang.

Until the late sixteenth century most small houses had no chimney. A fireplace in the hall was under a hole in the roof through which the smoke escaped. This blackened the roof timbers and one of the more certain ways of searching for evidence as to whether a particular house began its history as such a 'hall house' is to look for soot on the central timbers of the roof. To improve the dispersal of smoke, smoke hoods rather like cowls were built inside the hall. Such smoke hoods, or structural evidence for their existence, survive in a cottage at Southern Green in Rushden, in Gravelpit Hall at Wareside, and in houses at Barkway and Furneux Pelham. The building of a proper chimney and the insertion of a floor was the first great step in improving the comfort and privacy of those who lived in these houses. The thatched hall house in Great Hormead had such floors inserted in the late sixteenth and early seventeenth centuries. In the parish of Much Hadham several houses have late sixteenth century fireplace lintel beams, which are dated. Some of these fireplaces may have been built when floors were put into earlier hall houses, others may be in houses first built with two storeys. In either case the dates suggest that it was in the last quarter of the sixteenth century that two-storeyed houses began to be available for the middling ranks of farmers. New houses built with two storeys were of the axial-stack type, with "two fireplaces back to back and . . . this double stack in the middle of the house . . . You came in by the front door to find yourself opposite the stack wall, and had to turn one way into the hall or main living room, or the other way into the parlour". The screens passage disappeared. "Access to upper rooms was usually by a stair built against the stack on the opposite side from the door'. Barbara Hutton, in giving this description, comments that "This convenient and very sensible arrangement was popular in Hatfield at the beginning of the seventeenth century". The Rectory in Fore Street, the Forge Cottage at Coopers Green, and Brewhouse Cottage at Wild Hill are good examples.[13]

As the accumulated, detailed evidence for the county's timber-framed houses is carefully analysed no doubt regional differences will become apparent. There are already suggestive indications. Graham Bailey and Barbara Hutton's study of *Crown Post Roofs in Hertfordshire* distinguished between a western and an eastern style. In the west they found "remarkable arrangements of braces and tie-beams expressing a taste for curves". In the same area were the only six examples of a 'lower king-strut' which differs from the crown-post structure as the diagram (Fig. 22) shows.[14] Cruck building, in which the frame consists of curved timbers so that, in the simplest form, the wall and roof timbers are one, was mainly employed in the west, the Midlands, and north of Britain. But it extends into the west of Hertfordshire with one example surviving as far east as Rushden. In Offley there is a house with a cruck frame base and a crown-post roof superimposed.[15] On the other hand pargeting, the

[13] Barbara Hutton, *Houses—Hatfield and its People Book 10*, 1963, pp. 13–17.
[14] Especially pp. 3, 4, 12, and 17.
[15] N. W. Alcock, *A Catalogue of Cruck Buildings*, 1973, pp. 5 and 42 and information from Graham Bailey.

ornamental treatment of external plaster-work, flourished in Essex and extended into Hertfordshire, "notably the eastern part around Bishop's Stortford, which seems at one time to have been a flourishing centre for the craft".[16] However there is a splendid example of pargeting in Hertford on the corner of Fore Street and Market Place and pargeting

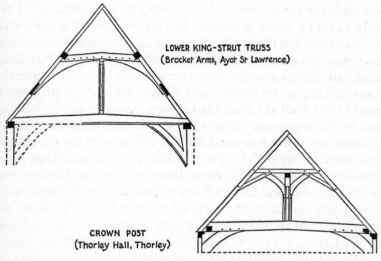

LOWER KING-STRUT TRUSS
(Brocket Arms, Ayot St Lawrence)

CROWN POST
(Thorley Hall, Thorley)

Fig. 22. *Left* Lower king-strut truss (Brocket Arms, Ayot St Lawrence). *Right* Crown post (Thorley Hall, Thorley). From *Crown Post Roofs in Hertfordshire* (Ch. 8 and 10) by Graham Bailey and Barbara Hutton.

extended at least as far west as St Albans and Wheathampstead where a great deal survived into the twentieth century which has now gone. Lastly the interval between the upright timbers, the studs, is close in timber-frame houses in the east of Hertfordshire, as it is in Essex, but much further apart in houses in the west of the county. Two houses, in Sandon and Nettleden, provide instructive contrasts. These

[16] Alec Clifton-Taylor, *The Pattern of English Building*, new edition 1972, p. 359.

differences hint at the existence of two cultural regions which met and overlapped in Hertfordshire. It is possible to associate this cultural frontier with the evidence for Roman-British survival in the west of the county or the fact that Hertfordshire was a frontier between Mercia and Essex or later between Wessex and the Danelaw. It seems more likely that the cultural influences travelled with the craftsmen and even with their materials. "The only building stone abundant in Hertfordshire" is flint and it "was used for the walls of most local churches". Royston cave may have begun its existence as a flint quarry. Pudding stone or conglomerate was occasionally used for church foundations, as at Sarratt and Great Munden, and it was used in the Hall at Great Gaddesden. Most stone, however, had to be imported. "From the end of the twelfth century Totternhoe stone was used almost universally for dressings and interior work" in Hertfordshire churches. This soft limestone, almost chalk, came from quarries at Totternhoe near Dunstable and Eileen Roberts has suggested that it may have been carted over much of Hertfordshire, perhaps in part along surviving Roman roads. A study of the work of Philip Lessy, a Totternhoe mason of the end of the fourteenth century, suggests movement along the Icknield Way. The churches in which this style is found are in north Hertfordshire, mostly just south of the Icknield Way. The furthest east are at Hinxworth, Wallington and Wyddial.[17]

Stone used in King's Langley in the south-west, however, came from quarries at Wheatley near Oxford, down the Thames and up the Colne and the Gade. Significantly the Hertfordshire churches, with stone from Barnack near Peterborough, are in parishes on or east of the Beane, with the single exception of St Albans Abbey. The stone could have come up the Cam (Rhee) to Ashwell or up other tributaries of the Ouse to Hitchin, and then been carted south and east,

[17] Eileen Roberts, 'Totternhoe Stone and Flint in Hertfordshire Churches' in *Medieval Archaeology*, Vol. XVIII, 1974, pp. 69, 71, and 74-5.

and floated down the rivers of east Hertfordshire.[18] The use of brick spread westwards from Essex and Kent. The original Moor Park built in 1425 was an early example of a brick building. Rye House gateway, of *c.* 1443 (Plate 32), is still standing. Brick was widely used in Hertfordshire later, replacing timber as in most counties south and east of the limestone belt. The brick was locally fired until the canals and railways brought bricks from the Bedfordshire brickworks into most parts of the county. It is only possible to speculate on the significance of these regional differences, but if a Totternhoe mason travelled with his stone, spreading a particular style, might not other masons have done so, and craftsmen in other materials have followed similar routes?

Parliamentary Enclosure

Canal building coincided with parliamentary enclosure, the last major transformation of the rural landscape apart from the very recent ploughing out of old field boundaries. It is too early to chronicle this latter ploughing up except to note that Hertfordshire, while affected, seems to have been changed less than its north-eastern neighbour, Cambridgeshire. Parliamentary enclosure, however, has left clear evidence on the landscape in certain areas of the county (Fig. 23) and in two different ways. In the south and west, where piecemeal enclosure had already transformed the arable, parliamentary enclosure was largely of waste, the surviving commons. In the north and north-east parliamentary enclosure was of arable open fields. Much of this latter enclosure was late, under the General Act of 1845, and even the enclosure by private act was not very early: the first acts, for Hexton and Walsworth in Hitchin, were of 1766 but there were only seven acts before 1795. North-east Hert-

[18] *King's Langley*, p. 32; *Inventory of the Historical Monuments in Hertfordshire*, 1910, pp. 262–4.

fordshire shared this pattern of late enclosure with its neighbour Cambridgeshire. Chauncy at the end of the seventeenth century had described Odsey and Hitchin Hundreds as Champion, that is open field; but, of Edwinstree Hundred, he wrote: "All

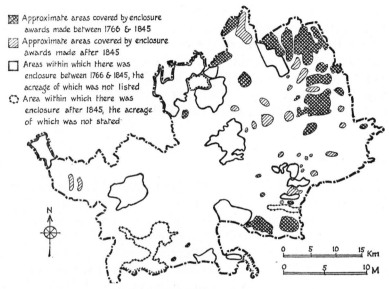

☒ Approximate areas covered by enclosure
   awards made between 1766 & 1845
▨ Approximate areas covered by enclosure
   awards made after 1845
☐ Areas within which there was
   enclosure between 1766 & 1845, the
   acreage of which was not listed
⬭ Area within which there was
   enclosure after 1845, the acreage
   of which was not stated

N

0   5   10   15 Km

0   5   10 M

Fig. 23. Parliamentary enclosure

this hundred (except the Parish of Barley, and Part of Barkeway) is enclosed".[19] Chauncy underestimated the extent of surviving open field. Enclosure acts covered no less than fifty-eight per cent of the area of Edwinstree Hundred, if the six parishes along the eastern border of the county are excluded. It was only here and in the southern parts of the hundred, near Ardeley, that the fields can have been really enclosed when Chauncy wrote. In contrast to this fifty-eight per cent, probably only forty per cent of the area of Odsey Hundred was affected by enclosure acts. Altogether some

[19] Vol. 1, p. 189.

27,000 of the 49,000 Hertfordshire acres specified in enclosure acts were in Odsey and the north-west part of Edwinstree Hundred. There were other parishes in the area, like Newnham, which must have been enclosed by private action sometime in the late eighteenth or early nineteenth centuries.[20]

Parliamentary enclosure which consolidated holdings into compact groups of fields led to the building of Victorian, brick farmhouses, sometimes with rows of labourers' cottages, in outlying parts of a parish. These buildings have had a short life. Modern transport makes it possible to live at some distance from the farmland and modern labourers and farmers, or their wives, dislike the isolation of these Victorian farm sites. South of the Icknield Way, between Royston and the Ashwell turn, there are several such abandoned or half abandoned farm sites. William Cobbett described another by-product of enclosure, a continuation into more desperate times of squatting on the waste. The "wretched hovels" which he saw at Cricklade were "stuck upon little bits of ground *on the road side*, where the space has been wider than the road demanded . . . It seems as if they had been swept off the fields by a hurricane, and had dropped and found shelter under the banks on the road side!"[21] Just south of Biggin Bridge, between Barkway and Hare Street, are four semi-detached cottages, seemingly of nineteenth or early twentieth century date, whose situation exactly recalls Cobbett's description. They are not hovels; one pair is brick, the other covered with pebble dash; but they may have replaced earlier buildings. The sites have been taken from the road side waste and the houses crouch half under the old hedgeline.

All the way from Barley and Barkway to Hitchin the

[20] I have used the tables in W. E. Tate's, 'A Handlist of Hertfordshire Enclosure Acts and Awards' in *E.H.A.S. Transactions*, Vol. XII, Part 1, 1954–6, pp. 18–31.

[21] William Cobbett, *Rural Rides* introduced by Edward Thomas, 1934, Vol. I, p. 18.

countryside bears the familiar marks of parliamentary enclosure: large, rectangular fields; hedges of thorn without timber or hedgebanks of any size; and straight roads from the village nucleus to the parish boundary with wide grass verges. This kind of landscape can be clearly seen in Norton (Fig. 28) north of Letchworth, and in the parishes between Norton and Ashwell, in Radwell, Newnham, Caldecote and Hinxworth. All the countryside to the east of Ashwell, from Kelshall to Barley has the same look.

There is a clear landscape frontier to the south. Norden's survey and map of Barley, of 1593–1603, makes the existence of this frontier very clear. Jack Wilkerson, the historian of Barley who has published Norden's survey, explains:

> The land to the south of the Chishill-Barkway road is heavy clay and was probably still covered with an oak forest at the time that the Open Field system of farming developed round the main village . . . when times were more settled and an expanding population needed more land, isolated farms would have been founded at Mincinbury and Abbotsbury on land cleared from the forest. It is significant that there is no evidence that open field farming was ever practised in the neighbourhood of these farms.

The present day observer would find it difficult to spot any great difference between the field shapes on either side of the divide, clear as the distinction is on Norden's map. The reason is an interesting example of the kind of exceptional phenomenon which can upset generalisations. Jack Wilkerson describes how Rider Haggard visited the area, in 1901, staying at Cockenach with Alexander Crossman who owned the land in the south of Barley. He was taken 'to see 2000 acres of derelict land' and describes Crossman's improvements: "Foul fields have been fallowed and drained, cottages built, pastures laid down and mended, ponds dug, roads constructed of burnt earth, fences erected, hedges trimmed and laid and plantations improved or reset". It seems likely that Crossman replanned and rearranged the whole pattern of fields and field roads as the Prouts had on their farms at Sawbridgeworth in the 1860s.[22]

While the frontier between the one-time open field landscape and its neighbour has been obliterated in Barley, it is still clear to see on the forward slope of the chalk ridge as it runs through Sandon, Wallington and Clothall. The Cat Ditch flows northwards, through a parliamentary enclosure landscape, to join the River Ivel. An older landscape of Greens and Ends, with winding roads and footpaths, climbs over the watershed to the south, past the head waters of the Rivers Beane and Rib. Perhaps it is no coincidence that it is precisely on this frontier, in Clothall, that strip lynchets survive on the north-east side of Bird Hill and on the north of Ashanger Hill. They are no longer so pronounced as they were in the recent past. While Hertfordshire lacks the obvious high back ridge and furrow of the Midlands, changes in the directions of furlongs can be seen in the middle of a field at Cumberlow Green. A fainter example is in the field alongside Chesfield Manor and ruined church, in Graveley parish. Neither of these areas, however, was enclosed by act of parliament.

Leland described the early sixteenth century landscape of west Hertfordshire, 'Chiltern-hilles', as 'baren, wooddy and ferne ground for the most parte'. Between Gaddesden and Berkhamsted there were 'very faire medowes' along the rivers but otherwise it was 'hilly, woddy, and much baren ground'. Between Luton and St Albans it was 'woody and enclosyd ground, to Barnet . . . like soyle'.[23] Large areas of

[22] Jack Wilkerson, *Two Ears of Barley*, 1969, pp. 16, 27 and 89–90; and ed. *John Norden's Survey of Barley, Hertfordshire 1593–1603*, 1974, p. 7; V.C.H. II, p. 138 and III, p. 333.

[23] Lucy Toulmin Smith, ed., *The Itinerary of John Leland in or about the years 1535–1543*, 1907, Vol. I, pp. 104–5, Vol. IV, p. 34.

manorial waste were left untouched by the centuries of en-closure by agreement. The parliamentary enclosure pro-cedure was followed to bring these areas into individual ownership. Pieces of waste and woodland were successfully enclosed in the Barnets, Elstree, Bushey, Watford, Rick-mansworth, Hemel Hempstead, Northchurch, Wigginton and Puttenham. Large areas of waste escaped enclosure and survive as common, in Berkhamsted, Harpenden, Hemel Hempstead, King's Langley and Wheathampstead for ex-ample. At the beginning of the 1960s 5550 acres, one and a quarter per cent of the county's area, were common; over one half was in the extreme west of the county; the greater part of this was in Aldbury and Berkhamsted.[24] The only large area of common in the rest of the county is Therfield Heath near Royston with its unique flora.

Local authorities control 1892 acres, 1780 remain under some form of common ownership, and 1508 belong to the National Trust; village greens cover 370 acres. Much of what was once manorial waste has become public property, of one kind or another. The stubborn Hertfordshire peasant may have been an encloser but he resisted enclosure by manorial lords, and to the extent that he was successful preserved the commons for later generations. There is a marked contrast between the yeoman or husbandman, whom Quarter Sessions Records so often present for nibbling away at the edges of the 'common highway', and the 'in-surrection in Hertfordshire for the comens at Northall (Northaw) and Chesthunt' of 1547–8 of which John Hales wrote.[25] While James Stretcher, husbandman of Willian, enclosed two perches of the highway from Weston to Hit-chin with a hedge and ditch in 1633, and Christopher Knight, yeoman of Cottered, ploughed up thirty perches of a foot-

[24] L. Dudley Stamp and W. G. Hoskins, *The Common Lands of England and Wales*, 1963, pp. 287–90.
[25] Elizabeth Lamond, ed., *A Discourse of the Common Weal of this Realm of England*, attributed to W.S. 1893, p. LVIII (from the Defence which John Hales sent to Somerset in Sept. 1549).

path to Royston in 1634, the tenants of the lord of the manor of Aldenham had taken him to court in 1576 because he wished to enclose some of the 1000 acres of waste.[26] The House of Commons was informed on 20 May 1643 of a riotous assembly on the Blackheath in Shenley which threatened to 'lay all the said grounds common'. The land had been enclosed and 'sown with wheat and oats' by Captain Edward Wingate, M.P. for St Albans and at the time a prisoner of the Royalists.[27] Similarly seventeenth century attempts to enclose pieces of Berkhamsted Common were stopped "by the generallity of the Inhabitants and Tenants being at least six thousand, by some of which the enclosures were throwne downe and lay'd open as before".[28]

Very slowly the manorial enclosers began to get their way and parliamentary enclosure sometimes completed the process. At the beginning of this century the Victoria County History wrote of Aldenham: "Inclosures were made from time to time till the date of the Aldenham Inclosure Act of 1801, when only 375 acres of common remained open, all of which were inclosed under this Act. There is now very little waste land in the manor beyond the green at Letchmore Heath." And of Northaw: "The south of the parish was once open common, which formed part of Enfield Chase, but the land is now all inclosed." Cuffley has grown all over the east of Northaw parish and Potters Bar at its south-west corner.[29]

In Berkhamsted, however, the manorial enclosers were finally defeated, not by countrymen but by the commuters who now demanded open spaces for their leisure. Nearly 1200 acres of bracken, gorse and trees on the high ground east of Berkhamsted remained unenclosed, manorial waste until 1865, when the second Earl Brownlow of Ashridge

26 Hertford County Records. Sessions Books, Vol. V, pp. 183 and 193.
27 Commons Journals, Vol. III, quoted in Alfred Kingston, *Hertfordshire during the Great Civil War*, 1894, p. 144.
28 G. H. Whybrow, *The History of Berkhamsted Common*, pp. 48 and 107–8.
29 V.C.H. Vol. II, p. 149.

enclosed about a third of the common with five feet high iron fences. Encouraged by his mother, Lady Marian Alford, he had bought out the rights of the manorial tenants, as Robert Cecil had done at Hatfield in the early seventeenth century. The people of Berkhamsted were offered ten acres for allotments and a thirty-two acre recreation ground. Augustus Smith, Lord of the Scilly Isles, of Ashlyns in Berkhamsted had not sold his rights. During the night of 7 March 1866 he imported 120 labourers from London who threw down three miles of railings. Supported by the newly formed Commons Preservation Society, Smith continued the battle in the law courts until 1870. The final judgment was that "there appears . . . to be as little justification now as there was in the seventeenth century" for the encroachment; "the tenants . . . enjoyed . . . in common the whole waste".[30]

The general public gained no rights through this judgment. What happened was that lords of manors now found waste an encumbrance. The National Trust was able to buy a considerable area of Berkhamsted Common after the First World War. In 1888 Sir John Bennet Lawes, faced with the need to police Harpenden Common against the undesirables who haunted it when race meetings were held, called a meeting of the commoners and proposed that in future a Harpenden Common Preservation Committee should take over the responsibility. During the twentieth century the Urban District Council gradually acquired most of the wastes and greens in the parish. This kind of change of responsibility took place in many parts of the county, but in others common ownership came to rest with a body of trustees. The Boxmoor Trust came into existence in the sixteenth century, to manage the commons of Hemel Hempstead on behalf of the inhabitants. An Act of Parliament of 1809 gave them new powers. In the late 1880s an elected Board of Conservators was created by government order to manage Ther-

[30] Whybrow, op. cit., pp. 107-8.

field Heath, balancing the rights of Therfield commoners with the needs of Royston for recreational space.

The last major changes in the rural landscape left as much variety as there had ever been. The woodland of the west had become commons, in many places; the open field arable of the north-east had been hedged; only in the secret landscape of narrow winding lanes and isolated farmhouses can much of the scenery as it was left by the first settlers be visualised. But each of these three landscapes is quite distinct although in so many places in the county they intermingle.

SELECT BIBLIOGRAPHY

Yaxley, Susan (ed.) *The History of Hemel Hempstead* (1973).
Young, Arthur *General View of the Agriculture of Hertfordshire* (1804,1971).
Forrester, Harry *Timber-Framed Building in Hertford and Ware* (1965).
Hutton, Barbara *Houses—Hatfield and its People Book 10* (1963).
Wilkerson, Jack *Two Ears of Barley* (1969).
Wilkerson, Jack (ed.) *John Norden's Survey* (1974).
Stamp, L. Dudley and Hoskins, W. G. *The Common Lands of England and Wales* (1963).
Whybrow, G. H. *The History of Berkhamsted Common* (1934).

8. The eighteenth century: Hertfordshire on the eve of transformation

The fields and their produce. Watermills. Maltings and breweries. The inns. The beginning of modern communications: turnpike trusts and navigations. The Grand Junction Canal.

The fields and their produce

BY THE MIDDLE of the eighteenth century the landscape of Hertfordshire was extremely varied. A map of Knebworth estate, made in 1731, perfectly illustrates what much of Hertfordshire must have looked like. The map extends from Knebworth into Stevenage and Shephall and shows pieces of land in other neighbouring parishes. The whole area was a mixture of small, irregular shaped fields, many but not all of which looked like enclosed furlongs, intermingled with surviving open field strips. Two typical areas are reproduced in Figs. 24 and 25: one to the west of Graffridge Wood, where Knebworth, Codicote, Kimpton and St Paul's Walden meet; the other in Stevenage, an area now in the middle of the New Town but not all built over. Many Hertfordshire Tithe maps, made just over a century later, show the same landscape pattern, those in Harpenden, Wheathampstead and Sawbridgeworth for example. In other places, like King's Langley and Tewin, the Tithe maps show no surviving strips, but many fields which had once been furlongs. None of these parishes was enclosed by act of parliament. Between twelve and nineteen per cent of the county's acreage was to be enclosed by act of parliament or contemporary private agreement. But in the mid eighteenth century open fields were still dominant in the north of the county and the area of unenclosed waste in the west was considerable.

With this mixture of field systems, and of farming in severalty with communal practices, the rapid spread of new farming methods was encouraged. Innovations tried out on privately controlled small fields could be widely copied in the surviving areas of communal farming. Ley farming was common in the county by the sixteenth century, as many field names indicate. Floating of water meadows was causing trouble with the county's millers in the seventeenth century; the ditches can still be seen in some of the meadows, as the riverside walk which is being opened along the upper Lea will reveal. New crops were being planted in the open field arable in the eighteenth century. George Cooke, who claimed that he was a Hertfordshire farmer, wrote in 1750 that three varieties of clover were 'cultivated in the open fields, for the use of cattle'.[1] Arthur Young gave several examples of rotations in the open fields round Baldock, Clothall and Hitchin: 'Turnips, Barley, Pease, Fallow, Wheat, Oats: this by agreement'.[2] The mixture of field systems in eighteenth century Hertfordshire may have played an important part in the county's undoubted prosperity. Hertfordshire farmers followed the most up-to-date practices in manuring and crop rotations. One of the first really popular agricultural writers, William Ellis of Little Gaddesden, drew much of his material from the experience of his neighbours in the early eighteenth century. Anyone who reads Ellis, instead of referring to the inaccurate and ill-informed life in the *Dictionary of National Biography*, will find that he had a thorough grasp 'of meliorating the different soils' by appropriate manures, of the need to select species of corn suitable for local soils, and of the

[1] George Cooke, *The complete English farmer; or Husbandry made perfectly easy in all its useful branches, c.* 1750, p. 6.
[2] *General View*, pp. 73–5.

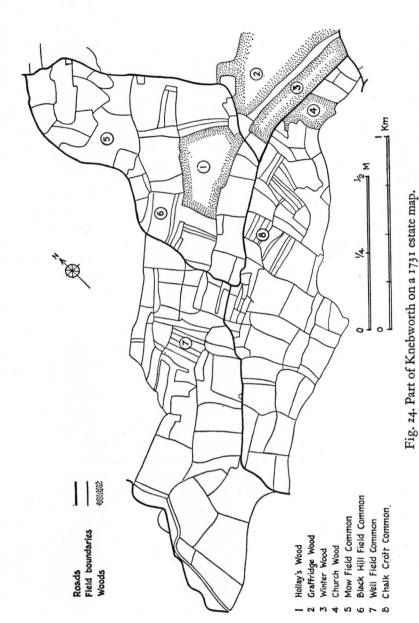

Roads
Field boundaries
Woods

1 Hollay's Wood
2 Graffridge Wood
3 Winter Wood
4 Church Wood
5 Mow Field Common
6 Black Hill Field Common
7 Well Field Common
8 Chalk Croft Common.

Fig. 24. Part of Knebworth on a 1731 estate map.

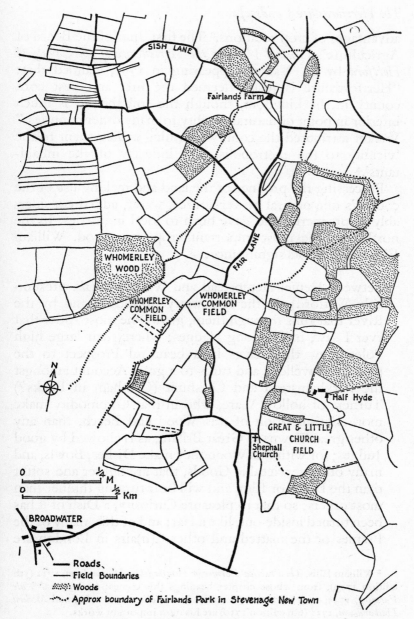

Fig. 25. Shephall and Fairlands based on an estate map of 1731.

Labels on map:
SISH LANE
Fairlands Farm
FAIR LANE
WHOMERLEY WOOD
WHOMERLEY COMMON FIELD
WHOMERLEY COMMON FIELD
Half Hyde
GREAT & LITTLE CHURCH FIELD
Shephall Church
BROADWATER
N

— Roads
— Field Boundaries
Woods
Approx boundary of Fairlands Park in Stevenage New Town

0   ¼ M
0   ½ Km

advantages of crop rotations.[3] The first draft of the Board of Agriculture's *General View of the Agriculture of the County of Hertford* by D. Walker, appearing in 1795, claimed that: "Hertfordshire is justly deemed the first and best corn county in the kingdom, though the soil therein is much inferior in point of natural fertility to many other counties." Walker attributed the county's farming achievement to the 'vicinity to the metropolis, and industry of the inhabitants'.[4]

Processing the produce of the land and making use of the county's one natural power source, water, added considerably to prosperity and gave birth to local industries. In the north-west the most important crop was wood. William Ellis described its significance:

> Between Hemel Hempstead and Waterford (*sic.* presumably Watford), in the low watry Meadows, and by the River that runs through them, grows the most Alder that ever I saw, in fine long Hedges; where their large high Poles shew themselves in a beautiful Prospect to the passant Travellers, and turns to a great Account amongst the Barkhamstead and Cheshunt (Chesham in Bucks?) Turners of hollow Ware, who in that Commodity make more Consumption of this Wood and Beech, than any other great Towns in Great Britain, as is allowed by good Judges; for with this Wood they make Dishes, Bowls, and many other serviceable Goods, that are lighter and softer than the Beech or Elm, and will bear turning thinner than most others; so that to pleasure Curiosity, a Dish of it has been turned inside-out, like a Hat; and of this, many of the Frames of the matted and other C(h)airs in London are

[3] William Ellis, *The Practical Farmer or Hertfordshire Husbandman*, 1732 (5th edition 1759), from whose chapter headings this comes; *Chiltern and Vale Farming*, 1733, 1745; *Practice of Farming in all Soils*, 1735, 1764; and *Modern Husbandman*, 1731 (6th edition 1750) are his most important works.
[4] pp. 25 and 30.

made; as are Pattens, Clogs, and Heels of Shoes; Gates, Hurdles and small Rafters.[5]

Except for the beech which flourishes around Ashridge and the alder which industrialisation has much reduced in the Gade valley, the only remaining physical evidence for this once flourishing industry is the surviving joinery firm of East and Sons Ltd in Berkhamsted. The furniture business shrank during the nineteenth century to concentrate on the other side of the Chilterns in High Wycombe.

Straw plaiting and straw hat making flourished over an even wider area in North-west Hertfordshire in the eighteenth and early nineteenth centuries. The plaiters used weak straw grown under hedges and this flourishing domestic industry was of considerable importance to the economy of agricultural labourers' families, but it made no lasting impact on the landscape. St Albans museum contains examples of plait, straw hats and the simple equipment used by the plaiters and hat makers.[6]

Watermills

Hertfordshire's many small rivers were full of watermills. At the end of the sixteenth century the county had been 'stocked beyond its needs with mills working for London'.[7] As the cloth industry which had never been very important disappeared and more grain was malted instead of being ground for flour, the mills turned to other uses. Papermaking was one of them. There were at least eighteen waterpowered paper mills in Hertfordshire in the eighteenth century. Since they were converted fulling or flour mills, often only temporarily converted too, they have left little trace, but their existence was important. For it was in paper

[5] *The Timber-Tree Improved*, 1745 (4th edition), Part 1, p. 108.
[6] John G. Dony, *A History of the Straw Hat Industry*, 1942.
[7] V.C.H. IV, p. 210.

making that the first modern industrial development in the county took place. Mill Green, Hatfield became a paper mill in the sixteenth century. Before that it had been a fulling mill. Converting a fulling mill into a paper mill was easier than converting a corn mill, for "the machinery for fulling consisted of great wooden hammers raised by the water-wheel which beat the dirt out of the cloth. They could equally well be used to pulp rags for paper, and at this time the pulping process was the only part of paper making to be mechanised." Thomas Vallance was making paper at Mill Green in 1788. In 1796 he bought Pickford Mill, on the Lea at Harpenden, which had been making paper since 1775 if not earlier. Mill Green continued to function as a paper mill until about 1838; it was later demolished. Pickford Mill lasted as a paper mill until 1849. The site is now a small industrial estate.[8]

Sometimes the very existence of a paper mill has been discovered by accident. The appearance of papermakers in every Redbourn militia list between 1758 and 1783 was only explained when a lease of Dolittle or Redbourn Mill was discovered. A 'water grist mill which is intended to be converted into a paper mill' was leased in 1753 to John Vowell stationer of London. In 1784 the mill was leased to a new tenant; it reverted to its original use.[9]

The other important industry for which water mills were used was silk throwing. Silk mills appeared between 1771 and the 1820s in Watford (Rookery Mill), Rickmansworth (High Street), St Albans (Abbey), Hatfield, Hitchin (Grove Mill), Tring (Brook Street), and Redbourn. Some of these began as converted water mills; other mills, at Rickmansworth and Redbourn, were built as steam mills. The paper mill at Mill Green, Hatfield had been converted to steam

[8] Henry W. Gray, 'Families and Trades—second part' in *Hatfield and its People*, 1964, pp. 69–71; Eric Thomas Finerty, 'The History of Paper Mills in Hertfordshire' in *The Paper-Maker and British Paper Trade Journal*, 1957, p. 510.

[9] Lionel M. Munby, ed., *The Story of Redbourn*, 1962, pp. 18–19 and 46. The lease is H.C.R.O. IID 42.43.

after Vallance left it. The transition from the old order to the new took place erratically. The Evans at Tring used both water power and steam. John Ransom seems to have undertaken corn milling and silk throwing at the same time in Grove Mill, Hitchin. The silk industry survives in one striking looking building, Kayser-Bondor at Baldock (Plate 33), though the factory was built for a firm of photographic chemists.[10]

Whatever their past and present uses, water mills and their sites are still an important part of the Hertfordshire landscape. In many towns and villages the site of a Domesday Book mill is still occupied by an industrial building and in a significant number of cases the building contains some remnant from its earlier history. In the middle 1960s three mills were using water power though not regularly: they were S. W. Cole's Hyde Mill in Wheathampstead near the county boundary, Moor Mill between Frogmore and Colney Street near St Albans, and Miss I. Hawkins' Redbournbury Mill, the "entire equipment (of which) appears to belong to the early nineteenth century, of wood construction often handsomely turned".[11] In 1975 Hyde Mill was still working intermittently; at Moor Mill (Plate 35) one wheel was still in working order, but the equipment to control the supply of water was not, so the wheel was not used. Redbournbury Mill was closed; the wheel was still there and the St Albans and Hertfordshire Architectural and Archaeological Society were undertaking restorations.

Ten disused mills contain iron wheels, as do some working mills. Kingsbury Mill at St Albans may well be on the site of a mill which was in existence long before the Norman Conquest, for it is in the old royal borough which the abbots destroyed. It is an Elizabethan building with a brick eighteenth century front and an iron undershot wheel; its con-

[10] W. Branch Johnson, *The Industrial Archaeology of Hertfordshire*, 1970, pp. 62–70.
[11] Ibid., pp. 47–52.

version into a water-mill museum, also containing old farm implements, won a European Architectural Heritage Year Award. The mill buildings at Moor Mill and Kingsbury still have their eighteenth century appearance; so does the working mill at Picott's End, Hemel Hempstead and the working mill in the centre of Wheathampstead. In other places, where the mill has gone, the millhouse often survives as a private house.

Branch Johnson, in his *The Industrial Archaeology of Hertfordshire*, described the sad state of the county's eight surviving windmills, some of which have been destroyed since he wrote. The post mill at Cromer has been restored; it is a striking landmark. Some of the tower mills have been converted to other uses and their working gear has gone.

Maltings and breweries

Much of the corn which brought wealth to Hertfordshire farmers was barley and the barley was turned into malt, chiefly in Bishop's Stortford and Ware but in many other towns as well. Maltings were as characteristic a feature of the Hertfordshire landscape as oast houses in Kent. Peter Mathias wrote of the Lea as "tapping some of the richest barley country in Hertfordshire . . . The region centred upon Ware, Hoddesdon and Stanstead Abbots was the oldest and most mature malting area in the country . . . even today the gentle valley of the Lea and Stort may be seen as the cradle of the industry in Britain."[12] Branch Johnson, when surveying the county's industrial monuments in the mid 1960s, examined some eighty sites in the county. There were twenty-two in Ware, seventeen in Bishop's Stortford, nine in Hertford, seven in Baldock, four each in Stanstead Abbots and Ashwell, and others in Berkhamsted, Bovingdon, Braughing, Furneux Pelham, Hatfield, Hitchin, Hoddesdon, Kimpton, King's Langley, Royston, St Albans, Sawbridge-

[12] Peter Mathias, *The Brewing Industry in England 1700–1830*, 1959, p. 437.

worth, Tring, Walkern, Watford and Wheathampstead.[13] While the square, tapering flues of the kilns, their characteristic domes and cowls, have not survived everywhere and most maltings are used for other purposes, they are still, as they were, very much part of the Hertfordshire landscape. They can be seen best along the Stort or at the waterfront of Ware (Plates 13 and 14). While most of the buildings Branch Johnson visited were of nineteenth and even twentieth century date, there is plenty of evidence for earlier buildings of the same kind on the same sites. F. & R. G. Grace's premises at Tring had been occupied by maltsters since the middle of the seventeenth century, at least, and a maltings on the corner of Charlton and Wratten Roads in Hitchin had, Branch Johnson found, sixteenth century brick in its base.

Much of the Hertfordshire malt went to London but a great deal was used in local breweries. Hertfordshire used to have breweries in every town and very many villages. Few are left. Simpson's fine eighteenth century brewery in Baldock's main street was destroyed in 1968. Fordham's 1839 yellow brick brewery and maltings at Ashwell (Plate 36) has, since 1969, been transformed. The kiln area has been converted into modern flats and cleaned. It stands by the little River Rhee, the infant Cam, looking most attractive. The rest of the brewery has been pulled down and modern houses built on the site, except for one building which stands derelict, perhaps awaiting conversion. The transformation earned an award in European Architectural Heritage Year. Rayment's little red brick brewery of 1860 survives by the crossroads at Furneux Pelham, an isolated situation in an unspoiled countryside. It carries a proud new sign 'Rayments Brewery' and sells its own draught next door with all the charm of an old country brewery though it belongs to Greene King Ltd. The only surviving, independent Hert-

[13] W. Branch Johnson, 'Hertfordshire Maltings' in *Hertfordshire Past and Present*, No. 6, 1966 and *Industrial Archaeology*, pp. 34–40.

fordshire brewer, McMullen, still work their large red brick brewery built in 1891 in Hartham Lane near the Old Cross, Hertford. Their offices and vaults on the site of the Green Dragon near the war memorial, with decorative tiles proclaiming the firm's name, are offered for development. McMullen's two sites symbolically mark the twin centres of historic Hertford. Benskin's Cannon Brewery at Watford, Ind Coope Ltd since 1957 and the largest modern brewery in the county, flaunts its Benskin sign where Watford High Street rises from the river; it dominates the bridge like the keep of a Norman castle.

The Inns

From the middle of the eighteenth century Hertfordshire breweries were actively engaged in creating tied houses; the free house has almost disappeared. But the pubs remain, buildings of many periods. Hertfordshire's inns have been so thoroughly recorded by the indefatigable Branch Johnson that it seems absurd to repeat what he has written.[14] However, they form an important element in the history of the Hertfordshire landscape and a number of general remarks must be made. A surprisingly large number of the older buildings in many villages have been inns, or at least beerhouses, at one time or another. Since inns changed their names frequently, tracking the history of an inn can be quite complicated. Thus the *Jolly Butchers* at Hare Street in Great Hormead began life as the *Dog's Head in the Pot* which it was in 1594. It changed its name when a butcher's daughter inherited it in the second half of the eighteenth century. Similarly the *New Inn* at Holwell started life as the *Dirt House* because it was built on land where the scavengers of Hitchin dumped their refuse. In 1791 it was the *Dirt House or Flower de Luce* and it was renamed after a rebuilding early in the nineteenth century. Bulls and Lions, of various colours, Bells

[14] *Hertfordshire Inns: part one East Herts*, 1962; *part two West Herts*, 1963.

and Crowns, combined with other objects or alone, are so common that in a place of any size there may have been two or three inns with the same name in different buildings. The sign could change too. The most attractive of modern inn signs may be misleading. An inn on Welwyn Hill called the *Steamer* has a horse on its "sign board (which) perpetuates the common fallacy that the name derives from the steaming extra horse that drew waggons and coaches up Welwyn Hill". In fact the inn was the *Steam Engine* "in 1850 (when the Great Northern Railway opened)".[15]

If the pub was the only building in the village which could vie with the church in importance, its sign often commemorates the local family of gentry, either with a full heraldic shield like the *Lytton Arms* at Knebworth or with heraldic animals or other symbols. Three inns at Hertford commemorate families who have fought for the borough's parliamentary seats: the *Dimsdale Arms, Duncombe Arms,* and *Salisbury Arms*. St Albans has many inns which have or claim to have had some connection with the abbey: the *Fleur de Lys*, the *King Harry*, the *Queen's Head* (once the *Chequers*), and the *White Hart* are certainly on sites that were occupied by inns before the dissolution of the monasteries. Not all inns have changed their names or moved their sites. The *Saracen's Head* in King's Langley is mentioned by name in a survey of 1619, and by implication in one of 1591 as a tenement adjoining 'a lane called dronken lane'.[16] It is still there.

Many of the county's inns had more than a local function. Because Hertfordshire lay across the main roads from London to the north, it had always been an area in which travellers stayed overnight. William Vallans hymned 'the guested town of Ware' in verse in 1589. The improvement of roads and road surfaces in the eighteenth century made possible greatly increased traffic. The Post Office organised a reliable mail coach system throughout the country, to precise

[15] *Hertfordshire Inns: part one*, pp. 102–3.
[16] H.C.R.O. 20113.

201

timetables. Naturally many of the coaches ran through Hertfordshire. Timebills of 1797 show that the coaches to Birmingham, Liverpool and Carlisle all stopped in Redbourn. They were only three of the more than seventy coaches which passed through Redbourn every twenty-four hours. The Edinburgh coach and the 'Wisbeach' coach took John Gilpin's road to Ware and on to Royston.[17] Alfred Kingston listed fourteen coaches which passed through Royston at the end of the reign of George III and two more which passed through Barkway just to the east. "Besides the coaches, 'fly-waggons' travelled up and down the North Road to and from London daily, conveying goods, . . . and occasionally passengers to whom the coach fares would have been prohibitive."[18]

Traffic like this, and there were many more mail coaches than these as well as other coaches and waggons, meant more trade for the inns. The wide doors which once opened into innumerable coaching inns can be seen in towns and villages on all the chief roads in Hertfordshire. Some have been filled and the space used for shops or houses. Others remain as inns. The bar lounge of the *White Lion* in Stevenage was once the entrance through which coaches proudly drove. The cosmopolitanism which developed around the inns can be seen in the presence of a Welshman among the servants at the Swan inn in Stevenage in 1760; 'Daved the Fly' is how the local constable spelt his name in the militia list. In 1764 a draper from Aldbury lodged in the *Saracen's Head* at King's Langley and lost 'five pieces of Gold Coin of the proper Coin of the Kingdom of Portugal, called Moidores, of the value of six pounds fifteen shillings'. The landlord, who may have been involved in the theft, had warned the draper against some 'lose Irishmen' in the house.'[19]

[17] Edmund Vale, *The Mail-Coach Men of the late Eighteenth Century* (1960), 1967, pp. 236–48.
[18] Alfred Kingston, *A History of Royston*, 1906, pp. 179–80.
[19] W. J. Hardy and William Le Hardy, eds., *Hertford County Records*, Vol. II, 1905, p. 100; Vol. VIII, 1935, p. 112.

The Beginning of Modern Communications: Turnpike Trusts and Navigations

The landscape of eighteenth century Hertfordshire was transformed by the development of communications (Figs. 26a and b). Just as the Roman roads fanning out from London had influenced the county's earlier history, so improved roads and waterways began a fundamental alteration in the county which railway lines and motorways were to carry further in the nineteenth and twentieth centuries. The beginnings were localised. The first turnpike trusts and the canalisation of the Lea and the Stort were local operations, although the need for them was indirectly due to London pressures. In both these enterprises Hertfordshire was something of a pioneer.

Each parish was responsible for the maintenance of its own roads and this put an intolerable burden on those parishioners who had to maintain main roads when traffic increased. The breaking point came on Ermine Street north of Ware. In 1629 Hertfordshire Quarter Sessions were told that the roads in Standon were too decayed to be repaired by the usual six days labour a year. In 1632 Quarter Sessions ordered what may have been the first traffic census, at Collier's End in Standon parish. Two people were paid to count 'how many waggons from Cambridge, Northwhich and St Edmondsbury' passed to and from London. In 1646–7 Standon people suggested to Quarter Sessions that taxes should be levied on loads drawn by five or more horses, to help with the cost of repairing Ermine Street. Springs appeared in the 'swallowinge clay' and the parish contained no stones or gravel suitable for road repair. Ware complained, at the same time, of "the great decay of all the ways" due to "the bringing of great loads of malt from both the Hadhams, Alburie, Starford, all the Pelhams and Clavering, . . . the teams often consisting of seven or eight horses".[20]

[20] *County Records*, Vol. V, pp. 111 and 161–2; I, pp. 82–3 and 86; VI, pp.

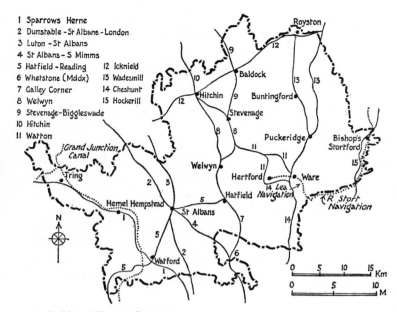

A. Turnpikes and waterways.

Key (left of map A):

1 Sparrows Herne
2 Dunstable - St Albans - London
3 Luton - St Albans
4 St Albans - S Mimms
5 Hatfield - Reading
6 Whetstone (Mddx)
7 Galley Corner
8 Welwyn
9 Stevenage - Biggleswade
10 Hitchin
11 Watton
12 Icknield
13 Wadesmill
14 Cheshunt
15 Hockerill

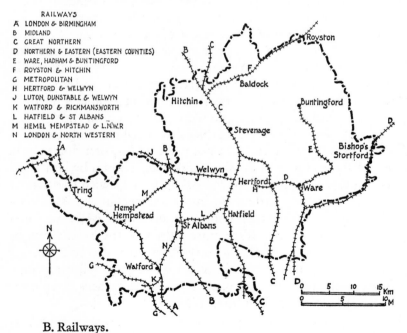

B. Railways.

Key (left of map B):

RAILWAYS
A LONDON & BIRMINGHAM
B MIDLAND
C GREAT NORTHERN
D NORTHERN & EASTERN (EASTERN COUNTIES)
E WARE, HADHAM & BUNTINGFORD
F ROYSTON & HITCHIN
G METROPOLITAN
H HERTFORD & WELWYN
J LUTON, DUNSTABLE & WELWYN
K WATFORD & RICKMANSWORTH
L HATFIELD & ST ALBANS
M HEMEL HEMPSTEAD & L.N.W.R
N LONDON & NORTH WESTERN

Fig. 26. The communication pattern developed between the eighteenth and nineteenth centuries.

Relief came in 1663: an act of parliament created the first turnpike trust in the country. The J.P.s of Hertfordshire, Cambridgeshire and Huntingdonshire were made responsible for the maintenance of Ermine Street through tolls on road users. The first turnpike tollgate was put up at Wadesmill just north of Ware. Fifteen different turnpike trusts, established between 1712 and 1769, covered most of the main roads in Hertfordshire. While they improved the roads considerably, they were developed erratically and covered too short sections of road. The Hertfordshire stretch of the Great North Road became the responsibility of no less than four separate trusts and they were set up at different dates. Only two of them were in existence when Daniel Defoe wrote, in 1725, of the appalling condition of the road between Baldock and Stevenage:

> Famous for being so impassable, that the coaches and travellers were oblig'd to break out of the way even by force, which the people of the country not able to prevent, at length placed gates, and laid their lands open, setting men at the gates to take a voluntary toll, which travellers always chose to pay, rather than plunge into sloughs and holes, which no horse could wade through.

The Stevenage-Biggleswade Trust had been established in 1720; so "this terrible road is now under cure . . . and probably may in time be brought to be firm and solid, the chalk and stones being not so far to fetch here".[21] Now that a motorway bypass has removed much of the traffic, it is possible to look at the old route and to imagine the improvements which the turnpike trust began, in the dip to Graveley and over Jack's Hill to the north.

127–8, 139, and many later entries under Wadesmill in Index. The quotation is taken from the printed Calendar, not from the original ms.

[21] Daniel Defoe, *A Tour through England and Wales, 1724–6*, 1948 Everyman Edition, Vol. II, pp. 122–3.

The improved roads meant improved transport and books of itineraries were published, showing main roads and the junctions with minor roads; the pattern they adopted is still used by the A.A. and R.A.C. Many milestones survive to commemorate the new system of main roads which developed; Branch Johnson counted seventy-eight still in position, though commenting that they were diminishing. Improvements to A1 over Digswell Hill and north of Hatfield have removed the last surviving Hertfordshire tollhouses. The major impact on the local landscape was made by the 'constant rerouting, straightening, widening' of roads which the turnpike trusts undertook. The road pattern south of Sawbridgeworth, past the High Wych turn to the bridge across the Stort, was completely refashioned by the 'Hockerill Highway' trust, the southern part being McAdam's work. Turnpike trusts were responsible for making the cuttings through the chalk hills to the east and south of Royston, which greatly eased the journeys of both local and long distance traffic.[22] John Loudon McAdam lived at Hoddesdon between 1825 and 1836; he became surveyor to many Hertfordshire trusts. He made many minor, local road improvements and planned a remodelling of the Great North Road which was never carried out. But acting for other trusts he remodelled the Holyhead road through Barnet and St Albans, creating a deserted hamlet in South Mimms in the process.

While the roads were gradually improved by turnpike trusts, Hertfordshire's two most important rives, the Lea and the Stort, were being made navigable. There had been many piecemeal attempts to keep the Lea open to shipping. The Lea Navigation Act of 1739 brought the river, more or less, under one control. It was scoured; obstacles were removed, and locks were built at Ware, Stanstead, and Broxbourne. John Smeaton was employed in 1765 to make new

---

[22] *Industrial Archaeology*, pp. 109 and 105–6. See also F. H. Maud, *The Hockerill Highway*, 1957 and Kingston, op. cit., p. 179.

cuts, more locks and a continuous towpath; Thomas Telford followed him. The Stort Navigation Act of 1766 led to dredging and the building of fifteen locks along the river's thirteen miles; eight locks remain. A local innkeeper, Thomas Adderley, and Sir George Duckett of Bishop's Stortford were responsible for the navigation. Four lock-houses still have a carved tablet with the initials G.D. and a hand, the badge of an Ulster baronet. The charming Saw-bridgeworth lockhouse shows them best. Sir George is better known under his own name, Jackson: as Secretary of the Admiralty he helped Cook on his voyages. The change of name came when he married an heiress.

The local impact of the navigations was considerable. Within a few years of the passing of the Lea Navigation Act no less than 5000 quarters of malt and corn a week were being sent by barge from Ware to London. There were no less than seventy maltings in Ware in the mid-nineteenth century, and most of London's breweries were supplied. The Militia Returns for Bishop's Stortford reveal that there was a sudden increase in the numbers of people working in local brewing at the end of the eighteenth century. This was because a new brewery, Hawkes and Co., had just been built. The brewery, on a large site between Water Lane and North-gate End, was the most considerable brick building which had been put up in the town. Not surprisingly there was also a noticeable increase in the numbers of bricklayers in the local Militia Returns. The traffic on the Stort Navigation doubled in the twenty years before 1807. Dwindling returns and the collapse of a lock forced its closure a century later, in 1909. But the Lea Conservancy reopened the waterway in 1924 and so *Kelly's Directory of Hertfordshire* for 1929 could still claim that "considerable traffic is carried on in malt, great quantities of which are made here, and in grain and other articles, which are sent to London".[23]

[23] V.C.H. IV, p. 243; *Sawbridgeworth*, pp. 30–31; Kelly, p. 54.

The Grand Junction Canal

Hertfordshire was the home of the canal duke whose monument, a Doric column with an urn on top, stands in Ashridge woods in Aldbury parish. But the Duke of Bridgewater built no canals in Hertfordshire, though he did have a far-sighted scheme for linking the Stort Navigation with the Norfolk canal system. Hertfordshire has only one canal, but an important one, the Grand Junction or Union Canal, which joined the Thames with the Midland canal system at Braunston. This was the first planned communication between London and the north since the making of the Roman roads. The Great North Road had grown; it was not planned. The Grand Junction canal, however, was a completely new venture along a new route and for the specific purpose of making a direct waterway link between London and Birmingham. It provided regular fast passenger transport; in 1806 troops were moved from London to Liverpool for embarkation for Ireland: "the men will be only seven days . . . it would take them above fourteen . . . to march".[24] But above all heavy goods, like coal, could be moved across country more easily. There was an immediate local impact. The price of London manure fell and one Hertfordshire farmer at least, Newman Hatley of the 500 acre Langley Lodge Farm in King's Langley, "opened a trade upon the canal, in order to give him a greater command of manure for his farm".[25]

The building of the canal was authorised by act of parliament in 1793; it was built from London outwards, reaching Boxmoor by 1798, Tring by 1799. Local landlords had to be pacified, with effects on the landscape which can still be seen. In Cassiobury Park the towpath crosses from the west to the east bank because the Earl of Essex was afraid that poachers

---

[24] *The Times*, 19 December, 1809, quoted in Charles Hadfield, *British Canals*, 1959, pp. 116–17.
[25] Arthur Young, *General View*, p. 16.

Plate 23 Ardeley Bury, Sir Henry Chauncy's home

Plate 24 Panshanger

Plate 25 Ayot St Lawrence, church

Plate 26 Great Hormead, The Old Swan at Hare Street

Plate 27 Anstey, Cottage at Snow End

Plate 28 Clothall, Luffenhall Farm

Plate 29 Great Hormead, Oak Cottage at Hare Street

Plate 30 Harpenden, Cross Farm

Plate 31 Thundridge, Fabdens

Plate 32 Rye House gateway

Plate 33 Baldock, Kayser-Bondor Factory

Plate 34 Letchworth, Borg-Warner Factory

might use it to gain access to his game preserves. Bridges in all kinds of materials and of many types survive. A humped bridge in Grove Park gives access to what was in 1800 Lord Clarendon's home. At Dixon's Gap and Wilstone, near Tring, two small, original bridges cross the arm of the canal that went to Aylesbury and which was opened in 1815. Some of the original lock keepers' houses still stand along the canal. On the county boundary, just beyond Tring, where the canal reaches its highest point, are four large reservoirs built about 1838. One consequence of building a canal, which was to be repeated at railway stations, was the opening of new inns. The Fishery Inn, across the canal from Boxmoor, is most picturesque though its original function was the utilitarian one of stabling barge horses. Percy Birtchnell described how "canal workers had their favourite public houses and shops and were especially fond of sheep's head and pluck for which Thomas Ashby, the Northchurch butcher, charged a shilling. The lock by New Road bridge was known to all boatmen as Sheep's Head Lock."[26]

The canal brought change to West Hertfordshire. The industrial revolution reached the county. In two paper mills on the River Gade, at Two Waters and Frogmore in Hemel Hempstead, the Fourdrinier brothers invented the endless web of woven wire which mechanised the production of paper, by making it in a roll. John Dickinson installed his own, improved, version of the Fourdrinier machine in Apsley Mill, Hemel Hempstead which he bought in 1809; paper had been made there since 1794. From Apsley Dickinson created a great paper empire along the Gade. The firm introduced silk thread as a protection against forgery, made the Mulready envelopes and Basildon Bond stationery. John Dickinson bought Nash Mills in 1811, began building Home Park Mills in 1825 and Croxley Mills in Rickmansworth in 1828. He leased Two Waters, Frogmore, and a mill at Batchworth in Rickmansworth. The situation of these mills, in

[26] Percy Birtchnell, *A Short History of Berkhamsted*, 1972, p. 85.

Hemel Hempstead, the Langleys, and Rickmansworth, near the River Gade *and* the canal was all important in their success. The river provided the considerable quantity of water needed in paper making; it was believed locally that chalky water was an advantage. By 1834 Telford was complaining to the House of Commons that Gade water could not be used for London's water supply: it was 'infected by the deleterious substances used for paper mills'. The new canal provided cheap transport both for the bulky raw materials, rags at first, then wood pulp and esparto grass, and for the heavy finished products. Steam power soon replaced water power; a steam engine was installed in Nash Mills in 1824. Around his Apsley and Croxley mills Dickinson built workmen's cottages. In 1819 Apsley was described as 'rather resembling a village than a manufactory'.

The Industrial Revolution brought a new social order. There was a strike in 1821 which Dickinson broke using unskilled local labour; it was said that he could 'make a papermaker out of a hedge'! A new type of businessman moved into the area. Dickinson, himself, lived at Nash Millhouse from 1811. When he moved to Abbots Hill in Abbots Langley, his partner, Charles Longman, a member of the great publishing family took over the millhouse. In turn Longman moved to Shendish in King's Langley, and Dickinson's son-in-law, Sir John Evans, came to Nash House. Sir John became a partner; one of his sons, Lewis, continued in the paper business and like Sir John became well-known as a local antiquary. Lewis' brother, Arthur, was far more distinguished in this line, for his work in Crete; while a sister, Joan, became a well-known art historian as well as chronicler of the firm's history.[27]

In effect the London–Birmingham canal brought the Industrial Revolution into Hertfordshire, along the Gade valley from Hemel Hempstead to Watford and Rickmans-

---

[27] Joan Evans, *The Endless Web*, 1955; *King's Langley*, pp. 98–9 and 113–15; *Industrial Archaeology*, pp. 55–61.

worth. It brought factories, and strikes, commuting businessmen and intellectuals, two middle-class groups more closely
related in the nineteenth century than today. This was a fore-
taste of the Hertfordshire which was to exist in the twentieth
century.

SELECT BIBLIOGRAPHY

Ellis, William *The Practical Farmer or Hertfordshire Husbandman*
    (1732).
Dony, John G. *A History of the Straw Hat Industry* (1942).
Johnson, W. Branch *The Industrial Archaeology of Hertfordshire*
    (1970).
Johnson, W. Branch *Hertfordshire Inns:* two parts (1962, 1963).
Maud, F. H. *The Hockerill Highway* (1957).
Evans, Joan *The Endless Web* (1955).

9. Railways and commuters

For and against the railways. The railway landscape. The Victorian townscape. Middle-class estates. The commuter in the countryside.

For and against the railways

THE CANAL FIRST brought those economic and social changes which were to transform the county's appearance. The railways became the main instrument through which people began to flood into the county. Four main lines from London to the north provided the framework around which a local railway system grew (Fig. 26b). Due to short-sighted government policies all but three of the spider's web of east-west lines which developed have been closed to passengers and the track of most of the other seven has been pulled up. The first main line to open was the London to Birmingham; it reached Boxmoor, from Euston, in July and Tring in October 1837. The last through line to open was the Midland, which reached St Pancras from Bedford in 1867; passenger traffic began in 1868. The Great Northern opened from King's Cross to Hitchin and beyond in 1850, and added a loop joining Cuffley and Stevenage in 1920. The Northern and Eastern from Liverpool Street to Bishop's Stortford and Cambridge was the fourth main line. The minor lines, which joined these four, were inadequate even at their maximum extension. The comment was made, in 1909, that

> with such a multiplicity of lines, it might well be imagined that railway communication between nearly all parts of the county would be well-nigh perfect. As a matter of fact,

this is by no means the case; and the journey by rail from the western to the eastern side, owing to changes and delays, is so slow and tedious, that it is frequently found convenient to hold important Hertfordshire meetings, like those of the County Council, in London.[1]

Lydekker's expression 'western to the eastern side' is revealing. He lived in Harpenden; his family were nineteenth century newcomers. Among other effects of the immigration which the railways brought was a reversal of the eastern predominance. R. E. Pahl, writing in the early 1960s, about 'the metropolitan fringe' in Hertfordshire, noted that "West Hertfordshire has developed more rapidly on account of its geographical position and accessibility. The broad frontier may be traced in central Hertfordshire. The far north-east of the county is still beyond the fringe as the recent figures of depopulation show."[2]

During the sixteenth and seventeenth centuries, statesmen and merchants had chosen to live in Hertfordshire. They continued to do so in the eighteenth and nineteenth centuries, and bankers joined them. Brocket Hall was bought in the middle of the eighteenth century by Matthew Lamb, the son of an extremely successful Nottinghamshire lawyer. Samuel Smith, a banker, bought Watton Woodhall in 1801. The Calverts came from Little Hadham, made fortunes in brewing in London, and bought property all over East Hertfordshire. All three families produced local M.P.s; Lamb's grandson became Prime Minister. By the beginning of the nineteenth century a new group of immigrants was arriving. Arthur Young wrote: "Property in Hertfordshire is much divided: the vicinity of the capital; the goodness of the air and roads, and the beauty of the country, have" made "this county a favourite residence" and attracted "great numbers

[1] R. Lydekker, *Hertfordshire* (Cambridge County Geographies), 1909, p. 132.
[2] R. E. Pahl, *Urbs in Rure*, 1965, p. 78.

of wealthy persons to purchase land for building villas".[3]
'Villas' needs explaining. The kind of property Arthur Young
had in mind is described in the introduction to the parish
history of Barnet in the Victoria County History:

> East Barnet contains many so-called parks, that of Oak
> Hill being the largest. It comprises about twenty acres,
> and occupies one of the highest points in the parish, from
> whence good views are obtained of the surrounding
> country. There are smaller parks at Belmont; Bohun
> Lodge, the residence of Mr William Allen Vernon; and
> Little Grove, the seat of Mrs Stern. Osidge Park, the seat
> of Sir Thomas Lipton, lies to the south of the parish, and
> Willenhall Park, now a building estate, is at the western
> extreme of the parish near Barnet Vale.[4]

The building of railways meant that it was possible to live
in Hertfordshire and go to work daily in London. So newcomers poured in. Arthur Young's 'wealthy persons' increased greatly in numbers as the parish introductions of the
Victoria County History make clear. The professions followed the businessmen and politicians; the clerks followed
the businessmen; and in the twentieth century came a mass
of wage-earners. The first arrivals clustered around railway
stations; after the First World War, with the help of the
motor car and bus services, settlement spread further into
the countryside. At first houses were built by individuals
according to their whims; then came private estates, whose
developers showed very varying degrees of consideration
for any other values than their own economic profit. Private
individuals acting cooperatively planned dream towns.
Local authorities built estates, and after the Second World
War the central government built New Towns.

Every group of new arrivals was resented by those already

[3] *General View*, 1804, p. 18.
[4] V.C.H. II, p. 337.

settled in the county, themselves sometimes of fairly recent arrival. William Lucas, a Quaker brewer of Hitchin, noted in his diary on 25 October 1846: "The Great Northern Railway Company have many men at work ... Heathcoat ... has driven the men from his land".[5] Samuel Heathcote had bought Wymondley Priory in 1806. Lucas, a businessman, was an exception: he commented that "if Hitchin could have been placed at the point of confluence of the South Midland, Great Northern, Cambridge and Oxford and Eastern Counties Railways we should be in a first-rate position for business ... the real cause of our not getting the Eastern Counties has been the opposition of the landlords"; Abel Smith whose family had acquired Watton in 1801 was an example.[5] Lucas had a flair: it was not purely coincidence that led Ebenezer Howard to site his First Garden City less than four kilometres from Hitchin. "Its obvious advantages were that it was no more than thirty-four and a half miles from London by rail, only two and a half miles from a main railway to the north, with the important Cambridge line running through it, and not far from the Great North Road."[6]

In the 1840s it was the new rich squires who opposed the railway lines; in contrast the Marquis of Salisbury exploited the opportunity. In 1897 opposition to new railways, the Metropolitan network, came from the very people whom the main lines had brought into Hertfordshire. "Rumours of railways penetrating into the heart of London's country are heard on many sides ... Professor Herkomer still speaks pathetically of the peace of his little art colony being disturbed by the new railway, although the present proposal is for a line further removed from the Professor's *sanctum*." Professor Herkomer's 'sanctum' was in Bushey, conveniently to the east of Watford's main line railway station. "The

[5] G. E. Bryant and G. P. Baker, eds. *A Quaker Journal*, 1933, Vol. II, pp. 383 and 391.

[6] C. B. Purdom, *The Letchworth Achievement*, 1963, p. 11.

influence of the Herkomer School pervades the village, and is noticeable in the colony of artists, the numerous studios, and in the design of many of the houses. The school was commenced in 1883 as an experiment, by Sir Hubert von Herkomer." The trouble was: "new railways that enable us for a time to get rustic rambles more easily, soon bring with them the means for destroying rusticity." So "the residents ... who value a rustic home and need it within easy reach of London (must) make up their minds not to sell their land for building".[7]

If others had acted like this earlier, Professor Herkomer's colony would not have existed. They did not: the second Marquis of Salisbury sold land on the other side of the new railway line from Hatfield House in the 1850s. The area became known as New Town and California, revealing names. The Great North Road which ran past his house and through his park was diverted to run near the railway line, with financial assistance from the railway company. The large scale expansion of Harpenden began when the Pym and Packe estate was sold in the 1880s and 1890s. Cowper estates in Tewin and Digswell were sold to pay death duties in 1919 and a whole area opened up for middle-class settlement. Where private sales did not suffice, compulsory purchase took over. The same cry of anguish as had convulsed Bushey in 1897, rose from Stevenage in 1945. "The development of a 'Satellite' town . . . would convert a pleasant market town into a dormitory for workers in London . . . bringing with it an urban population with entirely a different outlook, habits and behaviour to that to which the residents of Stevenage have been accustomed."[8] The author of this letter to the local press was lord of the manor of Aston.

The railways changed the county's appearance in two

---

[7] *Middlesex and Hertfordshire Notes and Queries*, Vol. III, 1897, pp. 4 and 167; V.C.H. II, p. 179.

[8] Letter in *Hertfordshire Express*, 20th October, 1945, quoted in Harold Orlans, *Stevenage*, 1952, p. 54.

ways: directly, because they 'manipulated the landscape on a grand scale'; indirectly, because of the population movement which they made possible.[9]

The railway landscape

Ruskin wrote of railroad mounds vaster than the walls of Bablyon. Hertfordshire, gentle county though it is, has its share of examples and its first railway has most to show. The tunnel, just north of Watford, with its ornamental portals cost many lives to build. It was only necessary because the Earl of Essex and Lord Clarendon opposed the easier route along the River Gade which would have cut through their parks. The bridge at Nashmills, near the paper works, was described by a contemporary as a wonderful 'oblique arch bridge' which 'all men of science' should visit. Users of the road today take a different view! To the north the route of the railway was deflected along the River Bulbourne, the Grand Junction Canal route, from the first suggested route up the Gade valley, because of local opposition. The new route entailed a series of cuttings and embankments between Apsley and Boxmoor, at Berkhamsted, and at Tring. These are major engineering works and they were almost as costly in lives as Watford tunnel. The newly opened West Herts Hospital had forty-three in-cases between July 1836 and July 1837 from accidents during railway construction, six of which were fatal. The hospital's governors were concerned at the 'numerous and dreadful cases'.[10] The Berkhamsted embankment was built over marshland. It runs, impressively, alongside the Norman castle (Plate 17). To build it steam pumps were working, day and night, for six months and there are more bricks in the foundations than in the superstructure. The first train to run on the line was employed

[9] *The Making of the English Landscape*, 1955, p. 198, 1970, pp. 256–7.
[10] Quoted in *History of Hemel Hempstead*, ed. Susan Yaxley, 1973, pp. 122 and 118.

moving soil from the Northchurch cutting and tunnel site to the Berkhamsted embankment. The engine was carried in sections by canal barge and assembled in a barn at Bourne End. The four kilometres long Tring cutting, through the Chilterns, is the outstanding monument on this line. One and a half million tons of earth were hauled up the sides by hundreds of labourers using wheelbarrows, horses and gears. The earth was used to make the nine and a half kilometres embankment on the Buckinghamshire side. The Tring cutting cost £144,000 as compared with £138,000 for an eight kilometres stretch which included the Watford tunnel.

The best-known monument of the early railways to be seen in Hertfordshire is Digswell or Welwyn viaduct, built between 1848 and 1850 by Thomas Brassey's workmen. One of them, Tom Sayers, was the undefeated English champion boxer in the days of bare-fist boxing. The designer of the viaduct was Lewis Cubitt; it has forty arches, the highest being thirty and a half metres above the River Mimram. The bricks were fired on the spot. There are several other Hertfordshire viaducts, none as visually dominating as the Welwyn one, but some quite striking. One seven-arch viaduct, twenty metres above the narrow lane which bears the historic name of Robbery Bottom, is separated from Welwyn viaduct by Welwyn North station and two tunnels. The lane was a hiding place for highwaymen waiting to pounce on travellers along the Great North Road at an awkward corner. The existing route of this railway is also not on the line first chosen by the Great Northern, which would have gone through Welwyn into the middle of Hitchin. The present route through Stevenage to the outskirts of Hitchin was forced on the company by the obstructive squires whom Lucas criticised. If it had not been for this kind of opposition, there would not have been so many remarkable railway earthworks in the county. *Howard's End* might have been set in some other town than Stevenage. Hitchin might have lacked its nineteenth century extension towards Walsworth and Stevenage New Town might have been near Whitwell, pressing up against the Queen Mother's birthplace at St Paul's Waldenbury. Such speculation is relevant if only because it brings out how much the future of Hertfordshire was determined by the routes which the railway lines followed.

Two later viaducts, each with seven arches, are on the Cuffley link line. One of them makes a striking view to the north of the popular by-road from Hertford to Hatfield. Two much older, five arch viaducts are south of Watford; one crosses the River Colne; the other, Bushey Arches, is just to its south. The traffic confusion which occurs at the round-about underneath makes it difficult to appreciate! The Metropolitan railway to Rickmansworth crosses two girder bridges near Watford whose brick abutments are so large they look like a viaduct. Many simple red brick bridges, which carried branch lines over country roads and fields to which farmers had access, are still standing in the county. There are two interesting skew bridges, at Bowling Alley in Harpenden and over A6, south of St Albans. In a few places the railway station still retains its nineteenth century appearance, or something of it. Berkhamsted's station, the second which was built in 1875, makes an effective picture with the canal in front of it (Plate 37). Hertford East station still conveys the feel of a railway system which knew no motor cars, sordid though its neglected buildings are. Branch Johnson's *Industrial Archaeology* has details of many other railway 'monuments' in the county from tunnels to station buildings, though some he mentions have gone in the ten years since his survey was made.

The Victorian townscape

Symbolic of the change which the railways heralded was the near contemporary description of the new station at Watford as sheltered from the rain by an elegant corrugated iron roof.

Ahead lay all the prosperity of Victorian England and the change it brought, particularly to the market towns of Hertfordshire. In the same vein the Post Office Directory of 1845 described Hitchin's new Town Hall as 'a very chaste and spacious building'. It has the simplest of classical façades. The 1851 Directory called Hitchin's new Corn Exchange 'a handsome building of brick with stone facings in the semi-classical style, with a cupola'. It is, in fact, much more ornate than the town hall. Public appreciation of Victoriana has grown so fast that we can begin to sympathise with these nineteenth century descriptions rather than laugh at them, though it seems unlikely that we will ever describe corrugated iron roofs as elegant. Berkhamsted's Victorian Gothic town hall, built in 1859–60, has been temporarily preserved from destruction due to the action of local schoolboys.

The first town in Hertfordshire to be much affected by the development of modern communications was Hemel Hempstead, although Watford was the town which was to be totally transformed. In 1801 Hemel Hempstead, including the chapelries of Bovingdon and Flaunden, contained 3680 people and Watford 3530. As late as 1861 Hemel had 9347 inhabitants to Watford's 7418. By 1901 the figures were 12,490 to 32,559; the decade in which the change took place was 1861–71, in which Watford's population jumped from 7418 to 12,071 while Hemel Hempstead's grew from 9347 to 10,100. Hemel Hempstead grew fastest in the first half of the nineteenth century, Watford in late Victorian times. The first expansion of Hemel Hempstead took place at Frogmore End and towards Marlowes. By 1843 the Tithe Map shows new building since 1807 at Two Waters and Boxmoor. The canal, new railway line, and the paper industry were attracting houses. But there was also a substantial growth along Marlowes towards Two Waters and at the back of the High Street, uphill to the east. The nineteenth century development along Marlowes could still be seen in the 1950s. Most of it has now been swept away by the New Town's town centre development, but a group of pleasant houses has been left on the east side between Midland Road and Queensway. The poorer housing between Two Waters and Frogmore can be seen on the hillside south of the London Road.

Watford grew fastest in the late nineteenth and early twentieth centuries. Its townscape reflects this, stretching from Benskin's eighteenth century brewery in the south to Odham's mid-twentieth century printing works in the north, with its copper covered lantern reminiscent of Stockholm Town Hall. Watford in the 1840s was little more than a continuous line of buildings strung out on both sides of the High Street from the ford over the River Colne to half way between St Mary's Church and the Nascot Cottage cross roads produced by the Rickmansworth and St Albans roads. There was another string of buildings on each side of Nascot Cottage but mostly to the north. The High Street south of St Mary's still has a faintly medieval appearance and there are a few old houses at various places along the street. The northern half of the High Street has been given what Pevsner, in 1953, called a 'twentieth century urban' landscape.[11] By 1975 this was much more marked since most of the area has become a pedestrian precinct with some very recent buildings.

Watford Junction station was well to the north-east of the cross roads and the Victorian expansion of Watford began around its new railway station (Fig. 27). To the north and west of the station, across the St Albans road, a residential district, the Nascot or Nascot Wood estate, came into existence from the 1850s. The area still has something of the feeling of a community in the countryside, although now completely surrounded by later building. Stamford Road contains two cottages in the local yellow brick, Newton dated 1867 and Myrtle dated 1869. On the other side of the road are some larger houses situated, rather extraordinarily,

[11] Pevsner, p. 267.

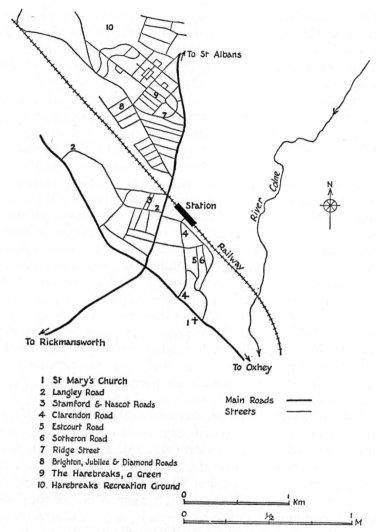

Fig. 27. Watford in the nineteenth century.

between two parallel streets which are very close together, Stamford and Nascot Roads. Langley Road, which they join, is the main road in the area and near its junction with the St Albans Road is a good example of the plaques with which the builder William Gough decorated many of the streets in Watford built by himself and Edwin Clifford after 1868 (Plates 38 and 39).

The station was linked to the High Street, rather as Hitchin and its station were joined, by another development which can be seen, strikingly, on the 1871 25″ Ordnance Survey map. This began when Clarendon Road was made in 1864. Estcourt and Sotheron Roads to the east were laid out by 1871 and houses were already in existence along them. Buildings in these and the neighbouring streets are dated between the 1860s and the 1880s (Plates 38 and 39). The whole area is an admirable example of late nineteenth century town development with churches as the only large buildings in the streets. Watford and its 'suburb' to the south, Oxhey, which was developing at much the same time, contain a variety of noticeable, and in some cases noteworthy, late nineteenth century churches. Alan Ball, until recently Watford's Borough Librarian, has made a thorough and most scholarly investigation into these nineteenth century developments, into the builders and into the street names, which is an invaluable source of information.[12] He points out that William Gough, who built so much of Watford at this time, came from Aynho in Northamptonshire. The street names which he, and other builders chose were of four main categories: builders' family names—Ashby, Carey, Clifford, Cole, Francis, Herbert, Judge, Percy, and Waterman; names with South-Midland connections, either of places or people —Aynho, Banbury, Clifton, Milton, Oxford, and Souldern; names of prominent local people such as Armand Blackley and Sutton Southeron Estcourt, both of whom gave more than one name to a street, while the Earls of Essex con-

[12] Alan W. Ball, *Street and Place Names in Watford,* 1973.

tributed Capell, Devereux, De Vere, Hyde, Malden and Villiers; and names of national figures, many of them royal—Albert, Alexandra, Cambridge, Cecil, Gladstone, Roberts, Victoria, for example. Many of these street names are still recorded in Clifford and Gough's plaques, some even containing human figures. But the most marked impact which Gough made on the Watford townscape was his preference for locally made "yellow stock brick with straight bands, geometric designs and sometimes dates picked out in red brick", and for two storey houses "of the type commonly found in small midland towns". As Alan Ball points out, "they are in marked visual contrast to" London houses of the same period, which were often three storey. "The traveller from the South . . . on entering Watford . . . has come to one of those regional boundaries, which even in twentieth century England are almost as marked as ever".[13] An indication that one is south of the boundary, in two different senses, can be seen on Sparrow's Herne Road in the middle of Bushey. A stark, square, red brick building of the nineteenth century proclaims itself the Metropolitan Police Station.

Watford building at the turn of the century can best be seen, just to the north of the railway line and west of St Albans Road, in rows of red brick cottages in the area of streets patriotically named Diamond, Jubilee and Victoria, and rather less appropriately Regent, Brighton and Sussex. The Harebreaks estate further to the north dates from after the First World War. It is beyond Ridge Street which was named for the builder's son, 'Ridge' for Reg. The history of this area is full of interest. In 1908 there was an ambitious project to develop here what was called the 'New Town' estate, with "sites of half an acre, well suited for the erection of picturesque villas, country cottages, shops and business premises". 'Villa' still had a snob implication though these villas would have been very much smaller than those Arthur

13 Ball, p. 11.

Young mentioned in 1804. The name, New Town, was chosen to associate the area with the earlier Nascot Wood development which had been called New Town after 1850 and to distinguish it from the working class housing, between the two New Towns, south of Ridge Street. This 1908 scheme never came off and in 1920 the area was bought by the Urban District Council. The Harebreaks estate is an early example of between-the-wars large scale council building. It follows almost exactly the lay-out published in 1920. The houses are not attractive to look at; they are predominantly pebbledash and have some strange shapes. But the arrangement is spacious, with a green in the middle, reminiscent in a small way of Welwyn Garden City's Parkway. There are other small open spaces, a recreation ground of some size, and streets planted with trees which are now mature; but there are no garages. The two areas, north and south of Ridge Street, provide an outstanding visual picture of the history of working class housing between the 1890s and 1930s.[14]

Middle-class estates

Alan Ball has much of interest to say about the contemporary architectural influence at work on the middle-class housing in the Cassiobury estate which was also developed between the wars, but there are many places in Hertfordshire where estates of this kind can be seen. Harpenden is, perhaps, the best. *The Official Guide*, published in the early 1950s, commented with justifiable pride, that "of the small residential towns lying just beyond the fringe of Greater London, few can equal Harpenden in attractiveness". With the opening of a main-line railway station in 1868, "development began; not a planned, but a natural development". Between 1891 and 1901 something like 270 new houses were built in the older area of the village; between 1900 and 1910 the new

[14] Ball, pp. 11, 14, 53–4.

Urban District Council approved about 450 new houses. While council house building began between the wars and within six or seven years of the end of the Second World War something like 300 council houses were built, mostly on the new Batford Estate, the most significant fact about local house building which emerges from the U.D.C. records is the extensive use made of the Small Dwellings Acquisition Act. Harpenden is a standing monument to the provision made in the first half of the twentieth century for the housing needs of the middle classes, for all the considerable range of income and occupation comprised in that omnibus phrase.

While this provision was not 'planned' in the sense that a public body employing 'planners' built the houses, there was only a limited amount of completely individualistic building. Builders were active as local councillors and very many of the plans submitted to the Council for approval came from builders. Most of the development of Harpenden took place on estates which were almost as planned in advance of construction as were the neighbourhood units in the New Towns of the 1950s and 1960s. The St Nicholas Estate is a good example of this. On the Tithe Map of 1843 the area between Amenbury Lane and Townsend Lane was fields. About 1895 the area was bought for development and plans produced in that year show the 'St Nicholas Building Estate' with the roads which exist today—Rothamsted Avenue connecting Church Green with the top of Amenbury Lane and Avenue St Nicholas and Salisbury Avenue leaving it at right angles. The roads between Rothamsted Avenue and Townsend Lane are laid out as we see them today, except that a Devonshire Road joins the top of Amenbury Lane and continues along the line of today's Longcroft Avenue, while the area west of this was not shown as available for development in 1895. This estate, which stands unchanged today, was laid out quite precisely as a unit, individual plots being offered for sale; many were in fact already sold or had been reserved when the 1895 plan was published. While it is quite true that the houses put up on the plots were not planned, nor all built by the same builder, it is quite obvious from looking at them that there was much common workmanship.

In much the same way, but rather earlier, plans were made to develop Bengeo as a middle-class 'suburb' of Hertford. There is a fascinating estate plan of 1867 in Hertford Museum which shows Warren Road with its oval cricket ground and New Road, as they were later built. The plan is by Arthur Evers, a London architect, for Hertford Villa Residence Company Ltd. It shows proposed plots on each side of Warren Road with elevations of the residences which it was suggested might be built on them. Some of the large, well spaced out brick houses in Warren Road stand in exactly the plots as drawn on the 1867 plan, but the houses do not resemble the fanciful elevations proposed by Mr Evers. One old house of very different appearance to those in Warren Road still stands in New Road. To the west of Bengeo Street is housing which catered for less affluent members of the middle class. Church Road has many individually designed houses, much smaller than those in Warren Park Road. While in Duncombe Road there are good examples of semi-detached 'villas', smaller still but with tri-angular pediments; the roof ridges, pediments and façades are tiled and ornamented to give character to these otherwise humble buildings.

Middle-class estates, of all kinds, began to be quite common in the county in the quarter century before the First World War. Their building has continued ever since. The long string of houses, which parallels the lower Lea from Hoddesdon to Cheshunt and Waltham Cross, contains a great many examples of this process. Knebworth is a special case. Like Harpenden it was transformed by the coming of the railway. The station at Knebworth was opened in 1884. Houses were built near the station, in Station Road and in

Westland Road before the end of the century. Pondcroft Road, parallel with and to the west of the Great North Road, was laid out in 1906. In 1910 Knebworth Garden Villages Ltd, with the second Lord Lytton as President and Edward Lutyens as architect, issued its prospectus. It was only seven years since Ebenezer Howard's First Garden City Limited had been formed; Lord Lytton was keeping up with the times. Eight hundred acres were to be developed with ample provision for recreational space and with large gardens allowed for; a new main road was suggested. In 1911 a Co-Partnership Tenant Society, Knebworth Tenants Ltd, was formed to build, let and maintain the houses. Lord Lytton was involved in this too. Lutyens had built the Golf Club house on Deards End Hill in 1908, some of the houses nearby, notably Homewood in 1900, and St Martin's Church on the A1. Pevsner described this as 'one of Lutyens's most remarkable churches'.[15] It is certainly striking to look at. But most of the ambitous scheme died with the First World War. New Knebworth, on both sides of the Great North Road, near the station and a kilometre east of old Knebworth, has some bits of Garden Village building but more of uncoordinated private development and council house building. It lacks the feel of a community, though now that the through traffic has moved to the motorway it may acquire more of it.

The finest area, in which to make a serious study of the fashions in middle-class house building of the first three-quarters of the twentieth century, is Harpenden. Its houses range from the remarkably well built and quite attractive to rather terrible monstrosities, though not everyone will agree on which houses they put in which categories. Both sides of Harpenden Common were developed between the wars; the development of the area behind West Common continued after the Second World War. East Common has a few large houses, so well spaced as almost to suggest that they stand

[15] Pevsner, pp. 150–1 and *Knebworth*, pp. 27–8.

in woodland or little parks. Mock Tudor is the fashionable style here and the golf course on Harpenden Common is, significantly, near at hand. West Common is laid out as an estate but a spacious one. The styles are more varied than on East Common. The popularity of Tudor building has meant that material from older buildings has been used in the construction of new ones. The recently built Moat House Hotel does incorporate an old house but much of it is quite new. One whole house, Flowton Priory, on West Common is a reconstruction of a house from Flowton near Ipswich, erected by the Priory of St John of Colchester in 1525, which was taken to bits and moved in the early 1930s. The architect made detailed drawings of the brick nogging and the house was rebuilt with the same brick patterns; the framing of the huge oak beams was rebuilt and is self-supporting. The house contains fine carving, including the Tudor Rose.

The commuter in the countryside

Almost anywhere in Hertfordshire examples can be found of ways in which developers have used available opportunities to meet the house hunger of the thousands who have poured into the county. They take the most varied and sometimes the strangest forms. Between Baldock and Bygrave there is a triangle of land which Lilian Redstone, in 1912, recorded as a 'ploughed warren'[16]; it is in 'the middle of nowhere' but now filled with houses, most of which appear to have been built between the wars, some since the Second World War (Fig. 11). Isolated and dull as this little, middle-class estate seems, it is, in fact, just two kilometres by road to Baldock station; and someone has planted a host of daffodils along the road verges at the bottom of the estate.

One of the more interesting forms of commuter settlement in Hertfordshire reminds us of the pioneer clearings of the first Anglo-Saxon colonisers and the medieval assart.

[16] V.C.H. III, pp. 212–13. Cp. Chapter 3, pp. 74–6.

Commuter houses in woods can be found in many parts of the county. They may be an extension of a built up area, as along Ruckolds Lane in the north of King's Langley. Ruckolds Lane starts opposite Nash Mills in an ugly little street of late nineteenth and early twentieth century buildings. A group of largish mock Tudor houses, one of which is dated 1906, is followed by rows of Council Houses, on both sides of the road; one is of the dreariest inter-war kind, the other a rather pleasanter post Second World War group. Then there is woodland on both sides of the road. For a considerable distance the wood on the northern side of Ruckolds Lane contains well concealed flint bungalows, mostly from between the wars, but a few of the larger ones are more recent. They were built by an enterprising 'amateur'.[17]

Many of these woodland settlements are quite remote as in Lady Grove south of Hudnall Common in Little Gaddesden. The wanderer, coming from Great Gaddesden past the site of St Margaret's, or Ivinghoe, nunnery along a minor road, is surprised by many large mock Tudor houses half hidden among the trees. They date, mostly, from between the world wars. Another surprising group of houses of all sizes and types and dates, from the 1920s to the 1970s, clusters along the sides of Robbery Bottom Lane between the viaduct and the Great North Road. The largest group of woodland houses in the county is not far from here, in the area where Datchworth, Digswell and Tewin parishes meet. Perhaps this is significant. Fuller described Hertfordshire as "forestry ground (which) would willingly bear nothing so well as a crop of wood".[18] It is at the edge of parishes that clearance would come latest.

Dury and Andrews' map of Hertfordshire, published in 1766, shows a large area of woodland stretching from Harmer Green to Burnham Green to Bull's Green; the Greens were clearings in the woodland. Much of the wood remains but

[17] *King's Langley Museum Society Newsletter*, No. 14, January, 1976.
[18] *Worthies*, p. 229.

today it is filled with houses. The stages in the development of this settlement, from its beginnings around Welwyn North, once Digswell, station, can be followed in the architectural styles of the houses. Just before the First World War the northern part of Digswell, north of the River Mimram, was described as follows: "the larger part of it has been developed by a syndicate, and is now covered with houses".[19] This refers to the elongated and irregular oval made by two more or less parallel roads through the wood which join at Harmer Green by a pond and farmhouse site and join again, to the south, at Digswell Water. Most of these houses are in red brick, substantial and comfortable, but not exactly inspiring to look at. The 'Red House' actually achieves an entry on the 1/25,000 map, but the really surprising house is a much more modern one, almost facing the Red House, of brick and stone, with a pillared portico, reminiscent in a way of Sir Lionel Lyde's church at Ayot St Lawrence. It is a remarkable building in the American 'Colonial' style (Plate 40).

Along the road from Harmer Green to Burnham Green are more houses which old fashioned estate agents would no doubt have described as in a 'sylvan setting'. From Burnham Green to Bull's Green there are more, but most of the building has been in Shankey's Wood and Tewin Wood to the south. The houses in Shankey's Wood and some of those along the road between Burnham and Bull Green may date from the 1920s but most are from just before the Second World War. One of the pleasanter contrasts in the Hertfordshire landscape is to find Queen Hoo Hall at the southern end of Shankey's Wood and Nancybury Gorse. For Queen Hoo Hall is a stark, but lovely, mid-Tudor, brick house of unusual design built by Edward Skegges, perhaps as a hunting lodge. Skegges was a newcomer, probably from the City of London, who bought Bramfield and Panshanger. Within twenty years the family had sold up and left Hertfordshire.

[19] V.C.H. III, p. 81.

Although the Tewin estate was sold in 1919, few houses were built in Tewin Wood until the late 1930s. By 1961 two-fifths of all the houses in the parish of Tewin were hidden in the wood and building was continuing. The result is that one can see here houses which range from rather dull builders' houses of the 1920s to some very charming examples of modern architecture, with mock Tudor and Scandinavian styles thrown in.

Why did people choose this kind of home? Is there anything in common between woodland dwellers of the twentieth and earlier centuries? Joan Thirsk has given examples of what seventeenth century writers thought about their temperament as contrasted with that of people who lived in 'champion' or open country:

> As Norden explained it: 'the people bred amongst woods are naturally more stubborn and uncivil than in the champion countries'. John Aubrey described the woodlanders as 'the mean people (who) live lawless, nobody to govern them, they care for nobody, having no dependence on anybody' . . . This independence of spirit was displayed in the revolts against disafforestation . . .[20]

Perhaps R. E. Pahl's comments can be put alongside. He wrote of "the development of social and spatial segregation". "The effect of (moving into such rural areas) is to heighten the social isolation of the immigrant middle class." But "a new type of community, associated with dispersed living, is emerging". While none of these descriptions may appeal to the people who live on woodland estates, they have one thing in common, an independence which looks for some escape from the herd. The very varied architectural styles of such areas may, indeed, reflect this 'independence of spirit'. The builders, the developers, recognise it in offering "a

[20] Joan Thirsk, ed., *The Agrarian History of England and Wales*, Vol. IV *1500–1640*, pp. 111–12.

choice of standard, split level and continental designs in woodland setting".[21] In woods it looks very different from the same kind of variety along a town street. Only the prejudiced would find it impossible to see at least occasional beauty here.

SELECT BIBLIOGRAPHY

Lyddeker, R. *Hertfordshire* (1909).
Pahl, R. *Urbs in Rure* (1965).
Ball, Alan W. *Street and Place-Names in Watford* (1973).

[21] Pahl, pp. 46, 48, 79 and 45.

10. Garden Cities and New Towns

Borehamwood and the New Towns. The Garden Cities. The New Towns. The future of Hertfordshire.

Borehamwood and the New Towns

GARDEN CITIES AND New Towns have focused international attention on Hertfordshire. Their true impact on the landscape can only be properly appreciated when it is compared with other surroundings into which people, coming from London, moved. There had been a scramble to move into Hertfordshire ever since the railways had opened up the county for settlement by Londoners. The First World War was followed by a great surge which became a flood after the Second World War. In 1960–1 67·25% of the land of Hertfordshire was still used for agricultural purposes, only ·5% for industry and ·22% for shops, offices and public buildings. But 7·6% of Hertfordshire land was used for residential purposes and 1% for schools and their playing fields; this figure excludes a further 4·9% under the control of the Development Corporations concerned with the four New Towns. In 1961 there were 787,850 people living in the county, an increase of over half a million since 1901.

While private developers had catered satisfactorily for the housing needs of the mass of middle class commuters, and would continue to do so, the much larger numbers of wage-earners were increasingly provided with homes only through council building. The Harebreaks estate at Watford was an enlightened example of inter-war development, but such estates could not provide for the flood moving out of

London after the Second World War. Between 1945 and 1951 the London County Council built 3500 dwellings at Oxhey. Between 1948 and 1952 they built even more at Borehamwood, on the Manor Way and Theobald Street estates. The New Towns were an answer to the problem which extramural building on this scale represents. Something more than council estate building, even more than large scale building by the L.C.C. in 'foreign parts', was needed if the population movement out of London was to be catered for. Hemel Hempstead and Stevenage only make sense when looked at in the light of Borehamwood. They were new ways of providing for something which was happening, whether or not the voters or the planners wanted it to happen.

Borehamwood is not very pleasant to look at, but it is extremely interesting. The main shopping centre, Shenley Road, is a straight, wide traffic highway with flower beds on the pavements, lined by uninspired buildings. It looks dull, and it cannot be pleasant for shoppers to have to deal with the traffic along a road which connects Watford, Bushey and Elstree with the Barnet by-pass. After the railway station was opened in 1868 at the western end of Shenley Road, new middle-class housing was built along Allum Lane, the continuation of Shenley Road beyond the station. The population of Elstree and Borehamwood rose from 525 in 1871 to 1323 in 1901. Early in the twentieth century terraces and small houses were built north and south of the western end of Shenley Road and in 1914 the first film studio was built in the village. After the First World War Borehamwood continued to grow, mostly to the south of Shenley Road, and more film studios moved in. Only in 1929, when the Barnet by-pass was built, was Shenley Road transformed from the new community's 'High Street' into a traffic artery. A new road, Elstree Way, was made connecting Shenley Road and the by-pass. In 1934 it was first suggested that the L.C.C. should build a council estate here. The two estates, which were built after the Second World War, kept Shenley

Road as their shopping centre, although it continued to be a traffic artery. The population of Elstree and Borehamwood rose from 1323 in 1901 to nearly 30,000 by the mid-1970s. As early as 1951 there had been 12,240 people in Borehamwood alone, of whom 7012 (56%) were insured workers. This was a higher percentage than in Watford; only two urban centres in Hertfordshire had higher percentages, Hatfield and Welwyn Garden City!

What do these L.C.C. estates look like? The Manor Way estate, south of Shenley Road and Elstree Way, seems more traditional than parts of the Theobald Street estate to the north. The two estates are, however, very similar. The housing is mixed: there are semi-detached houses, terraces, and flats in a great many styles but none are imaginative. There are square open spaces, much grass, some quite developed trees, schools, churches, and shops on the corner of some streets. At the weekend cars clutter up all the roads, for the houses have no garages, though some lock-ups have been built. The houses, though conventional in appearance, have something of the relative roominess of the best inter-war council housing and there is more privacy than in some of the almost claustrophobic Stevenage Radburn layouts. Though Borehamwood looks uglier and has not the facilities of the New Towns, some people may prefer to live in these houses. The front gardens and frontages are, in many cases, roomy enough to park a car in the garden without completely blocking the front window. For some time the only considerable employment here must have been in the film studios but there is now an industrial estate, with factories of many kinds, along Elstree Way. In 1951 Hertfordshire county planners looked forward to the consequences of the building of the estate and the factories: "it does not seem unreasonable to assume that an increasing number of people living on the London County Council estate will find local employment instead of travelling daily into London."[1]

[1] *Hertfordshire: survey report and analysis of county development plan*, 1951, p. 43.

Some of the supposed virtues of the New Towns are already present in Borehamwood: schools and shops on the estate, homes and work near together; Borehamwood need not be a dormitory. But something is missing. Comparison of the main shopping centres of Borehamwood, Hatfield, Hemel Hempstead and Stevenage is revealing. All three New Town centres, in their different ways, look like town centres; Shenley Road does not. Hemel Hempstead's centre is along a main road too, and one with too much traffic on it, but there are first floor catwalks for pedestrians in places and a footbridge over (Plate 42). There are car parks at the end of Marlowes and a beautifully designed, parallel side road with gardens along the River Gade. This was in 1945 a revolting mess of back gardens, scruffy huts and stagnant water. Whether one does or does not like the architectural styles and the detail, Marlowes looks like the High Street of a town that is proud of itself. Shenley Road, like all of Borehamwood, looks like a piece bitten off the edge of suburban London and dropped in the countryside near an arterial road. Stevenage has an entirely different type of town centre, a rectangular pedestrian precinct partly covered and built in a more delicate, less imposing manner than Marlowes. There are car parks at the back, bus stops in front, and larger buildings in an outer rectangle—a Mecca ten pin bowling alley, library, towerblock flats and hotel, parish church and swimming pool. Hatfield's New Town centre is closer to Stevenage's than Hemel Hempstead's in concept. The inner pedestrian, shopping precinct is quite attractive but from the outside the area still looks untidy. Stevenage's market square already looks like a town centre and Hatfield's is beginning to do so.

The Garden Cities

The difference between estates like Borehamwood, however well built and however many facilities they contain, and the

New Towns arises from the differing intentions of their builders. Controversy over private and public enterprise and emotive feelings about planners have made many people forget that any considerable building of homes today has to be planned by someone, somehow. An end result has been intended, though sometimes the result does not match the intentions. Most building in the past has been concerned with producing homes for people and with creating whatever were thought to be the necessary ancillary provisions. The Development Corporations set out to build new communities, not merely houses or shops or factories or schools or pubs or churches. The inspiration came from the Garden Cities which were built in fulfilment of Ebenezer Howard's dreams, and both the Garden Cities are in Hertfordshire.

Ebenezer Howard's little red book, *Tomorrow: a Peaceful Path to Real Reform* was published in 1898. The Garden City Association was founded a year later. In 1902 Ebenezer Howard's book was reissued as *Garden Cities of Tomorrow* and on 1 September 1903 the First Garden City Limited company was registered with a capital of £300,000. The Letchworth area had already been chosen for development; the area consisted of nearly 4000 acres in the parishes of Letchworth, Norton and Willian; only 566 people lived in these three parishes in 1901. Development began immediately; by 1919 the population had reached 10,000; in 1961 it was 25,515. The estate owned and developed by First Garden City Limited was transferred to the Letchworth Garden City Corporation on 1 January 1963. This Corporation was set up by act of parliament and consists of a member appointed by the U.D.C., a member appointed by the County Council and a chairman and three members appointed by the Minister of Housing and Local Government, as he was then. The Corporation was given the statutory responsibility of continuing the management of the estate along the lines on which it has been established.

What sort of place is this town of 25,000 people, built by

enthusiasts in what had been 'an entirely rural area'? It is a landmark in the history of twentieth century city building and town planning, but it does not look like this. The most striking thing about Letchworth is that there is nothing striking to see. Even C. B. Purdom, one of the great Garden City pioneers and enthusiasts, had to admit to 'the short-comings in architecture and planning of a pioneer enter-prise'.[2] The shopping streets of Letchworth are like those of many suburbs built in the inter-war years, except that they meet at a roundabout opposite the railway station. This is an unusual focus for any small town, even a pioneer. There is neither the grandeur of a well proportioned High Street nor the intimacy of a small village or medieval street. Facing the station and running away from the streets of shops are some public buildings and beyond them a charming rose garden which does give an open space in the middle of the town. A larger and more traditional type of park with play and games spaces is roughly parallel to this to the east, dividing shops and houses from the industrial area.

There are no architecturally interesting buildings in Letchworth though many pleasant, if rather uninteresting, simple houses. One of the proud achievements in the early days was building three-bedroom 'cottages' at twelve to an acre, a low density for working-class housing before 1914. Raymond Unwin, one of the two architects, boasted of 'nothing gained by overcrowding'.[3] The sense of space which this produced was one element in the *garden city* idea. Others were the preservation of existing trees, the planting of new ones, the width of the streets, and the grass in front of the houses. Some of the middle-class houses in Letchworth are almost as embedded in trees as those in Tewin. The difficulty about appreciating Letchworth is that so many things which were done there for the first time have become common-place since. Pevsner put it succinctly: "to the younger generation they have become a matter of course, but it

2 Purdom, pp. 11 and 104.   3 Purdom, p. 23.

should not be forgotten that they were for the very first time systematically followed at Letchworth."⁴ Allowing for all this it remains true that Barry Parker and Raymond Unwin's town lacks the spark which lit up parts, at least, of Louis de Soissons' Welwyn Garden City.

What the architects of Letchworth did achieve was to embody Howard's dreams in a workmanlike plan which could become the basis of a town in which people lived more comfortably than elsewhere. Howard's first principle was that land values increased enormously when streets of houses, shops, factories and public buildings were built on agricultural land, and that this increment should benefit the community so created rather than the lucky or speculative original owner of the land. If this principle was followed through, it should be possible to build a new community from scratch which would be integrated and harmonious in its parts. So much has been written about Howard's ideas and about town planning that to do more than explain the essence would be tedious. Letchworth's example was soon followed at Welwyn Garden City. In 1919 Ebenezer Howard bought 1688 acres of the Cowper estate in Digswell, Hatfield and Welwyn parishes. This was part of the same estate, the sale of which opened up Tewin Wood for private developers. In 1920 Welwyn Garden City Limited was formed on the pattern of the First Garden City Limited and in December the first house was occupied in Handside Lane. The population was about 400; in 1951 it was over 18,000. The area was handed over to a Development Corporation in 1948, when Welwyn Garden City and Hatfield were designated New Towns.

Welwyn Garden City Limited appointed Louis de Soissons as its Town Planner and Architect in 1920, and Welwyn Garden City is very much his town, although other architects have contributed notably to its building, A. W. Kenyon and P. Mauger for example. The 'campus' area, the

⁴ Pevsner, p. 154.

Plate 35 Colney Street, Moor Mill

Plate 36 Ashwell, Fordham's Maltings

Plate 37 Berkhamsted, canal and railway station

Plate 38 Watford, Alma Terrace

Plate 39 Watford, Souldern Street

Plate 40 Digswell, New House in American 'Colonial' style

Plate 41 Welwyn Garden City Broadway, French influence

Plate 42 Hemel Hempstead, Marlowes New Town Centre

Plate 43 Hemel Hempstead, Old High Street

Plate 44 Near Little Wymondley, electricity pylons 'stride across the countryside . . . like Martian invaders'

Parkway with its Coronation Fountain, Welwyn Stores, the White Bridge and the recently built public buildings near it, is a notable centre for the town, with something of the dramatic impact, on a small scale, of the Parisian boulevards and gardens like the Tuileries (Plate 41). The streets and shops between the Stores and the railway station, east of Parkway, are, in contrast, disappointingly trivial. The visual success of Welwyn, as compared with Letchworth, is not only due to its grandiose centre; there are many streets of attractive housing. The predominant style is 'a quiet comfortable Neo-Georgian', with de Soissons' favourite round window like a mason's mark on houses of different types and sizes.[5] Curving streets dominate Welwyn, as they do Letchworth, and are one of the contributions garden cities have made to the twentieth century town landscape, breaking away from the Roman grid pattern of so much urban building. These are not the geometrically regulated curves of Regency crescents but rather more like the artificial wildness of Capability Brown's landscapes. It is not easy for a stranger in Welwyn to retain a sense of direction; the points of the compass seem to shift! The architectural treatment of these curving streets is interestingly varied. In some of the older areas of middle class housing, around Handside Lane for example, the general effect is of detached suburban housing of good quality with considerable gardens, roomy streets and much greenery. In some of the newer areas, on the other side of the railway line, to the east along Howlands the effect is rather more like that of eighteenth century crescents in a modern idiom. There is plenty of variety in Welwyn Garden City's housing but it is nearly all harmonious. One striking feature is the straight line of houses along Knightsfield. This is exactly on the crest of the hill to the north of the White Bridge, overlooking the Mimram valley. The line of buildings is parallel with the crest and the skyline is serrated; it looks like some enormous battlement.

[5] Pevsner, p. 272.

241

Welwyn Garden City may be more pleasing to look at than Letchworth but it is visually marked with the English disease, social snobbery reflecting class division. In spite of brave efforts by the pioneers to mix people in different economic and social situations in the same street, the Garden City became socially divided by the railway line. To the west is Parkway, the shopping centre and middle-class housing; to the east are the factories and working-class housing. Much of this housing, which was built before the Second World War, is conventionally dull; in some ways the earlier, and more romantic, cottages in Letchworth are pleasanter to look at though not necessarily more comfortable to live in. Only partially in the New Towns, in a less class-dominated, post-war society, has some successful social mixing in housing been achieved.

The New Towns

Stevenage was designated a New Town on 11 November 1946; it was the first New Town in the United Kingdom. Hemel Hempstead followed on 4 February 1947, Hatfield and Welwyn Garden City on 20 May 1948; the membership of Hatfield and Welwyn Development Corporations was identical. The sites chosen for these New Towns differed in their existing local government status and in population. Hemel Hempstead was a Municipal Borough containing 23,437 people in 1951. Welwyn and Stevenage were U.D.C.s with 1951 populations, respectively, of 18,804 and 7168. Hatfield was a civil parish; the area that became a New Town held 9256 people in 1951. By 1971 the four New Towns had been transformed: Hemel Hempstead contained 70,380 people, Stevenage 67,080, Welwyn 40,450 and Hatfield 25,360. By 31 March 1971 19,029 new houses or flats had been built in Stevenage, 13,992 in Hemel Hempstead, 6593 in Welwyn, and 4473 in Hatfield. There had been a parallel building of new shops: 354 in Stevenage; 305 in Hemel

Hempstead; 133 in Welwyn; and 110 in Hatfield. These figures give some idea of the enormous changes in the local landscape produced, since the Second World War, by a government decision.

The four New Towns not only began as very different places, they have also developed in different ways. Welwyn Garden City has, in essence, continued along the lines laid down by the Garden City company; the Development Corporation took over Louis de Soissons as its town planner. At neighbouring Hatfield, Lionel Brett was the Corporation's architect. The site made a garden city type of development impractical. Hatfield New Town site was constricted. To the east the railway line, with the old town and Hatfield House just beyond it, set a limit on expansion. The Barnet by-pass with De Havillands' aircraft factory, built in 1934, and its airfield alongside it restricted expansion to the west. The London green belt lay to the south and Welwyn Garden City to the north. The need to house De Havillands' expanding labour force was a main influence in the decision to build a New Town here. Unlike other New Towns, Hatfield was a one-industry centre and the industry was already there. The 'green belt' between Welwyn and Hatfield, which has become a sports park, was not built on because the decision was made that there were to be twin towns, rather than one expanded town. So Lionel Brett planned Hatfield New Town with many more urban-type buildings than was usual in most of the first generation New Towns; terraces, low-rise flats, and closely knit housing units are frequent. Some of the later New Towns and cities have followed this pattern.

Although Hatfield is divided into neighbourhood units, it is only in Hemel Hempstead and Stevenage that one is really conscious of this. The idea was to build up the new town out of a group of smaller 'village' communities, each with its own local shops, pubs, churches and schools. In Hemel Hempstead the natural landscape has made this easier, for

243

Adeyfield, Bennetts End, and Chaulden each have an innate cohesion from the hills on which they lie. Adeyfield is effectively divided from Bennetts End by the St Albans road, which leads from M1, past the new industrial area, downhill to the imposing entrance to Marlowes, the town centre. The road follows a natural valley which has been deepened in places; a combination of devices has been used to make this road an effective break between the two communities. On the Bennetts End side a large green area has been left open; the houses on the Adeyfield side turn their backs to the road with gardens behind them and an unscalable fence keeps the children off the main road. Main roads like this are even more important in Stevenage where the natural landscape does not provide convenient areas for neighbourhood units; the roads provide a skeleton. They not only divide neighbourhood units but they bind them together, conducting people from their homes to the town shopping centre and to the factory area. Along these main roads are segregated footpaths and cycleways with underpasses. The roads also provide fingers of green in the urban landscape, for the neighbourhood units are designed with schools and their playing fields on the outer edges along the main roads. Woods and even farmland have been preserved inside the town.

In both Hemel Hempstead and Stevenage the street pattern is as curvaceous as anything in the Garden Cities. Chaulden neighbourhood unit has been built around a roughly shaped D; it is surprisingly easy to drive twice round the D before finding the way out! Neighbourhood units are distinctive. By employing different architects, a variety of building materials, and numerous house types the dull uniformity of the worst nineteenth century terraces and of twentieth century council estates has been avoided, but only rarely has the harmony of an eighteenth century townscape or the charm of a medieval one been approached. Stevenage has some attractive areas. Broadwater, in south Stevenage, displays a pattern of black and white buildings blended with the green of young trees and grass which can be quite delightful in the spring sunshine. Some of the Radburn areas of Stevenage have their own individual charms. The 'Radburn' idea came from the U.S.A.; it consists of planning an area so that cars can be driven into garages near to the backs of the houses while there is only pedestrian access to the front. It is then possible to walk through the whole of a large area without ever being on a road used by motor cars. The Bronte paths in Chells have a Dutch air about them, while the Sishes area of Pin Green has something of the feel of almshouses round a secluded village green. But just across Verdon Road, also in Pin Green, is a windblown empty space which makes the surrounding area seem desolate. The idea is splendid, the achievement remarkable and occasionally beautiful, but the congestion is reminiscent of an ant heap as is so much modern town building. The Cockaigne scheme at Hatfield has the same mixture of qualities. A staggered line of closely packed boxes strikes the eye from the road. Though apparently packed like sardines they are visually attractive. These are twenty-eight single storey houses built on two point six acres of land which also contains a community house, tennis court, and children's play areas. The twenty-eight householders own the housing association to which the whole group of buildings belongs. The houses and their courtyard gardens have complete privacy and great internal flexibility within the elongated corridor of which each house consists. People like living here. It was originally proposed to build twelve detached houses on these two point six acres; now there are twenty-eight homes of different sizes. While the trees and the grass have survived from Letchworth, Raymond Unwin's 'nothing gained by overcrowding' has been lost.

The New Towns in Hertfordshire have few individually outstanding buildings. It is not easy to achieve architectural glory with small two- and three-bedroom houses. There are no new cinemas or theatres; the pubs and most other new public buildings are on a small scale. Ironically, in a secular age, the best buildings are churches and, perhaps, the two swimming baths in Stevenage and Hatfield whose roofs have miniature butterfly wings like Sydney Opera House. There are many churches of very different appearances, from the green glass of Hemel Hempstead's Roman Catholic Church of Our Lady on the St Albans Road to the glass and concrete of Stevenage's St George. This latter is the largest parish church to have been built in England since the war and it is disappointingly colourless save for its delightful little Lady Chapel in the crypt with a charming bronze Madonna and Child made by Gwendolin Williams in 1902. Hatfield has the two best churches in the county's New Towns. The most outstanding, and one of the newest, is Roman Catholic. It has a superb site, on a piece of ground around which roads joining old and new Hatfield meet. The church is circular, reminiscent in a small way of Liverpool's Roman Catholic Cathedral but in its own idiom, plain, lit by light from a louvre and through dazzlingly colourful windows. A much smaller Anglican church, serving the South Hatfield neighbourhood unit, has the same quality. St John's is like an upturned Viking ship, in plain wood and brick, with nuggets of coloured glass in its windows. The area it serves is a sad one. Alongside the church is a squat building, Hilltop, an experimental marriage of the local pub with a community centre. An ugly semicircle of shops shut in St John's and Hilltop, but it does not shut out the wind which usually has plenty of waste paper to play with. Across the road, Bishops Rise, is a group of houses with flat roofs sloping in one direction, many of which were removed by a gale in the night of 3 November 1957. This hill top is an appropriately symbolic place at which to stand and weigh up the mixture of idealism in conception with cheeseparing economies and bad workmanship in some of the execution which makes up the New Towns. A feeling for beauty has had to struggle with a petty trader's lack of imagination. A genuine humanitarian desire to do good to others has not always been based on an understanding of what 'the others' want. This, and a great deal more, can be seen in the local landscape by those who have eyes to see.

Before leaving the Garden Cities and New Towns, one subject must be touched on. It would not be too unkind a parody of much public opinion about planned towns to represent it as believing that they were creations of architects and bureaucrats who wiped away all traces of earlier occupation so that they could build their monuments in a landscape which was totally of their own creation. From this standpoint it might well seem irrelevant to have devoted so much space in a book on the history of the landscape to contemporary building. But the assumption behind this belief is wrong. When Letchworth was built, important features from the old village of Norton were preserved and incorporated in the new Garden City (Fig. 28). A comparison between the 1796 enclosure map for Norton and the modern town plan reveals what happened. The road called the Icknield Way which runs across the north of Letchworth does not curve because of any architect's whim; it is on the line of the old Icknield Way which was the southern boundary of Norton parish. Wilbury and Norton Roads, which are on the same axis but to the north, are the old main road which led to the village centre. In fact most of the roads radiating from the old village centre, Green Lane, Croft Lane and Norton Road, are as they were on the enclosure map. What was the Commoners' allotment in 1796 survives as an open space, with a swimming pool, Norton Common. Most of the buildings in this part of Letchworth lie in what were two open fields and the surviving roads still outline their boundaries.

Stevenage New Town covers the area of the old parishes of Stevenage and Shephall, with some additional pieces of land from neighbouring parishes, chiefly Knebworth. The village green of Shephall has been 'encapsulated', to use the horrible jargon of planning, in a new neighbourhood unit called Shephall. This triangular green was not a beauty spot. Just before the First World War the houses round it were described as 'largely poor except the vicarage'. Shephall-bury, in a small park to the south, is "a Gothic building of red brick faced with Bath stone, built about 1865".[6] Yet all

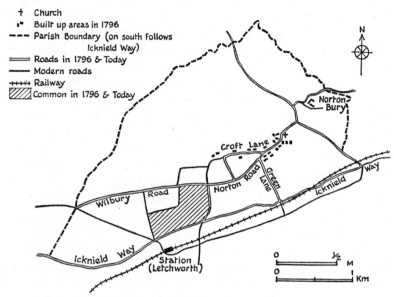

Fig. 28. Norton in Letchworth.

this has been preserved and, indeed, improved. The scheme earned a commendation in European Architectural Heritage Year. The village green is, in a sense, more secluded than it was, for the road at its southern end has been blocked. It is still possible to enter and leave Shephall by car, but not to drive through it. The village church has obviously become popular with New Town inhabitants for Saturday afternoon weddings. The outside of the church has, recently, been restored and a rather hideous new church room built on; the

6 V.C.H. II, pp. 443-4.

churchyard with its old yews is very tidy; but the porch and
church doors are battered and the door is, ominously, kept
locked. The vicarage, an interesting brick building of many
periods, survives. The old irregular building line round the
green has been well preserved with a remarkable mixture of
modern buildings, dull nineteenth century brick cottages,
and a few earlier houses of brick and half-timbered. A new
motor through-way crosses the open country to the south,
leaving pedestrian access by subway to the park and surviving manor house which had become a school long before the
New Town was thought of. A trespassers' board warns that
this is now County Council property.

To the west of Shephall is Stevenage's lung (Fig. 25), the
great open valley which the planners are, rightly, proud of
having preserved from buildings even in the face of governmental pressure. Fairlands Valley is a substantial open space,
two and a half kilometres from north to south with a substantial bulge in the middle where Six Hills Way cuts across
it from west to east. Schools with playing fields are on its
edges in the northern half. There are sports and recreation
grounds in the middle, and much open grassland in the
south. Before the New Town came it was almost all farmland. In 1731 it was part of Knebworth estate and much
more divided than it is today. The southern area was
Whomerley Common Field, in which enclosure was beginning. Although there is no surviving ridge and furrow, nor
any balks, the area is today more open than it was in 1731.
To the west Whomerley Wood and its southern continuation, Monk's Wood, survive with much the same boundaries
as in 1731. The tree growth shows that this wood was once
coppiced. The fields to the west of the woods have, however, disappeared. While the outer shape of this area of local
roads and houses conforms to that of 1731, the whole
interior pattern has been changed. There is no trace left of
the individual field boundaries.

The most attractive blending of the new and the old is in

the centre of Hemel Hempstead. Marlowes has been referred to already, several times; it is an old street, new made, in which a few striking buildings from earlier periods have been incorporated in the New Town 'High Street'. These range from pleasant early nineteenth century classical houses, through shops of the 1920s and 1930s, to a full scale mock-Tudor pub and a just pre-New Town 'Georgian' post office. Somehow the whole street has been given a unity, while the River Gade which runs parallel to it has been developed in a series of water gardens to give it breadth. But the really imaginative achievement is in the linking of the new Marlowes with the old High Street (Plates 42 and 43). This used to be a through-road. While the High Street has not been turned into a pedestrian precinct or even made a one-way street, the cross roads at its junction with Marlowes has been developed so that much of the traffic avoids the High Street. Pevsner called it 'one of the most agreeable streets in Hertfordshire' in 1953.[7] It is more agreeable now, quieter and with its buildings cleaned and redecorated; the inns, restaurants and shops flourish in a new elegance.

The future of Hertfordshire

Before men came to Hertfordshire it was wood, all trees. The question which has to be asked today concerns the future: is the county to become a concrete, glass and metal jungle of houses, shops, public buildings and factories criss-crossed by motorways? Was Robert Browning right when he put the following words into the mouth of the young David, singing to *Saul*?

Carouse in the past.
But the licence of age has its limit; thou diest at last.
As the lion where age dims his eye-ball, the rose at her height,

[7] Pevsner, p. 120.

So with man—so his power and his beauty for ever take
flight.

It might seem so. The first motorway in Britain, M1, runs
through west Hertfordshire. It is ugly and abrasive, cutting
ruthlessly through the older landscape. M10 branches off it,
south of Hemel Hempstead, linking the motorway with
Watling Street and, via A405, with the end of A1 (M) at
Hatfield, the county's second motorway. M11 will affect the
extreme east of the county and dual by-passes are being built
on A10. Puckeridge, Ware and Hoddesdon are already by-
passed. The motorway builders did not face so effective an
opposition as did the railway builders. These were not
private enterprise projects; the power of the state was
behind the county councils and the construction companies.
The building of M1 attracted as much local interest, however, as did railway building. Luton citizens turned out on
Sundays to see what had been done the previous week.
Critics of M1's failings have forced improvements in later
motorways, but all motorways are so new that it is difficult to
see them in perspective. Will future generations come to
sentimentalise over motorways as we now do over the railways? A journey along M1, south from Luton, is not too
encouraging. Like a similar railway journey one is sometimes above the surrounding landscape, sometimes in a
cutting, but unlike the railways always mesmerised by the
speed and noise of other traffic. This motorway journey
shows little of Hertfordshire; it gives the impression of flat,
open country with occasional woods. The most important
landmark as one approaches Hemel Hempstead is a towering
silo on the horizon. Neither Hemel Hempstead nor St
Albans can be seen; from M10 there is only the briefest
glimpse of St Albans Abbey sited finely on the hillside
across the Ver. A1(M) between Baldock and Hatfield has
more attractive bridges than M1 and goes through more
varied scenery. But the overall effect of motorway driving in

Hertfordshire is monotonous. One sees neither the towns and villages nor the small scale beauties of the countryside.

Perhaps the only beautiful scene from a motorway is of the lights of Stevenage seen from the south on a clear night. This does suggest that there may be beauty in the work of modern man. There are other examples. Around Little Wymondley and Stocking Pelham electricity pylons stride across the countryside in all directions (Plate 44). They leave their nests like H. G. Wells' Martian invaders, from a pit near Bury Wood in Little Wymondley by the road to Titmore and Redcoats Greens, and from an even larger enclosure south-east of Crabbs Green in Stocking Pelham. To many people, no doubt, they seem invaders indeed but in fact these modern pylons have a Regency grace; glistening in the sunshine or glowering in a storm they add a new dimension to a countryside which is after all entirely man made.

There are many twentieth century factories in Hertfordshire, mostly but not all in the planned industrial areas of the Garden Cities and New Towns. Although some industrial buildings, in particular power stations, can add to the landscape the twentieth century equivalent of a cathedral or a country house,[8] Hertfordshire lacks such. But there is a real difference between the new factories and the old. The new are clean, light, airy and surrounded by flowers, grass, trees —and acres of cars! At their best they are functionally simple, like the Borg-Warner factory at the entry to Letchworth's industrial area on the road from Baldock to Letchworth (Plate 34) or Automatic Transmissions on the industrial estate in Hemel Hempstead.

From the outside some of Hertfordshire's new factories remind one of William Morris' description of "A Factory as it might be": "our factory stands amidst gardens"; the "buildings will be beautiful with their own beauty of simplicity". But how often does the inside meet Morris'

[8] See the examples in G. E. Kidder Smith, *The New Architecture of Europe*, 1961, pp. 53–6, 58–62 and 64–70.

requirements? "Our factory which is externally beautiful will not be inside like a clean jail or a workhouse; the architecture will come inside in the form of such ornament as may be suitable to the special circumstances."[9]

The public buildings in which the dreams of William Morris have been most nearly fulfilled are the schools. The county's education and architects' departments united to plan a school building programme for the years of expansion after the Second World War. They used as a basic unit a module of 8' 3", later of 3' 4", and ordered materials in bulk from suppliers. The savings in costs and times so achieved made it possible to equip many schools with unusual 'ornaments'. The Barclay School in Stevenage had William Morris wallpaper on its dining hall wall and Henry Moore's *Family* in front of the entrance. Hatfield Technical College, as it was called in 1952 when opened, had a Barbara Hepworth sculpture and two decorative panels by Ben Nicholson. While these were not the only examples in the county, the really important benefit which accompanied the County Council's advance planning was that the building 'bricks' were combined sensitively to produce schools which were good-looking places in which to work, set in open spaces. The schools built in Britain since the Second World War have an international reputation and many Hertfordshire schools rank high in any list of Britain's best modern school buildings. Perhaps it is some guarantee for the future of the local landscape that an increasing proportion of Hertfordshire's adult voters have been educated in such an environment.

In spite of the giant strides which industrialisation and urbanisation has made in Hertfordshire during this century, far more countryside remains to be enjoyed and studied than many of the county's inhabitants realise. Travelling along narrow roads across the county's main communication routes, from east to west or west to east, takes one through

---

[9] *William Morris*, centenary edition, ed. G. D. H. Cole, Nonesuch, 1934, pp. 647, 648 and 654.

every variety of countryside. There is a marked contrast between the dull, open view from motorways and the attractive glimpses of a different, secretive world seen from winding lanes. But this rural Hertfordshire was man made. The landscape of Hertfordshire, rural and urban, is more of a piece than many believe. None of it is natural: town and country, industry and agriculture, interpenetrate. A remote little village like Furneux Pelham contains Rayment's brewery of 1860 in working order. Stevenage New Town has preserved and opened out Fairlands valley. Change is not simply in one direction. Perhaps it is symbolic of the everchanging use and appearance of the county's surface that the Lea valley, which in 1931 boasted a new glass house industry booming when the rest of agriculture was depressed, became in less than forty years a derelict area within which it is now proposed to create a recreation park for Londoners and the commuters of Hertfordshire. Nor is this new use completely new, for a century ago the Rye House, in this very area, was flourishing as a tourist resort, managed by J. Teale and Co. Their guide book, *Nether Hall and the Mysteries of Rye House*, first appeared in 1848 when the author commented in his opening 'Address' that "so numerous have been the visitors to this pleasant place, that the Directors of the Great Eastern Railway Company have erected a station within a few yards of the spot".

SELECT BIBLIOGRAPHY

Howard, Ebenezer *Garden Cities of Tomorrow* (1902).
Macfadyen, Dugald *Sir Ebenezer Howard and the town planning movement* (1933).
Purdom, C. B. *The Letchworth Achievement* (1963).
Report of the Royal Commission on the distribution of the industrial population (Cmd: 6153) (1940).
Orlans, Harold *Stevenage* (1952).
Successive versions of the county plan for Hertfordshire.

Index

Map references follow most place names. They refer to the parish church in most villages and towns or to the site of a building. In a few cases, in parks where there is no surviving building or in urban areas where there is no geographically relevant parish church, the relevant grid square or squares is given.

Index

Index

settlement patterns: prehistoric and Roman, 34, 42–9, 52–64, 84; medieval 37–8, chaps. 3 and 4; scattered settlement, 73–4, 76, 78–81, 84–9, 107–12, 115–16, 126, 129, 153, 166, 184, 189, 229–33; ends and greens, 84–7, 107, 109, 129, 166–9, 185, 230–1; nucleated villages, 73–4, 81, 85–6, 109–16; street villages, 86–7, 126–7; green villages, 73, 87–9, 248–9; changing layout, 74–6, 78–81, 86–9, 106, 108–10; woodland settlement, modern, 230–3; village greens, 26, 186

Shaw, G. B., 162

Shenley (190 004), 187; Blackheath, 187; Salisbury, 119

Shephall (257 230), 45, 190, 247–9; Shephallbury, 248

Shrimpton, John, 95

Skegges, Edward, 231

Smeaton, John, 206

Smith, Augustus, 188

Smith, G. E. Kidder, 252

Smith, John T., 38, 174

Smith, Lucy Toulmin, 185

Smith, Samuel and Abel, 213, 215

soils, 26, 30–3, 45, 49, 52–3, 61–2, 78, 93–4, 114, 165, 184

South Mimms (222 012), 206; Castle, 116; Kitts End, 129

Spence, Joseph, 171

Stageman, F. D., 45

Stamp, L. Dudley, 186

Standon (396 222), 27, 77, 106, 112–16, 203; Balsams, 115; Barwick, 116; Biggin's Farm, 116; Bromley Hall Farm, 59–60, 64; Colliers End, 115, 203; Friars, 115; High Cross, 115; Latchford, 115; Lordship, 142; Marshalls, 115; Mentley Farm, 60, 115; Popeshall, 115; Rigery Farm, 116; Ralph Sadlier School, 54; Skeleton Green, 54; Sutes, 119; Wickham Field, 55, 58, 60; Wickham Hill, 64; Youngsbury, 60, 64, 112, 148,

156–7; *see also* Puckeridge

Stane Street, 59–60, 82

Stanstead, 206; Abbots (39 12), 37, 81, 85, 198; Rye House, 181; St Margarets (38 12), Bridge of Thele, 81, 104

Stead, I. M., 52, 57, 59, 98

Stenton, F. M., 62, 65, 67, 74, 84–5, 88, 108

Stephen, King and Matilda, Queen, 95, 117–18

Stevenage (2322–2626), 25, 29–30, 34, 63, 99–100, 106, 109, 123, 170, 190, 205, 212, 216, 218–19, 234–7, 242–9, 252–5; Barclay School, 253; Broadwater, 170; Bury, 99; Chells, 245; churches, 99–100, 246, 248–9; Fairlands, 249, 254; inns, 202; Middle Row, 100, 105–6; Monk's Wood, 249; Pin Green, 245; Six Hills Way, 249; Southend Farm, 177; Whomerley Wood, 249; *see also* Shephall

Stone, Jeanne and Lawrence, 140–1, 144, 147, 151

street patterns (towns), 59, 81–3, 92, 95, 97–106, 220–5, 226–7, 235, 237, 239, 241–5, 247, 250

strip lynchets, 185

Stroud, Dorothy, 157, 159

Styles, Benjamin, 148, 157

Summerson, John, 144

surveys; *see* maps

Swift, Jonathan, 161

Tate, W. E., 183

Taylor, Christopher, 67

Telford, Thomas, 129, 207, 210

Temple, Sir William, 150, 157

Tewin (268 143), 46, 67, 190, 216, 230–3; House, 142; Marden Hill, 142; Nancybury Gorse, 231; Queen Hoo Hall, 231; Shankey's Wood, 231; Water, 143, 158–9; Wood, 231–2, 240

Theobalds (355 012), 140–4, 148, 152–4